New

A MAGAZINE OF MARXIST POLITICS AND

NUMBER 11   1998

Contents

EDITOR Mary-Alice Waters

MANAGING EDITOR Steve Clark

CONTRIBUTING EDITORS Jack Barnes, Sigurlaug Gunnlaugsdóttir, Carl-Erik Isacsson, Steve Penner, Ron Poulsen, Jean-Louis Salfati, Samad Sharif, Jonathan Silberman, Mike Tucker

Michel Prairie, editor, *Nouvelle Internationale*
Martín Koppel, editor, *Nueva Internacional*
Catharina Tirsén, editor, *Ny International*

The articles that appear here in English are also available in French, Spanish, and Swedish. All four publications are available from New International, 410 West St., New York, NY 10014

Cover photograph: Andrea Brizzi. Reproductions of mural by permission of Pathfinder Press.

Cover design: Eva Braiman

New International is distributed internationally by Pathfinder Press:

Australia (and Asia and the Pacific):
    Pathfinder, 176 Redfern St., Redfern, N.S.W. 2016
    Postal address: P.O. Box K879, Haymarket, N.S.W. 1240
Canada:
    Pathfinder, 851 Bloor St. West, Toronto, ON, M6G 1M3
Iceland:
    Pathfinder, Klapparstíg 26, 2d floor, 101 Reykjavík
    Postal address: P. Box 233, IS 121 Reykjavík
New Zealand:
    Pathfinder, La Gonda Arcade, 203 Karangahape Road, Auckland
Sweden:
    Pathfinder, Vikingagatan 10, S-113 42, Stockholm
United Kingdom (and Europe, Africa except South Africa, and Middle East):
    Pathfinder, 47 The Cut, London, SE1 8LL
United States (and Caribbean, Latin America, and South Africa):
    Pathfinder, 410 West Street, New York, NY 10014

RONIC, IS IT NOT? In East Europe, the victims of communism tear down images of Marx and Engels; in the arts capital of America, their portraits go up [and] Fidel Castro rises over the Westside Highway," wrote right-wing demagogue Patrick Buchanan in his nationally syndicated column in late November 1989. Buchanan's vitriolic comment was in reference to the Pathfinder Mural, pictured on the front and back cover, which had been unveiled in New York City several days earlier, on November 19, 1989.

In fact, there is nothing "ironic" about it, as readers of "U.S. Imperialism Has Lost the Cold War," the 1990 Socialist Workers Party resolution featured in this issue of *New International*, will be well equipped to understand.

Buchanan was seconding a provocative call to assault the mural, launched the very day of the dedication itself. The November 19 issue of the *New York Post* had carried an editorial headlined, "Off the wall — that's where it belongs." Tarring the mural as a "bizarre celebration of totalitarianism," the editorial concluded with the real point, an incitement to act: "The mural should be removed."

An ultrarightist squad responded to these calls a few weeks later, defacing the mural with five paint bombs during the night of December 20. Artists rallied to repair the damage. And from that day forward, the mural, and the Pathfinder Building whose wall it covered, was defended — successfully — around the clock by a roster of volunteers who gave up a night's sleep once every few weeks to be part of teams doing guard duty.

The fact of the completed mural, and its impact, caught the right wing by surprise, and they were never able to effectively respond.

Many revolutionary and communist leaders discussed in this issue, whose writings and speeches are published and distributed by Pathfinder, are portrayed on the mural, which was painted on the six-story south wall of the Pathfinder Building in lower Manhattan. The mural was a joint endeavor of communist workers and youth and of artists from around the world who volunteered their talent and their time, and who in addition helped raise the funds to purchase paint, erect scaffolding, and cover other costs. The November 19 dedication drew some four hundred participants: artists, supporters of the Cuban revolution and of the antiapartheid struggle in South Africa, students, and workers — including unionists on strike against Eastern Airlines and United Mine Workers members supporting the hard-fought strike against Pittston coal company. Two and half years in the making, this work of art was truly an expression, to paraphrase the Communist Manifesto, of "an existing class struggle, of a historical movement going on under our very eyes."

The centerpiece of the mural is a large printing press, with the words of Cuban president Fidel Castro — "The truth must not only be the truth, it must also be told" — imprinted on a paper roll. The press is churning out books on which the featured portraits appear. Starting at the top left of the mural, and tracing an inverted "S" across and down the front and back cover of this issue, readers will find the following portraits:

Karl Marx and **Frederick Engels,** the founding leaders of the modern communist workers movement (artists: Aldo Soler — Cuba; Marjan Hormozi — Iran);

Five central leaders of the Communist International (from left to right), **Gregory Zinoviev, Nikolai Bukharin, Leon Trotsky, V.I. Lenin,** and **Karl Radek** (artist: Malcolm McAllister — New Zealand) — *now flipping to the back cover;*

U.S. socialist and labor leader **Eugene V. Debs** (artist: David Fichter);

United Mine Workers union organizer **Mother Jones** (artist: Eva Cockcroft);

Rosa Luxemburg, internationalist leader of the workers movement in Germany and Poland (sketch by May Stevens, painted by Mike Alewitz);

Black rights leader and author **W.E.B. Du Bois** (artist: Seitu Ken Jones) — *now returning to the front cover;*

Nicaraguan revolutionary leader **Augusto Sandino** (artist: Arnoldo Guillén — Nicaragua);

U.S. working-class and communist leaders **Farrell Dobbs** and **James P. Cannon** (artist: Bob Allen);

Carlos Fonseca, founding leader of Nicaragua's Sandinista National Liberation Front (artist: Arnoldo Guillén — Nicaragua);

Black rights fighter and revolutionary leader **Malcolm X** (artist: Carole Byard);

Ernesto Che Guevara, the Argentine-born communist and leader of the Cuban revolution (artist: Ricardo Carpani — Argentina);

Maurice Bishop, the central leader of the Grenada revolution (Maxine Townsend-Broderick);

Thomas Sankara, leader of the revolutionary government in the West African country Burkina Faso (Lynne Pelletier — Quebec; Luis Perero);

African National Congress leader and later president of South Africa **Nelson Mandela** (artist: Dumile Feni — South Africa); and

Fidel Castro, the central leader of Cuba's socialist revolution (artist: Aldo Soler — Cuba).

FROM THE "BREAKER BOYS" gathered around a mine portal at the foot of the mural (child laborers exploited by Pennsylvania mining bosses in the early twentieth century, some of whom later joined in the bloody struggles to unionize coal); to the battle flag carried into combat against the British colonizers of New Zealand by Maori warrior Te Kooti, flying across the mural's peak; to the fighting workers and peasants scaling the classics of Marxism — the mural depicts the struggles of working people over the past 150 years. Among the multitudes are portraits of other working-class leaders and fighters for national liberation and social justice the world over. Some can be seen more clearly in the detail from the mural on the facing page.

Eighty artists — volunteers all — from twenty countries participated in creating the mural. Many painted scenes of working-class and national liberation struggles from their countries, or portraits of leaders of those struggles.

The mural's first project director was Mike Alewitz, and the work was carried through to completion by Sam Manuel, who cut the ribbons to unveil the mural at its 1989 dedication. Manuel continued as director following that ceremony, overseeing work to restore sections of the mural damaged by right-wingers, fighting a disciplined if inevitably losing battle against the effects of weather, and keeping in contact with the artists and others whose collective efforts brought the mural into being.

THE MURAL REMAINED on the wall of the Pathfinder Building for seven years, attracting visitors, tour groups, and press coverage from across North America and around the world. From the start it won a supportive reception, and often the admiration, of workers and residents in the Manhattan neighborhood it overlooked. It was viewed by literally millions driving north on the heavily traveled Westside Highway, or enjoying riverboat cruises along the New York City shoreline. A number of figures portrayed in the mural who could not visit it had this work of art described to them in detail by others who had been able to view it directly.

A full-color poster of the Pathfinder Mural can be ordered by consulting the ad printed on page 9.

By 1996 the mural had faded and the underlying surface had crumbled beyond repair from the effects of sun and weathering. The wall it covered had suffered similarly and was badly in need of structural repair.

Detail from Pathfinder Mural. Depicted are scenes from the Chinese revolution and India's independence struggle; South African antiapartheid protesters; U.S. abortion rights activists; several of the Haymarket martyrs; Mexican revolutionary leaders Emiliano Zapata and Pancho Villa; Paris communard Louise Michel; American Indian leader Leonard Peltier; U.S. antislavery fighters John Brown, Sojourner Truth, and Harriet Tubman; Puerto Rican independence fighter Lolita Lebrón; Irish Republican martyr Bobby Sands; 19th century revolutionist August Blanqui and Marx collaborator Joseph Weydemeyer; Socialist Workers Party leaders Joseph Hansen and Evelyn Reed; Congolese liberation leader Patrice Lumumba; gay rights activist Leonard Matlovich; Industrial Workers of the World leaders "Big Bill" Haywood and Frank Little; and numerous others.

Following a June 1996 celebration outside the Pathfinder Building — participated in by artists and others involved in its creation, as well as workers, young people, and neighbors — the mural, in the process of structural restoration of the south wall, was covered over with a light yellow protective paneling. That surface stands invitingly for a new generation of socialist workers, at a future junction in the class struggle, to organize the next artistic representation of Pathfinder, the publishing house that was born with the October revolution.

The rendering of the mural wrapped around this issue of *New International* was made possible by the collective work of Eva Braiman, the cover designer, and Toni Gorton, who provided invaluable consultation. They collaborated with the editors while working opposite shifts in factories in different cities. The workers in Pathfinder's printshop took the design and, with painstaking care for quality, transformed it into the magazine you now hold in your hands.

The editors express appreciation for all these efforts, which will help get this issue of *New International* into the hands of workers, farmers, and youth around the world. We hope it is a fitting tribute to those who created and defended the mural, and to those who today continue to guard the space that will serve as the site of the next one.

Steve Clark
September 1998

October 17, 1997, homecoming ceremony in Santa Clara, Cuba, at which remains of Ernesto Che Guevara and six other guerrillas from Bolivia, Cuba, and Peru killed in 1966–67 Bolivian campaign were interred. "Revolutionary internationalism is the wave of the future not the last vestige of a bygone era. This future will be marked by class struggles, popular revolutions, national liberation movements, and civil wars." (From "U.S. Imperialism Has Lost the Cold War")

OURS IS THE EPOCH OF
WORLD REVOLUTION

by Jack Barnes and Mary-Alice Waters

"We cannot think about the world clearly today without the beginnings of motion toward a youth organization. Why is this so? Because in addition to the working-class experience, composition, and continuity without which any communist organization will go off the rails politically, there are also points in history at which so much is changing so rapidly that even the best fighters will be disoriented unless they can break from habits of thought developed in the past and see the world through the eyes of a generation just awakening to political life."

These words from the featured article in issue no. 10 of *New International*[1] are also at the center of the "Young Socialists Manifesto," the opening piece in this issue. This document was drafted by members of the Young Socialists chapter in Los Angeles, California, in April 1998. It is the product of several chapter discussions in the course of which they put down working notes to clarify for themselves the character and activity of

---

1. "Imperialism's March toward Fascism and War" by Jack Barnes, published in issue no. 10 of *New International*, had been discussed and adopted by delegates to the Socialist Workers Party's August 1994 national convention.

their organization and the necessity of its political relationship to the Socialist Workers Party, the communist vanguard party of the working class in the United States.

The brevity, clarity, and freshness of the document are a testimony to the hard work and collective effort of its authors, as well as evidence of its insight.

The "Manifesto," as others soon named it, became the center of discussion at a West Coast Young Socialists regional conference held in San Francisco, September 5–6, 1998, hosted by the California YS chapters. Participants in that conference, acting on the request of the National Executive Committee of the Young Socialists, issued a call for the third national convention of the organization to be held in Los Angeles, December 4–6, 1998. They decided YS chapters around the country should begin work to build the convention by discussing the manifesto, along with the "Young Socialists Organizer" adopted by the second national convention of the Young Socialists in March 1997. The opening section of that document, too, is printed here.

The "Young Socialists Manifesto" brings into focus what this issue of *New International* is about: understanding the depth of the political, economic, and social changes reshaping our world, and forging the kind of working-class parties whose units are capable of *acting* in a politically centralized manner, with speed and effectiveness, as we are confronted with the unpredictable challenges and opportunities created daily by capitalism's accelerating world disorder.

WITHOUT THE TRAJECTORY the YS Manifesto traces for the new generation just beginning to move toward the working class politically, the other contents of this issue of the magazine might still have historical and analytical merit. Alone, however, they would not constitute a communist course for today. Marxism is a guide to revolutionary practice. As the founders of the modern working-class movement put it so succinctly more than 150 years ago: the point is not to interpret the world, but to change it.

The opportunities for organizations of communist workers and of youth to act together along the lines presented in the pages that follow have been expanding at least since early 1997. The evidence continues to accumulate that the working class in the United States and most other imperialist countries has emerged from the period of political retreat that followed the short, brutal — and demoralizing, because largely uncontested — imperial assault on the people of Iraq in 1990–91. Signs of renewed defensive action are all around us — more numerous strike actions reflecting the tenacity and resistance of the embattled ranks; a noticeable growth in the confidence and determination of women in industry; the increased weight of Black leadership in labor battles and struggles of working farmers; an upswing in the Puerto Rican independence movement; more actions in defense of immigrants' rights. Such developments prepare the strengthening of working-class leadership in these struggles and increase the potential of the unions "to act deliberately as organizing centers of the working class in the broad interests of its complete emancipation."[2]

It is at moments such as these, above all, that the vanguard party of the working class and revolutionary-minded young people who seek to build a proletarian youth movement must march together, deepening their understanding and organizing their work within the history and line of march of the modern communist movement. That is the precondition for carrying out effective mass work and recruitment to both organizations — not in the long-run, but today. It is the only way to implement a proletarian course, responding in a timely way — free of political hesitation, abstention, or ultraleft missteps — to the accelerated resistance bred by capitalism's deepening crises.

---

2. From "Trade Unions: Their Past, Present and Future," the founding trade union document of the communist movement. Drafted by Karl Marx for discussion and adoption by the First International in 1867, it is published in the book *Trade Unions in the Epoch of Imperialist Decay* (Pathfinder, 1990).

"Theory is not dogma, nor an IOU. It is the living generalization of the line of march of a class, of the strategic political lessons our class has learned through bloody sacrifice and struggle," states the document cited by the Young Socialists in their manifesto. "These lessons are the most valuable asset of the communist movement, our most valuable weapons. It is the absorption of these lessons into the day-by-day, week-by-week political practice of an organized world communist movement that makes it possible, when the crunch comes, for millions of individual communists to think and act in a disciplined way to do the necessary."

That is the course the Young Socialists Manifesto charts, and that the Young Socialists will be moving along as they build toward the third national convention of their organization in Los Angeles. That is why their manifesto deserves its leading place in this issue of *New International,* and the attention of every revolutionary-minded person, regardless of age or years of political experience.

"U.S. Imperialism Has Lost the Cold War," the document featured in this issue of *New International,* was discussed and adopted by delegates to the 35th national convention of the Socialist Workers Party in the United States, August 8–12, 1990. The resolution was put before convention delegates by the National Committee of the Socialist Workers Party. As the resolution was being discussed and debated in party branches across the United States and by communist organizations in other countries, the historic events that marked the end of Stalinist regimes across Eastern Europe and the Soviet Union, and the disintegration of the power of the Communist Party apparatuses in those countries, were unfolding day by day. The imperialist rulers had begun to loudly proclaim the defeat of communism and the birth of a "new world order" — even the end of history itself — with themselves supposedly heading toward undisputed control at the world's helm.

At the very time delegates to the SWP convention were deliberating, the U.S. government opened a drive toward war against Iraq that culminated five months later in six weeks of massive, devastating bombing, a 100-hour invasion of that country, and the slaughter of some 150,000 Iraqi men, women, and children.

Plans to rapidly edit and publish the resolution adopted at the August 1990 convention were temporarily put aside, as the branches and trade union fractions of the Socialist Workers Party and chapters of the Young Socialist Alliance, along with communists around the world who shared the political conclusions of that document, turned to the immediate tasks campaigning against the approaching war. U.S. imperialism was to prove unable to achieve its goals in the Iraq war, however. The "grand coalition" engineered under the baton of President George Bush began to come apart even as the guns blazed, obliging the U.S. rulers to stop short of establishing the protectorate they need in that region. The outcome of the Gulf War was among the first striking confirmations of the sharpening interimperialist conflict that would mark the post–Cold War world, sounding a minor-key chord in the midst of paeans to U.S. hegemony in the new world order. The consequences of that outcome for U.S. finance capital are still being played out today.

THAT "U.S. IMPERIALISM Has Lost the Cold War" would be published by *New International* only some eight years after it was written and adopted was not foreseen or intended. But its appearance now is perhaps fortuitous. What is printed here has not been rewritten with the benefit of hindsight: it is published as it was presented in the *Discussion Bulletin* of the Socialist Workers Party in May 1990, incorporating the changes decided by the delegates to the convention that adopted it. The resolution has been edited only to eliminate unnecessary repetition, digressions, and ambiguities, and to footnote facts and references that the passage of time has left dated or unclear. We read the document today with different eyes, however. The perspective of a few short years allows us to appreciate the enormity of the consequences that followed from imperialism's historic loss, and the speed with which some of the most fundamental linchpins of world politics in the post–World War II era have changed and are changing.

• Far from the "relative strengthening of German finance capital within the imperialist system" and the formation of a European Union "increasingly dominated by German finance capital," long-term trends noted by the resolution, the German bourgeoisie, and its previously solid currency, the mark, have been politically and economically weakened by the traumatic nine-year attempt to swallow and digest the east German workers state. The resolution accurately points to the manifold contradictions inherent in the coming reunification of Germany. But it stopped short of indicating the probable consequences, since they were at such variance with the previous period marked by a sharply separated "East" and "West" Germany, as well as by a long capitalist wave of expansion.

OFFICIAL UNEMPLOYMENT rates matching those not seen in Germany since the eve of Hitler's installation as chancellor of the Third Reich, sharpening political polarization with rising fascist currents, and German finance capital's heightened vulnerability to the destabilizing consequences of Russia's economic disintegration — these are among the most visible manifestations of the new reality in capitalist Europe.

This relative weakening of the German bourgeoisie vis-à-vis its rivals, especially imperialist France, has been the single biggest shift in world politics since the resolution was drafted. Together with Tokyo's accelerated decline over much the same period, it has altered the popular misconception — which was reaching its zenith among bourgeois commentators leading up to 1990 — that Germany and Japan, with their respective "economic miracles," were the "real victors" in World War II.

But only a new interimperialist slaughter, with new powers emerging victorious, can change the balance of forces established with the outcome of the last world war. And such a contest is being prepared.

The real victor in World War II, we should never forget, was not only U.S. finance capital, which emerged largely unchallenged among the imperialist ruling classes. The "American century" remained a sad delusion of Washington liberals, much to their surprise, due to the checkmate imposed by the working class internationally, the other victor in that world conflagration. The toilers' victory resided in the fact that the dictatorship of the proletariat in the Soviet Union, however weakened and deformed, was not destroyed. The working people of the Soviet Union, at an enormous material and human cost, with the support of workers and farmers worldwide, turned back the imperialist invasion and began to reconstruct. The economic foundations laid by the October 1917 revolution survived. And the oppressed nations and peoples of Asia, Africa, and Latin America seized the moment created by the weakening of the imperialist system to unleash powerful national liberation struggles that changed the face of world politics and the relationship of class forces internationally to the detriment of finance capital.

• The first war on the European continent in almost fifty years had not yet begun in 1990. But for seven years now, since early 1991, it has been sometimes smoldering, sometimes exploding, throughout the lands of Yugoslavia and across the Balkans.

On the blood and bones of the Yugoslav people, the United States government has established itself as the major "European" power. As the rival national capitalist classes of Europe, wrapped in the United Nations flag, wore themselves out in futile attempts to displace one another as the "winner" in the new Balkan wars, Washington unfurled its NATO banner in 1994 and decisively moved in. Despite demagogic rationalizations, the U.S. rulers' aim is not to stop "ethnic cleansing" or to impose "democracy," but to establish U.S. supremacy in Europe and create conditions that one day will facilitate the restoration of capitalist social relations throughout the Yugoslav workers state.

• The growing strains within the reactionary NATO alliance "from intensifying interimperialist competition and shifting alignments" noted in the resolution have sharpened, not diminished. But under the guiding hand of a U.S. ruling class far from unanimous on the fateful consequences of its course, NATO is being expanded to encompass even more explosive contradictions; its center of gravity is being shifted sharply to the east. The encirclement of the Russian workers state is being tightened along its entire perimeter, from Central Europe, through the oil-rich Caucasus, and deep into Asia along the historic Silk Road to the south. This ring of fire will be fanned into raging flames with increasing frequency, as the capitalist powers seek to advance their interests. The uncontrolled forces set in motion will grow. That is the actual perspective at the dawn of the twenty-first century.

STEP BY STEP, U.S. imperialism is preparing, with cold-blooded awareness, for what it is convinced must eventually be done. What was opened by the October revolution in Russia cannot be finessed out of history. Capitalism can only be established in those lands through bloody counterrevolution. The toilers in the former USSR will have to be taken on directly. Though weakened and betrayed by decades of misrule of the bureaucratic caste of opportunists, assassins, and other anti-working-class parasites, now shattered into countless warring camps, the state power of the working class must still be overthrown by military might.

As the resolution affirms, "The workers states and their proletarian property foundations have proven stronger than the castes."

• In August 1990 the skeletal forms of the Union of Soviet Socialist Republics still existed. Mikhail Gorbachev was president of the Soviet Union and general secretary of the Communist Party. The Moscow regime still sought to justify its legitimacy by claiming to represent the continuity of the Bolshevik-led October 1917 revolution. None of that remains the fact today.

The disintegration of the bureaucratic castes, abandoning all pretense to speak for communism or represent the interests of the working class and its allies internationally, has removed an enormous roadblock that for decades stood in the way of revolutionary fighters finding their way to Marxism. Millions were diverted instead onto a course that was in reality a counterrevolutionary negation of what the historic leaders of the modern working-class movement, including Marx, Engels, and Lenin, fought for. But today neither tottering Russian president Boris Yeltsin and his collaborators nor their factional opponents — to say nothing of imitators throughout the various former Soviet republics — have the capacity to influence and disorient any revolutionary fighter anywhere in the world.

Gone with the roadblock is also the glue that for decades served to structure the milieu broadly referred to as "the left" throughout the world. Since the Stalinist initiation of the Popular Front "strategy" of class collaboration in the mid-1930s, "the left" has derived its political line and coherency, and often its resources, from identification with and loyalty to the actually existing castes that dominated the workers states. The attractive power of the existing fact was enormous — hence the crisis of "the left" that swept 'round the world when, as Cuban president Fidel Castro put it, "one day the sun did not rise at 6:00 a.m., nor at 7:00 a.m., nor at 10:00 a.m., nor at noon."[3] The mettle of all those calling themselves socialist or communist began being tested anew — a test that is deepening and broadening today.

---

3. Speech to the congress of the Union of Writers and Artists of Cuba (UNEAC), November 1993. See "Defending Cuba, Defending Cuba's Socialist Revolution" by Mary-Alice Waters in *New International* no. 10, p. 30.

Currents claiming to be revolutionary no longer have any power in the workers movement outside themselves to blame, or to credit, for whatever they prove capable of doing, leading, and becoming.

• At the beginning of 1990, the superinflated Japanese stock and real estate markets had just collapsed. That this marked the opening of a world deflationary crisis is only today — belatedly, and in more and more panicky tones — beginning to be acknowledged in certain quarters of bourgeois public opinion. Contrary to expectations, the recovery never occurred. The crisis has only continued to deepen.

Eight years later, as the "Asian crisis" spreads and the international collapse of capitalism's banking system looms threateningly on the horizon, no one yet knows if we are in fact already living through what will soon be universally recognized as the first year of a new world depression. Will 1998 be looked back on as a new 1929? Yes or no, the answer changes little. What is incontrovertible is that we are witnessing the last desperate and feeble efforts of the capitalist rulers to stave off the inevitable.

And what is coming will be more devastating for the world's toilers than the aftermath of 1929. This time it will be of truly global dimensions.

Dᴜʀɪɴɢ ᴛʜᴇ ᴡᴏʀʟᴅ depression of the 1930s, capitalist social relations were marginal throughout most of colonial Asia and Africa — and even parts of Latin America. For the huge peasant majority under colonialism, the economic and social consequences of colonial superexploitation meant life on the knife's edge. But subsistence and survival took place largely outside the reach of the world capitalist market, and conditions of life for the majority of the world's toilers were often not qualitatively worsened by the Great Depression. Today, capitalism has penetrated agriculture more deeply in most of these countries, and an industrial working class of wage-labor that is not always small has developed in many of them.

The peoples of the Soviet Union, protected in the 1930s from the ravages of world depression by the revolutionary conquests of October that laid the economic foundations of nationalized property and a planned economy, are now infinitely more vulnerable.

The fate of the toilers everywhere has been drawn much more tightly into the workings of the world capitalist market. Hopes for a better tomorrow are just beginning to be dashed.

This world of the twenty-first century, born prematurely in the closing hours of the twentieth, may be rudely disorienting for many whose lives and consciousness were shaped by the upheaval and consequences of World War II. For the generation coming to political life today, however, this is the only world they have ever known. For all of us, "U.S. Imperialism Has Lost the Cold War" implies practical tasks and perspectives that fit well today's growing working-class resistance and put in political relief the forces that will shape the titanic battles that are approaching. Above all, it explains to us why — bourgeois propaganda notwithstanding — the historic odds in favor or the working class internationally have been strengthened, not weakened.

"A Havana-Washington axis of conflict will be at the center of world politics in the 1990s. It is the most direct manifestation of the international conflict between imperialism and the dictatorship of the proletariat."[4]

With the implosion of the bureaucratic castes, regimes, and parties of Eastern Europe and the Soviet Union, the U.S. imperialist rulers hoped the government of the workers and farmers of Cuba would become easier pickings. They failed to understand — as they have from the days of the revolutionary

---

4. From part 2 of "U.S. Imperialism Has Lost the Cold War."

war against the Batista dictatorship — that the leadership of the revolution in Cuba is not a tropical variant of Stalinism, but a truly revolutionary internationalist party that is blood and bone of the Cuban toilers.

The U.S. rulers anticipated that the sudden, brutal slashing of the standard of living in Cuba — the result of the abrupt end in 1990–91 of preferential trade agreements with the Soviet Union and Eastern European workers states, accounting for 85 percent of Cuba's foreign trade — would starve Cuban working people into submission, or at least create fertile conditions for the overthrow of the revolutionary government.

The world political perspective presented by Cuban Communist Party leader José Ramón Balaguer in "Socialism: A Viable Option," published in this issue, confirms the error of this view. "In the present international conditions, we reaffirm that socialism is a necessity," Balaguer told participants in the international conference on "Socialism on the Threshold of the Twenty-first Century," held in Havana, October 21–23, 1997. "Not only is it the logical result of the development of the productive forces on an international scale, it is the only alternative to guarantee the survival of humanity."

Referring to the "collapse of socialism in Eastern Europe and the USSR," Balaguer noted "it is not socialist truth that failed." Rather, what occurred there was "the crumbling of a dogmatic and vulgar type of Marxism, which in those countries was raised to the status of official theory, burying many of the central principles of our classics and elevating to the position of universal law certain doctrines that served only to rationalize political positions and had virtually no scientific basis."

THE INTERNATIONAL CONFERENCE of representatives of political parties at which Balaguer spoke, and in which some of the editors of *New International* participated, including the authors of this article, was hosted by the Central Committee of the Communist Party of Cuba. It was one of several events over the past two years that confirmed the Cuban revolution has conquered the worst days of what they refer to as the Special Period — the economic and political crisis precipitated by the abrupt disintegration of the governments and parties with which they had maintained the closest ties for more than a quarter century. A crisis deliberately compounded, of course, by intensified economic warfare waged against Cuba by the U.S. rulers.

Other events have included:

• The fifth congress of the Communist Party of Cuba, held in Havana, October 8–10, 1997, which reaffirmed the political course of the revolution, knitting the lines of continuity between the rectification process begun in the mid-1980s and the policies of the Special Period. Among other decisions by the delegates, the congress strengthened the party leadership, resolutely cutting the size of the Central Committee from 225 to 150 members, while incorporating some 50 new members from the younger generations bearing the direct weight of day-to-day leadership in every arena. The congress registered the reality that the transition in leadership in Cuba, the topic of much speculation by the revolution's enemies abroad, lies not in the future, but is ongoing in the present.

• The commemoration in the fall of 1997, and throughout that year, of the thirtieth anniversary of the revolutionary campaign waged by Ernesto Che Guevara and his comrades in Bolivia, reaffirming the proletarian internationalism that has been and remains the heart and soul of the Cuban revolution.

• The solemn and unifying welcome home given what Cuban president Fidel Castro in October 1997 called Che's reinforcement brigade, as the mortal remains, along with the "immortal ideas" of Che and his comrades returned to Cuba "to reinforce us in this difficult struggle we are waging today to save the ideas for which you fought so hard, to save the revolution, the country and its socialist conquests — the part of your dreams that have been fulfilled."

• The hosting in August 1997 of the 12,000-strong World Festival of Youth and Students by the Union of Young Communists and other youth organizations of Cuba, as part of the political battle to reach out and find the new generation of fighters around the world attracted to the example of the Cuban revolution.

• The "Declaration of the Mambises of the Twentieth Century," initiated in February 1997 by the generals of the Revolutionary Armed Forces and signed by 250,000 officers and troops, as well as, over the next few months, by more than 5 million other Cubans. Linking up with the continuity of the Mambises — the Cuban independence fighters of the late nineteenth century who fought Spanish colonial rule — the declaration repudiates the crude and insulting attempts of U.S. president William Clinton to foment divisions among the officers and ranks of the military with offers of aid in return for overthrowing the revolutionary government through which Cuba's workers and farmers exercise their political power.

• The welcome extended to Pope John Paul II on his state visit in January 1998, during which the revolutionary leadership set an example for working people the world over of courtesy towards religious believers and nonbelievers alike — while taking the moral high ground for the proletariat and speaking the truth to the world about the historical role of the Catholic Church hierarchy as an instrument of scientific obscurantism, racial prejudice, oppression of women, colonial conquest and slavery, and reaction in all its forms. The pope's visit was an event from which the working people of Cuba emerged more confident in themselves and their leadership, and more certain that their class, not the representatives of capitalism or feudalism, will be the bearers of culture in the forward march of humanity.

• The seventeenth congress of the Central Organization of Cuban Workers (CTC), held April 27–30, 1996, which registered the confidence of the working class in Cuba as it brings its direct weight to bear in determining the future of the revolution, and its capacity to surmount the enormous obstacles to increasing production under the conditions imposed by the

Special Period. As the theses adopted by the delegates expressed it, the organized working class of Cuba met to determine what they could do "to assure, under whatever circumstances, the revolutionary power of the workers, by the workers, and for the workers."

"One day we may have to erect a monument to the Special Period!" Fidel Castro noted in remarks to congress delegates. In meeting the challenge of the most difficult years of the revolution, the Cuban working class has emerged stronger and more self-confident than at any time since the Special Period began.

Each of these events required substantial material and leadership resources that would have been impossible to muster in Cuba during the darkest hours (literally as well as metaphorically) of the Special Period. Taken together, as Cubans jokingly remark, they clearly demonstrate that the revolution is now out of the intensive care unit — that it is no longer necessary to devote every fiber of being to the battle for survival alone. Cuban working people can now enjoy the luxury of directing some energy to thoughts of recovery and how to advance the international revolutionary struggle in today's world.

Socialism on the Threshold of the Twenty-first Century" was perhaps the most important such gathering to take place in Havana in more than thirty years — since the international leadership initiatives in the 1960s that culminated in the Tricontinental conference in January 1966 and the OLAS (Organization of Latin American Solidarity) gathering in August 1967.

Political conditions were vastly different then, of course. The heroic example of the Vietnamese national liberation struggle was galvanizing millions into action worldwide, as hatred for U.S. imperialism's murderous war against the Indochinese peoples deepened and spread. A wave of anti-imperialist struggle was rising throughout Latin America, borne on the crest of the Cuban revolution. Support for the Palestinian people and their struggle against dispossession by the state of Israel was exploding throughout the Arab world. The forces attracted to Havana's initiative then were substantially larger. In their big majority they were young and ready for action. Despite the political disparities, however, the objective place and weight of the leadership initiatives taken thirty years apart are similar: to reach out around the world and find the forces ready to chart a revolutionary strategy to move forward and to apply it.

In Balaguer's opening presentation to the delegates, there was no talk of tragedy having befallen Cuba or other revolutionary forces in the world. There was no bemoaning globalization, nor cowering before the relationship of class forces that has allowed the implementation of neoliberal policies throughout Latin America. Instead, there was a scientific examination of the world class struggle in the closing years of the twentieth century — with eyes fixed on the coming battles being born of the imperialist reality — and a program that constitutes a necessary and sufficient starting point for revolutionary action:

• No, to any variant on theories of globalization and super-imperialism that lead to undervaluing the struggle for state power against our own bourgeoisies. "Socialism will not appear on the historical scene through a modernization of present society, but through a revolutionary transformation of its dominant structures. In this sense, the question of the seizure of power remains a basic requirement. . . ."

• Yes, to the political course of rectification and the Special Period, as opposed to the "model of economic management copied, in large measure from the Soviet experience . . . that diverted the construction of socialism onto paths that had nothing to do with being revolutionary."

• No, to any policy of alliances that is not built "from, by, and for the ranks," or that demands revolutionaries renounce "conviction and firmness of principles."

• Yes, to the fight to take the moral high ground, to "show

not only the possibility and viability of socialism but also its desirability. . . . For us, socialism is the only possible, the only valid option for placing social relations on a moral footing," said Balaguer. "We cannot relax our efforts to demonstrate — on a theoretical level, and on a practical level — its clear superiority in shaping the highest of human values: justice, equality, fairness, freedom, democracy, respect for human rights, national sovereignty, solidarity. This socialist society continues to be a clear alternative not only to capitalism, but also to the failed experiences of Eastern Europe and the USSR."

THE SOCIALIST WORKERS Party resolution, "U.S. Imperialism Has Lost the Cold War," underscores that "the leadership of the Communist Party of Cuba is the first since the Bolsheviks to give communist guidance to the development of a workers state." At the helm of the Cuban government, and in the face of U.S. imperialism's unrelenting economic, political, and military pressures, they have maintained a revolutionary course for forty years. "This 'subjective factor' — the genuinely internationalist character of the proletarian vanguard guiding the workers state in Cuba — is the most important *objective* outcome and contribution of the Cuban revolution."

This is even more true today than it was in 1990. The objective weight in world politics of the only living example of a fighting, confident dictatorship of the proletariat — one with a seasoned combat leadership that has proven its capacity year after year for more than four decades — has grown not diminished. For revolutionary fighters the world over, it is not enough to recognize that imperialism really has lost the Cold War. That alone does not allow revolutionists to chart a way forward. They need the living example of Cuba, as well.

This is just as true for new generations of revolutionary-minded fighters inside Cuba as for young people elsewhere in the world. The real history of the Cuban revolution — the stories of the men and women who overthrew the Batista dictatorship, stood down the Yankee empire at the Bay of Pigs and during the October "missile crisis," and served in volunteer internationalists missions from Latin America, to Africa, Asia, and the Middle East — is a vital link in the revolutionary continuity that must be traced.[5]

A *strategy* of attempting to build socialism in one country — even in a country as vast and rich in resources as the Soviet Union, let alone a Caribbean island with a historical legacy of centuries of colonial and imperialist domination — can only mean the abandonment of proletarian internationalism, the demoralization and demobilization of the fighting vanguard of the toilers, and certain defeat. But communist workers assume no a priori limits on the capacity of Cuban working people to resist and survive, to hold off the imperial enemy until reinforcement brigades of the international class struggle arrive, to maintain the foundations of their state power, and to keep strengthening their internationalism and advancing their class interests.

That is a practical question, not an analytical one, where the example of Cuba itself weighs heavily in the balance.

"A more than ten-year offensive by the employers has failed to drive the labor movement from the center stage of politics in the United States."

Those opening words of "U.S. Imperialism Has Lost the Cold War" place in historical perspective the growing resistance in 1989–90 by workers in the United States to the bosses' union-busting drive that marked the period when the resolution was drafted. The high point of those defensive battles were two overlapping and intertwined strikes — the twenty-two-month strike by the International Association of Machinists against Eastern Airlines that began in March 1989, in the

---

5. For a powerful example, see *Secrets of Generals,* interviews by Cuban journalist Luis Baez with forty-one top officers of the Revolutionary Armed Forces (Havana: Si Mar, 1996), distributed by Pathfinder.

course of which the ranks successfully forced the hated boss Frank Lorenzo into bankruptcy and then liquidation, rather than allow his carrier to operate nonunion; and the eleven-month strike against Pittston, settled in February 1990, that set back the coal barons' drive to break the United Mine Workers of America in the eastern coalfields.

Those hard-fought conflicts — in which the ranks put their stamp on the strikes' leadership — and the example they set for the entire labor movement, foreshadowed bigger class battles to come at the beginning of the 1990s. Communist workers organized in industrial trade union fractions of the Socialist Workers Party — who had participated in and been transformed by the Eastern and Pittston struggles — confidently looked forward to the opportunities to respond as new tests developed, better prepared as a fraction of the fighting vanguard of the working class.

As the resolution notes, the end of the third "dog days" in the history of the communist movement in the United States seemed to be in sight. Those days had begun with labor's retreat in the wake of the deep 1981–82 recession. They extended through the rout that began to be reversed only with the resistance mounted by packinghouse workers in the Midwest in 1985–86. They coincided with the heavy blows dealt by imperialism against revolutionary advances in Nicaragua, Grenada, and elsewhere.

CONTRARY TO EXPECTATIONS when the resolution was adopted in 1990, however, the dog days for the working class in the United States (and the majority of other imperialist countries) lasted for another half-dozen years. The U.S.-organized military buildup and murderous war against Iraq between August 1990 and March 1991 marked all of politics for more than a year. The outcome of the war was a debacle for Washington, but the patriotism and triumphalism promoted by the U.S. rulers before, during, and after the largely uncontested assault on Iraq dampened working-class combativity for a period longer than the war itself.

The U.S. capitalist economy went into recession during the eight months of the buildup and war. The subsequent upswing in the business cycle was so sluggish that official unemployment continued rising during the first year of the "recovery." Evidence grew that a world deflationary crisis for capitalism was looming.

Labor was pushed toward the wings; the retreat was extended.

The Eastern and Pittston battles, it turned out, prepared communist workers in the immediate period not for bigger defensive strikes and other labor battles, but for the test of imperialist war. *New International* no. 7, "Washington's Assault on Iraq: Opening Guns of World War III," documents how well that test was met by communist organizations around the world, as they carried out a disciplined, centralized campaign, on the job, in working-class neighborhoods, in the unions, and on the campuses against the brutal war orchestrated by Washington.

IN THE AFTERMATH of the Iraq war, communist workers rose to the challenge of applying in practice their understanding of the world that was coming into being. The war in Yugoslavia, the Mexican "peso crisis," the political rise of Patrick Buchanan and character of his incipient fascist current in the United States, the challenge of building communist youth organizations as the first signs of renewed struggle by young people appeared on the horizons — all were among the elements of the political reality that unfolded in the half decade following adoption of the resolution presented here. They are dealt with in Pathfinder Press's forthcoming book, *Capitalism's World Disorder.*[6]

Since early 1997 the evidence has grown that the dog days are now indeed receding. Signs of resistance, from Caterpillar to the airlines, from the United Parcel Service workers strike in 1997 to the five-week strike by General Motors workers in

---

6. Available December 1998, by Jack Barnes.

1998, changes taking place among coal miners, organizing efforts by the United Farm Workers in the fields of California, and new forms of leadership initiative by workers who are Black and by women in the plants — all attest to rising opportunities for communist workers to turn toward mass work on a level that was simply not possible for a number of years.

The opening section of the 1990 resolution, entitled "Labor Movement Remains at Center Stage," can now be read, not with disclaimers that conditions are different, that much of what is written there may not be a useful guide to action today, but with confidence that the opposite is more and more true.

The six-story-high Pathfinder Mural, a reproduction of which appears on the cover of this issue, was unveiled in November 1989 in downtown Manhattan, a few blocks from the world financial center of U.S. imperialism. Only days after the Berlin Wall came down, and the capitalist masters of the world were trying to convince us all that they had emerged victorious in a historic battle against the toilers of the world, the ribbons were cut on that work of art celebrating the past, present, and future of the struggles waged by the modern working class and its allies on the road toward emancipation. That timing was an accident of history, but the symbolism could not have better captured the reality of our times. What the Pathfinder Mural depicts is the theme of this issue of *New International*.

Ours is the epoch of world revolution.

September 1998

Unions Their past, present, and future

The Eastern Airlines Strike

ACCOMPLISHMENTS OF THE
RANK-AND-FILE MACHINISTS

Ernie Mailhot, Judy Stranahan, and Jack Barnes
The story of the 686-day strike in which a
rank-and-file resistance by Machinists
prevented Eastern's union-busting onslaught
from becoming the road toward a profitable
nonunion airline. $9.95

The 1985–86 Hormel Meat-Packers Strike in Austin, Minnesota

Fred Halstead
The hard-fought strike against Hormel opened a round of battles
by packinghouse workers that—together with strikes by paper
workers, cannery workers, and western coal miners—marked a
break in the rout of U.S. unions that began with the 1981–82
recession. $3.50

Trade Unions in the Epoch of Imperialist Decay

Leon Trotsky

FEATURING "TRADE UNIONS: THEIR PAST, PRESENT,
AND FUTURE" BY KARL MARX

The trade unions must "learn to act deliberately as organizing centers of the working class [and] convince the world at large that
their efforts, far from being narrow and selfish, aim at the emancipation of the downtrodden millions." —*Karl Marx, 1866.*
In this book, two central leaders of the modern communist
workers movement outline the fight for this revolutionary
perspective. $14.95

Labor's Giant Step

THE FIRST TWENTY YEARS OF THE CIO: 1936–55

Art Preis
The story of the explosive labor struggles and political battles in
the 1930s and 1940s that built the industrial unions. And how
those unions became the vanguard of a mass social movement
that began transforming U.S. society. $26.95

From Pathfinder

Capitalism's world disorder

Working-class politics in the 21st century

by Jack Barnes

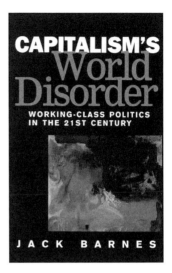

IT IS OFTEN SAID that great historical crises are only resolved in struggle; that's true. But what is not said as often is that the odds — the probability of victory or of loss — are determined long before these class battles themselves break out. The odds depend on the self-confidence, political clarity, and previous combat experience of the cadres of disciplined proletarian organizations who are already among the fighters in the labor movement, and who know that what they do *beforehand* will be decisive when the working class moves toward revolutionary action.
Jack Barnes, April 1993

Four talks by the national secretary of the Socialist Workers Party. Jack Barnes discusses . . .

■ **Capitalist Deflation and Debt Slavery** ■ **Stalinism versus Communism** ■ **Buchananism: What It Is and How to Fight It** ■ **Washington Lets Yugoslavia Bleed** ■ **The 'Bell Curve': the Scandal of Class Privilege** ■ **Socialism and Lifetime Education** ■ **Cuba's Socialist Revolution** ■ **Youth and the Communist Movement** ■ **New Openings for Mass Work and the Struggle for a Proletarian Party**

Available From Pathfinder, December 1998

Ernesto Che Guevara

Episodes of the Cuban Revolutionary War, 1956–58

A first-hand account of the military campaigns and political events that culminated in the January 1959 popular insurrection that overthrew the Batista dictatorship in Cuba. With clarity and humor, Guevara explains how the men and women of the Rebel Army and July 26 Movement led by Fidel Castro forged a political leadership capable of guiding millions of workers and peasants to open the socialist revolution in the Americas. Introduction by Mary-Alice Waters. $23.95

Pombo: A Man of Che's *guerrilla*

With Che Guevara in Bolivia, 1966–68

A never-before published account by a participant of the revolutionary campaign in Bolivia led by Guevara. Written by Pombo—Harry Villegas—who in his 20s was a member of Guevara's general staff and is today a brigadier general in Cuba's Revolutionary Armed Forces. $21.95

At the Side of Che Guevara

Interviews with Harry Villegas (Pombo)

Villegas worked and fought alongside Guevara in Cuba, the Congo, and Bolivia. In these interviews he talks about the struggles he has taken part in over four decades—including the defeat of South Africa's apartheid army in Angola, and he explains the importance of Guevara's political legacy for a new generation of fighters around the world. $4.00. Also available in Spanish.

Available from Pathfinder. See page 2 for addresses.

YOUNG SOCIALISTS MANIFESTO

Young Socialists and members of the Socialist Workers Party in San Francisco joined March 29, 1998, demonstration in support of United Farm Workers drive to organize strawberry workers in California. "More young people today are becoming interested in politics and are willing to fight. They hate the consequences of capitalism — the racism, the police brutality, the attacks on women's rights, the destruction of the environment, the unemployment, the wars and threats of war."

YOUNG SOCIALISTS
MANIFESTO

A. What does it mean to be a part of a functioning chapter of the Young Socialists in Los Angeles?

1. Political context provided by Jack Barnes in *New International* no. 10, "Imperialism's March toward Fascism and War."

    a. In recent past, harder for young fighters "to see how they could link up with a social force, with the working class and labor movement, that had the power to bring about change . . . harder yet for them to connect up with a broader tradition of struggle" in the working class (p. 222). But today there exists an open field where the YS can function as a revolutionary youth organization.

    b. ". . . more young people today . . . are becoming interested in politics and are willing to fight. They hate the consequences of capitalism . . . the racism, the police brutality,

---

This document was written in April 1998 by members of the Young Socialists chapter in Los Angeles, California. It is a set of working notes, the product of several chapter discussions, drafted as the members clarified for themselves the character and activity of their organization and the necessity of its political relationship to the Socialist Workers Party, the communist vanguard party of the working class in the United States.

The "manifesto," as it was soon named, became the center of discussion at a West Coast regional conference hosted by the California Young Socialists chapters in San Francisco, September 5–6, 1998.

It is published here together with the "Aims of the Young Socialists," the opening section of a document entitled the "Young Socialist Organizer," adopted by the second national convention of the Young Socialists in Atlanta, Georgia, March 28–30, 1997.

The California regional conference called the third national convention of the Young Socialists, to be held in Los Angeles, December 4–6, 1998, and placed both documents before the Young Socialists to initiate preconvention discussion in every chapter.

the attacks on women's rights, the destruction of the environment, the unemployment, the wars and threats of war. . . . Wherever there is resistance to oppression and exploitation, they want to join the battle" (p. 225).

c. ". . . seek to politically convince every young rebel we can, before he or she becomes committed to crank ideas, is pulled toward the radical right, or simply comes to terms over time with capitalism and sinks back into workaday life in bourgeois society" (p. 235).

d. ". . . I am raising something different: that we cannot *think* about the world clearly today without the beginnings of motion toward a youth organization. Why is this so? Because in addition to the working-class experience, composition, and continuity without which any communist organization will go off the rails politically, there are also points in history at which so much is changing so rapidly that even the best fighters will be disoriented unless they can break from habits of thought developed in the past and see the world through the eyes of a generation just awakening to political life" (p. 236).

e. YS attempting to understand our place within this context as a real, functioning chapter that is increasing its level of political activity and recruitment.

B. Increasing political activity of the Los Angeles chapter of Young Socialists

1. Political involvement with youth and students

   a. Community, plant-gate, and campus sales teams: California State University, Los Angeles (CSLA), University of California, Los Angeles (UCLA), United Airlines, door-to-door subscription drive campaign for the *Militant* and *Perspectiva Mundial*

   b. Hands Off Iraq political work: Occidental College, UCLA, and picket lines

   c. YS Class Series: weekly classes at bookstore and Occidental

   d. Welcome Back from Kosova, Havana, and Cairo Conference: bringing interested youth to the conference to dis-

cuss talks by party and YS leaders, and involvement and
responsibility, including financial, by YS members

e. Socialist Workers campaign: upcoming campaigning for
SWP candidates, one of whom is a YS member from LA

f. Jobs and the proletarianization of the Young Socialists

C. Building a stronger YS chapter: Recruitment and contacts

a. How to win youth to a working-class perspective: "Take advantage of any political opening. . . . Join demonstrations and
other protests that take place; take part in whatever resistance
there is on the job; go onto campus to meet whoever we can;
get socialist literature around as broadly as possible. . . . to
present the socialist alternative. . . . [and] basing what we do
on an objective, thought-out understanding of politics

b. and a disciplined and sustainable, a proletarian, approach to
organization. [Otherwise] we will end up frittering away our
accomplishments and disorganizing our work" (p. 228).

1. by taking a more conscious approach at being a part of
building a variety of youth-led actions

2. YS classes/education: Pathfinder arsenals, *Militant*, and
Perspectiva Mundial

3. Steady, patient political work to win new members

4. Maintaining focus within broader youth and student
coalitions

c. Clarity in defining the Young Socialists

1. YS is not a "turn" organization

2. Fast-track vs. quality political recruitment

d. How does the YS function in relation to the party?

1. Committee work with SWP

2. Different and auxiliary organization

3. Working on *Militant* articles with comrades

e. Campaign for Socialist Workers Party candidates

*"For the young Marx and Engels, joining this organization of revo-
lutionary-minded workers was a necessary step in recognizing themselves as actors in history who, in order to be effective in politics,
needed to be part of the vanguard movement of a class" (p. 231).*

AIMS OF THE
YOUNG SOCIALISTS

T HE CENTRAL aim of the Young Socialists is to participate in the fight to establish a workers and farmers government that will abolish capitalism in the United States and join in the worldwide fight for socialism. The YS strives to win young fighters to our political perspective, that of revolutionary socialism. We educate ourselves and other fighters with the history and lessons of the working class and apply these to the skirmishes and small-scale struggles that break out today in preparation for the major class battles ahead of us. Our political program and activity stem from 150 years of the modern class struggle and the principles developed by the revolutionary workers movement.

We also recognize that a youth organization cannot lead workers and their allies in the overthrow of the capitalist class and the conquest of a workers and farmers government. A mass revolutionary party of the Leninist type is needed. Our work is aimed to help facilitate the building of such a party. To that end, we collaborate and have fraternal relations with the Socialist Workers Party, the nucleus of such a party in the United States.

The Young Socialists is organizationally independent and politically subordinate to the Socialist Workers Party. We look to the Socialist Workers Party and its experience and continuity in the class struggle, which can be traced back to Marx and Engels, for political leadership. The Socialist Workers Party, along with the Young Socialists, make up the nucleus of the proletarian vanguard in this country. The SWP and YS have a structured, formal, organizational relationship, conducted through our respective National Committees and their elected executive bodies — the SWP Political Committee and the YS National Executive Committee. On a local level, Young Socialists chapters and branches of the SWP coordinate our work through the elected leadership bodies of the chapters and branches — the executive committees of those organizations.

The way we organize ourselves flows from our political aims. In order to effectively carry out our goals, the YS must be a cohesive and disciplined organization. We have adapted democratic centralism, used by the vanguard party, to the needs of the YS as the method for carrying out our aims.

Democracy is a method of reaching decisions, which requires organized discussion, debate, and a vote. The positions adopted by majority vote are the positions all YS members carry out in a centralized way. Majority rule is fundamental to the concept of democratic centralism. The minority may maintain its disagreements and raise them at the appropriate time within the organization, but is bound by the majority decision and the YS engages in political activity united and with a common purpose. This maintains both internal democracy and the ability of the organization to act with unity. This is based on fundamental agreement with the political program and principles of the YS, laying the foundation for discipline.

Membership is based on political agreement with the principles of the YS and active participation in the work of the organization. Responsibilities of membership include attending weekly chapter meetings, payment of monthly dues, and carrying out the work of the chapter on a weekly basis.

FROM PATHFINDER

Puerto Rico: independence is a necessity

BY RAFAEL CANCEL MIRANDA

"Our people are becoming aware of their own strength, which is what the colonial powers fear," explains Puerto Rican independence leader Rafael Cancel Miranda. In two interviews, Cancel Miranda—one of five Puerto Rican Nationalists imprisoned by Washington for more than 25 years until 1979—speaks out on the brutal reality of U.S. colonial domination, the campaign needed to free 16 Puerto Rican political prisoners, the example of Cuba's socialist revolution, and the resurgence of the independence movement today. In English and Spanish. $3.00

Rosa Luxemburg Speaks

EDITED BY MARY-ALICE WATERS

From her political awakening as a high school student in tsarist-occupied Poland until her murder in 1919 during the German revolution, Rosa Luxemburg acted and wrote as a proletarian revolutionist. This book takes us inside the political battles between revolution and class collaboration that still shape the modern workers movement. $26.95

A Packinghouse Worker's Fight for Justice

The Mark Curtis Story

NAOMI CRAINE

The story of the victorious eight-year international defense campaign to defeat the political frame-up of union activist and socialist Mark Curtis, sentenced in 1988 to twenty-five years in prison on trumped up charges of attempted rape and burglary. $6.00

See front of magazine for addresses.

READ

THE
MILITANT
A SOCIALIST NEWSWEEKLY PUBLISHED
IN THE INTERESTS OF WORKING PEOPLE

Perspectiva mundial
MONTHLY SPANISH-LANGUAGE SISTER
PUBLICATION OF THE MILITANT

The Militant and PM . . .

❖ provide firsthand coverage from the picket lines and other workers
battles in North America, Europe, and elsewhere

❖ tell the truth about the spreading capitalist economic and financial crisis

❖ dissect, lie by lie, Washington's rationalizations for its
war moves

❖ follow the efforts by Cuba's workers and farmers to
defend and advance their socialist revolution

❖ report on the rise of struggles for national
independence from Puerto Rico to Ireland and Quebec

❖ cover fights against cop brutality and racism, and for
women's equality

❖ offer a socialist alternative that can be achieved along
the line of march of fighting workers worldwide

News and Views from Cuba
Subscribe Today!

Granma   *La Gaceta*   **CUBA** SOCIALISTA
                  DE CUBA

Granma International	La Gaceta de Cuba	Cuba Socialista
Weekly news and commentary from Cuba. Includes speeches by Fidel Castro and other Cuban leaders, public statements by the Cuban government and Communist Party, and news and features on the steps being taken by Cuba's workers and farmers to defend the socialist revolution. Also available in Spanish and French.

$40/year | Journal in Spanish published six times a year by the Union of Writers and Artists of Cuba. A forum for discussion on culture, politics, and the challenges facing the Cuban revolution today.

Individual rate: $40
Special student rate: $28
Institutional rate: $75 | Published in Spanish four times a year, Cuba Socialista addresses many of the challenges facing the Cuban revolution today, as well as topics under debate among revolutionaries around the world. Journal of the Central Committee of the Communist Party of Cuba.

Individual rate: $28
Institutional rate: $40 |

SOCIALISM:
A VIABLE OPTION

The U.S.-backed Batista dictatorship in Cuba fell at the opening of January 1959 on the crest of a series of military victories by Rebel Army forces led by Fidel Castro and a countrywide insurrection and general strike. Above, Castro speaks to residents of Colón, January 7, 1959, the day before his column reached Havana. "Socialism will not appear on the historical scene through a modernization of present society but through a revolutionary transformation of its dominant structures. The seizure of power remains a basic requirement."

SOCIALISM: A VIABLE OPTION

by José Ramón Balaguer

CONTEMPORARY CAPITALIST SOCIETY
Once again the bells are pealing, triumphantly proclaiming the deification of capitalism, this time under the banner of the wonders of "globalization" — a fashionable term used to try to explain and justify many things. Both academic analyses and reports by governments and international organizations give us a picture of this intricate and multifaceted process, the axis of which is the globalization of the world economy.

Under the rubric of a future "global village" — which reminds us of early twentieth century arguments regarding "super-imperialism"[1] — we are told of a new world economy, the result of the end of the Cold War, where an atmosphere of permanent harmony will be possible, both between countries and within them. Moreover, it is assumed that nation-states have virtually dissolved and national sovereignty has lost its meaning, the result of universal tendencies that have been standardizing how the system functions.

To be sure, there has been an enormous growth in world trade, in the international movement of capital, especially in the form of money capital and its derivatives — growth at rates

Opening speech by José Ramón Balaguer Cabrera, member of the Political Bureau of the Central Committee of the Communist Party of Cuba, at the international workshop on "Socialism on the Threshold of the Twenty-First Century," held in Havana, Cuba, October 21–23, 1997. A report on the conference by New International *editor Mary-Alice Waters and Socialist Workers Party national secretary Jack Barnes appears in* Celebrating the Homecoming of Ernesto Che Guevara's Reinforcement Brigade to Cuba, *distributed by Pathfinder. Footnotes have been prepared by the editors.*

FOOTNOTES FOR THIS ARTICLE BEGIN ON NEXT PAGE.

so much higher than the rate of increase in production.
Moreover, it is not necessary to reiterate that there is a higher
degree of interpenetration of national economies. They have
been brought closer together by virtue of the revolution in the
means of transport. They are in closer contact due to the revolution in the means of communication and transmission of in-
formation. They are integrated through a transnational network woven by a capital that today has an international
mobility enormously greater than that of its great-grandfathers
of the last century.

Marxism long ago alerted us to the fact that the expansion
of capitalism's international economic relations is an objective
process of that system. Capital's tendency to move across borders — one of its defining features — made it possible for
capitalist rule, as one of its ingredients, to establish a world system, the first, to be exact, in the history of humanity. That
same tendency, reinforced today by colossal advances in science and technology, has resulted in a very high degree of in-
ternationalization of capital.

But is globalization equivalent to a universal and definitive
victory of capitalism, as some insist? Does it mean the abolition
of contradictions between social classes, countries, and regions?
Does it signify an end to crises of the system? Does it exclude the

1. Karl Kautsky, a leader of the centrist forces in the German Social
Democratic Party and Second International who capitulated to the German bourgeoisie at the opening of World War I, wrote in 1915: "Cannot
the present imperialist policy be supplanted by a new, ultra-imperialist
policy, which will introduce the joint exploitation of the world by internationally united finance capital in place of the mutual rivalry of national
finance capitals?" Bolshevik leader V.I. Lenin replied in 1916 that the
"real, social significance of Kautsky's 'theory' is this: it is a most reactionary method of consoling the masses with hopes of permanent peace
made possible under capitalism, by distracting their attention from the
sharp antagonisms and acute problems of the present times, and directing it towards illusory prospects of an imaginary 'ultra-imperialism' of the
future." (*Imperialism: The Highest Stage of Capitalism*, in V.I. Lenin, *Collected
Works* [Moscow: Progress Publishers, 1985] vol. 22, pp. 293–94.)

possibility of revolutionary transformations? Does it mean that all countries will be forced to adopt, like a straitjacket, a certain pattern of conduct in domestic and foreign policy?

Reality has dashed to bits these fantasies about globalization, in a dramatic way.

We are witnessing a crisis in the world capitalist system. This is expressed in the long-term tendency toward lower rates of economic growth, as well as in sharpening business cycles that have included steep slumps in the mid-1970s and at the opening of the 1980s and of the 1990s. Low rates of investment, generalized indebtedness, socially unsustainable rates of unemployment, and a decline in the rate of profit are just a few of the symptoms of the delicate health of the system.

Nor should we forget the volatility and instability represented by enormous masses of money capital moving erratically, without any real regulation, and with enormous destructive capacity, able to throw national economies and governments into crisis in a matter of hours. The dizzying separation of the mass of speculative capital from actual production, as an expression of the parasitic nature of capitalism, does have limits.

GLOBALIZATION does not provide an automatic mechanism for solving the contradictions and the unevenness that have accompanied the development of capitalism; even less does it mean the end of history. To the contrary, the disappearance of the socialist camp; the reassessment on the part of the industrialized countries of the relative weight of economic and political factors in defining their foreign relations strategies; the present and foreseeable development of economic blocs and of competition among them — all these aspects taken together appear to be raising interimperialist rivalry to a new level.

The law of uneven development has become clearer than ever, with the resulting tendency to reproduce, on a broadening scale, the North-South differences that historically have accompanied the development of capitalism. Today, however, levels of scientific and technical development have reached such heights that they cry out for social use and controls. Private ownership and domination over these developments poses a contradiction not just in terms of the class struggle, but of the survival of the species — both in terms of coexistence in social relations and of the continuation of life in a sustainable ecological environment.

Our Latin American and Caribbean region, along with Africa and a part of Asia, has, to an extreme degree, become marginalized in relation to the dynamics of the world economy and to a presence in the global functioning of the system. In practice, our place in that world system is limited to the simple payment of debt service to the international private banking system.

NEOLIBERAL ECONOMIC policies, stamped with the emblem of the International Monetary Fund and its formulas, have undoubtedly played a role in creating this grim picture of insecurity and inequality. Almost the entire underdeveloped world has been homogenized through total privatization and lowering of trade barriers at any price — as if these were the sole possible formulas for economic success. Nonetheless, those who give speeches exalting and proposing such formulas from the platforms of government, academic, business, and international agencies have carefully taken their distance from them in practice.

This intellectual and political capitulation has relegated to oblivion efforts to work out theories and policies of development conceived from the point of view of the underdeveloped countries and suited to them. For the Third World, the consequences of this capitulation are impossible to quantify. The tragedy, however, is plain to see: there is an overabundance of poverty, hunger, and injustice in the wake of privatization and the "dog-eat-dog" nature of the perfect market.

Today we witness an abysmal gap between wealth and poverty. This is true not only between the developed and under-developed countries, but also in niches of the Third World that are growing up inside all the economically developed countries, niches that are enlarged, among other things, by a migration of the poor. Efforts are being made to check this migration by means of racism, xenophobia, and repression, in other words by throwing gasoline on the flames.

In 1960 the richest 20 percent of the world's population had an income thirty times greater than the poorest 20 percent. Today the richest 20 percent have an income sixty times higher. This comparison measures the distribution of income between developed and underdeveloped countries, but if one considers the unequal distribution within the various countries, then the richest 20 percent have an income at least one hundred fifty times greater than the poorest 20 percent.

Another way of expressing this tragedy is that the richest 20 percent receive 82.7 percent of the world's total income, while the poorest 20 percent receive 1.4 percent.

In Latin America, which is the laboratory of choice for neo-liberal policy, 84 million people are indigent, a degree of poverty difficult to overcome. In other words, one out of every five persons in Latin America is statistically classified as indigent — even after some fifteen years of sustained application of neoliberalism, which, it was claimed, would eliminate the inefficiency of the state and advance development by unleashing the uncontrolled market and private initiative.

Nor can neoliberal globalization claim to have brought about political stability following the disappearance of the Soviet Union and so-called actually existing socialism.

To the contrary, the powerful wave of ethnic explosions, territorial disputes, religious fundamentalism, and the disappearance and emergence of states in the heat of local wars — all these factors underline that the momentary triumph over socialism did not eliminate capitalism's inherent tendency toward conflict. The exploitation, exclusion, and injustice that sprout from capitalism's deepest roots not only take forms that are new and surprising but also reappear in those that are old and dangerous, such as the rebirth of fascism.

Not only is the world more unstable, more prone to disintegration, and more politically explosive than ever, but the environment itself is being destroyed. It is not difficult to demonstrate that plunder of the environment and neoliberal capitalist globalization go hand in hand, inexorably united for reasons that have more to do with the search to maximize profits in the market than with reason.

The collapse of socialism
in Eastern Europe and the USSR: Some assessments

Under these conditions we have not the slightest doubt that the world has two roads to choose from: either the continuation of capitalist barbarism or the search for alternatives to this state of things. For us Cubans, as for millions of human beings, the alternative continues to be socialism.

It is not socialist truth that failed. The failure was of those who bore the historic responsibility to carry that truth forward, to guide it on the basis of daily creative work and concrete experience. This is a very delicate matter, since the future of humanity is at stake.

I have no desire to spend time analyzing the collapse of socialism in Eastern Europe and the USSR. I can point out, however, that the so-called domino effect did not reach our country.

In addition to imperialism's efforts to undermine and exert control over socialism in Eastern Europe and the USSR, its liquidation had historic, socioeconomic, and political causes, which we have been clarifying among ourselves. But one thing has been well demonstrated: that process in Europe did not signify the failure of socialism as a system.

Nor did it mean that Marxism and Leninism are useless as guides to action. It did mean the crumbling of a dogmatic and vulgar type of Marxism, which in those countries was raised to the status of official theory, burying many of the central principles of our classics and elevating to the position of universal law certain doctrines that served only to rationalize political positions and had virtually no scientific basis.

We all know that the classics did not present us a blueprint of socialist society; rather they developed fundamental ideas. The socialism that succumbed had been moving away from the socialist ideal envisioned by Marx, Engels, Lenin, and other Marxists. That model was mechanically copied to the countries that made up Comecon,[2] transplanting schemas that were perhaps valid in one situation but not others, and ignoring national realities and traditions.

When socialism collapsed in Europe and the USSR, the retreat of the revolutionary forces in those countries reached its most extreme point, one that had international reverberations. At that time, Cuba was going through a process of rectification of errors and negative tendencies initiated in 1986 by the leadership of our party. We had concluded that the model of economic management, copied in large measure from the Soviet experience, had to be fundamentally transformed.

That model, which permeated all of Cuban society, had led us to errors and negative tendencies that diverted the construction of socialism onto paths that had nothing to do with being revolutionary.

We began a social process that started in the economic arena and spread to the political life of the country. We began a process of rectifying and perfecting our socialism, based on socialist positions. This process was cut short with the disappearance of the socialism existing in Europe and the USSR. We were faced with the evaporation of the world with which we conducted 85 percent of our foreign trade, and from which we received fuel and basic raw materials for our industry and agriculture, financing for development, and many other benefits.

---

2. Comecon was founded in 1949, at Moscow's initiative, with the stated purpose of coordinating trade and investment policies of the Soviet and Eastern European workers states. Cuba joined Comecon in 1972.

We were starting off on an uncharted path. We began a period in which we adopted a series of economic measures aimed at saving our country, the revolution, and socialism.

Today those of us who make up the progressive forces are experiencing a new situation in world politics. It is one in which imperialism — the United States — seeks to establish a new world order, where the principles and values of capitalism would reign supreme. A new world order in which the United States would exert such dominance that it could subject the rest of the world's peoples to its designs, directing at will the affairs of the world.

Socialism as a system

In the present international conditions, we reaffirm that socialism is a necessity. Not only is it the logical result of the development of the productive forces on an international scale; it is the only alternative to guarantee the survival of humanity. The continual sharpening of global problems today provides more and greater proof than any other argument of the historic limitations of capitalism.

It is already clear that these global problems, along with domestic class contradictions, are weighty factors on a world scale pushing forward the struggle for a new social order. The contradiction between capital and labor is increasingly being internationalized, requiring even more that socialism, as well, broaden its scope beyond national borders and contradictions, and confirming the relevance of that classical slogan of Marxism: "Workers of all countries, unite!" Far from being outdated, that slogan could be extended, drawing in other social sectors and movements that are subjected to the barbarity of capital.

This aspiration transcends class and national boundaries to become a necessity of the world community.

The foregoing does not mean once again falling into the old error of designing a single abstract model of socialism for all countries. The aim must be a socialism that develops based on the specific characteristics of each nation or region.

In light of the generalized crisis of values worldwide, it becomes critical in charting new paths to emancipation to show not only the possibility and viability of socialism but also its desirability. Social change will not be possible unless the *objective* values that such a change is aimed at bringing about are first recognized on a *subjective* level as desirable values.

For us, socialism is the only possible, the only valid option for placing social relations on a moral footing. We cannot relax our efforts to demonstrate — on a theoretical level, and on a practical level — its clear superiority in shaping the highest of human values: justice, equality, fairness, freedom, democracy, respect for human rights, national sovereignty, solidarity.

This socialist society continues to be a clear alternative not only to capitalism, but also to the failed experiences of Eastern Europe and the USSR. The errors, deviations, and excesses that took place there under the name of "actually existing socialism," together with the exaggerations of them by the transnational media, have debased, in an extreme way, the image of socialism in the consciousness of workers and the oppressed of the world.

It is necessary to project a new, fresh image of socialism, based on a society full of justice and freedom. Taking into consideration the specifics of each situation, such a society entails an appropriate relation between plan and market, equality and efficiency, centralism and democracy, instilling in workers a true sense of ownership and respect for the means of production. It respects differences and takes them into account; it pays attention to the natural environment; and it is the genuine expression of popular will.

In sum, it should be what Comrade Fidel emphasized when he declared: "For me socialism is a total change in the lives of the people, the establishment of new values, of a new culture. This change has to be based fundamentally on solidarity between human beings, and not selfishness and individualism."

Socialism will not appear on the historical scene through a

modernization of present society, but through a revolutionary transformation of its dominant structures. In this sense, the question of the seizure of power remains a basic requirement, although it may take on different forms under the conditions of each country or region of the world.

The socialist alternative has never been more necessary. The paradox of our day, however, lies in the fact that capitalism has succeeded in taking advantage of the recent defeat. It still maintains a consensus that must be reversed by the forces of the left.

The Cuban revolution and its socialist development

Cubans have a history that is a living memory of far-reaching events, marked by heroism and resistance. We initially fought Spain to win independence and rid ourselves of colonial slavery, and almost simultaneously confronted the intervention and interference of the United States. Patriotism and anti-imperialism have been two organic forms of struggle present in the course of the revolution, from 1868 when the first effort for emancipation was begun, until today.

In his political testament José Martí denounced U.S. plans for expansion and warned of the danger that loomed over the peoples of Our America.[3]

----

3. José Martí, Cuba's national hero, was a noted poet, writer, and journalist who founded the Cuban Revolutionary Party, which launched Cuba's 1895 independence war against Spain. Martí was killed in battle during that war. The term "Our America" was coined by Martí, who had lived in exile in the United States for a number of years and understood the Cuban independence struggle to be part of the broader struggle against rising U.S. imperialist domination and pillage of Latin America as a whole. In an unfinished May 18, 1895 letter — begun the day before his death and since then often referred to as his political testament — Martí wrote: "I am in danger each day of giving my life for my country and for my duty — which I understand and am willing to carry out — of preventing the United States, as Cuba gains her independence, from extending its control over the Antilles, and consequently falling with that much more force upon our countries of America. Whatever I have done till now, and

Long years in the history of our homeland, some of them crucial years, reveal the dimensions of the battles the Cuban people have had to wage against this powerful neighbor who has not let up in attacking it, dominating it, occupying it by force, and destroying its wealth and culture. Nevertheless, this neighbor has not been able to add us as another star to its flag, much less make us surrender by means of economic, psychological, or biological warfare.

It will soon be one hundred years since the Yankees' first imperialist war, in which they stripped the independence fighters of their right to govern themselves, imposed the Platt Amendment[4] that curtailed the sovereignty of the country, and installed themselves by force on a piece of national territory, brazenly turning it into a U.S. naval base at Guantánamo, a base that has continued to exist to this day.

Obviously, in the logic of the patriotic consciousness of Cubans, anti-imperialism became an expression of defense of the Cuban nation and its identity, in face of the dangers to it.

Socialist Cuba broke with the ominous scheme of "Manifest Destiny" in the Western Hemisphere.[5] It has never been forgiven for this historical boldness, which some of the hemisphere's most prominent academics saw as "an error of U.S. policy toward the

---

whatever I shall do, has been with that aim. . . . I have lived within the monster and know its entrails; my sling is the sling of David."

4. The Platt Amendment was incorporated by the U.S. Congress into a U.S. military appropriations bill in 1901. The Cuban government established during the U.S. military occupation of the island following the Spanish-American War incorporated the provisions of the Platt Amendment in the new Cuban constitution. Washington was given the right to intervene in Cuban affairs at any time and to establish military bases on Cuban soil. Cuba eliminated these provisions from its constitution in 1934, in the wake of a revolutionary uprising the previous year.

5. Manifest Destiny was a term promoted by the rising U.S. capitalist class in the mid-nineteenth century to present westward expansion across the North American continent as the new nation's "destiny." The term was maintained and used as an ideological justification for U.S. imperialist domination in Latin America.

insurrection that descended from the Sierra Maestra."

On January 1, 1959, through the action of the guerrillas in the mountains and the combatants of the cities, the revolutionary insurrection triumphed amid the most intense class struggle. Power was now in the hands of the working people and their Rebel Army.

The oligarchy and its parties were left without a stage and their press was left without readers. Without any law to shield them, the multiparty regime of the bourgeois-landowner bloc succumbed forever.

The leaders of the revolution warned that the most difficult and dangerous moments were soon to come. The confrontations with the Yankee imperialists and the counterrevolution serving them were beginning.

Under those circumstances the unity of the revolutionaries was more necessary and urgent. They agreed to work together toward forming a single party, the path that could ensure the unity of the people.[6]

The victorious revolution not only united the nation around its program of social and national liberation. It also unleashed social forces whose actions wrote chapters of true human heroism, of unprecedented enthusiasm, and of total revolutionary selflessness — factors that characterized a people forging itself in the midst of its own history of struggle and combat.

With absolute firmness, Cubans have defended their sovereignty, independence, and right to self-determination. These are principles — universally valid for all states — that Yankee imperialism wants to take away from Cuba, with alleged plans

---

6. Following the victory of the revolution, the July 26 Movement led by Fidel Castro took the initiative to integrate the leaderships, and eventually fuse, with two other organizations that had joined in the struggle against the Batista regime: the student-based Revolutionary Directorate, and the Popular Socialist Party (PSP), the old Communist Party in Cuba. In 1961 the three groups formed the Integrated Revolutionary Organizations (ORI). This was the first step in the process that resulted, by 1965, in the establishment of the Communist Party of Cuba.

for a peaceful transition to capitalism. The truth is, they resort to terrorism and other acts of aggression in their efforts to impose that transition.

The basis of the Cuban revolution's political support has not changed. Far from retreating, Cuba continues transforming itself amidst the escalation of the U.S. blockade and hostility. It does so without renouncing its principles as a sovereign nation — one that chose to advance toward greater social justice and create the foundations for constructing a socialist society.

ENRICHED BY THE BEST traditions of revolutionary thought, Marxist and Leninist ideology reinforces the thinking and action of Cuban revolutionaries. Together with Martí's body of ideas, which is both our own and at the same time universal, it constitutes the ideological strength of our people and its party.

Fused with the seed of socialism that permeated the roots of Cuban revolutionary thought, internationalism — the expression of identification with struggles of the exploited in other corners of the world — is inseparable from the Cuban revolution. There are countless examples, but it is sufficient to recall two beautiful instances of this sentiment of our people: Martí and [Antonio] Maceo[7] could not conceive of Cuban independence without Puerto Rico's, and the Cuban revolution repaid a historic debt to its brother peoples of Africa.

In the task of educating new generations in these ideas, the internationalist deed and word left by Ernesto Che Guevara provide an undying and exemplary lesson.

Patriotism, internationalism, and socialism — both as historical tradition, and as our political principles — have been fused together into inseparable concepts that express the strength of the society we are building and defending.

The ideals of human dignity, self-respect, and social equal-

---

7. Antonio Maceo was a prominent military leader in Cuba's wars of independence from Spain. He was killed in battle in 1896.

60   *José Ramón Balaguer*

ity — in short, the desire to build the most just and advanced society in history — these are the rights that Cubans demand in the midst of the skepticism, imperial pressures, and political confusion that exist in today's world.

In the platform and program of the Cuban Revolutionary Party, founded by Martí to organize the war of 1895, one can see the profoundly humanistic content, the demand for a transformation of society, codified in the call for a republic "for everyone and for the good of everyone."[8] That sentiment of social justice was at the center of the revolutionary ideas that characterized the discourse of the liberation movement in Cuba.

The liberating message of our history includes the ideological adherence of socialists of the caliber of Carlos Baliño, founder of Martí's party, and of Julio Antonio Mella, founder of the first party of Cuban communists.[9]

THOSE IDEALS GREW to be the political strength of the working class and other progressive sectors during the neocolonial republic. When the revolution triumphed in 1959, the ideas of socialism were not alien to the content of that historic process, nor to the consciousness of its main protagonists. Our socialism is neither imported nor imposed from outside. The society we are building starts with Cuban reality, with our material conditions, and with the spiritual life of the people.

In the Cuban conception of socialism, revolutionary human-

8. José Martí, "Con todos, y para el bien de todos" (For everyone, and for the good of everyone), November 26, 1891, in *Obras escogidas* (Havana: Editorial de Ciencias Sociales, 1992), vol. 3, pp. 8–17.
9. Carlos Baliño, a leader of the Cuban workers movement, had been a member of José Martí's Cuban Revolutionary Party that fought for Cuba's independence at the end of the nineteenth century. In 1925 he was a founder of the Communist Party of Cuba. Julio Antonio Mella, a student leader of the struggle against the Machado dictatorship, became the founding leader of the Communist Party of Cuba. He was assassinated in Mexico in 1929 by agents of Machado.

ism — applied creatively at each stage according to concrete
conditions — has been and continues to be fundamental. We
continue to be loyal to Che when we describe our society as "a
Marxist, socialist system, harmonious, or more or less harmonious, in which man is put at the center, the individual is
talked about, man is talked about along with his importance as
the essential factor of the revolution."[10]

Capitalist and market elements have been introduced in our
country, without changing its socialist essence. This represents
a risk that we know how to face with intelligence and modera-
tion, without being dazzled by the deceptive recipes of enslav-
ing neoliberalism.

Under today's conditions, in spite of the difficult economic
conjuncture, the essential features of our socialism are being
maintained. These consist of the dominance of socialized
property relations, social justice, and policies that benefit the
great majority; the resolute leadership exerted by the party in
society; and the structure and functioning of the socialist state
and of the mass organizations, which help promote economic
development, the improvement of living standards, and the revival of social development programs. In short, this means a
struggle to maintain and consolidate the values of the material
and spiritual life of socialist society.

The reforms introduced into the Cuban economy have not
included layoffs of workers, privatizations, the loss of social security, or the closing of schools and hospitals, although we
have not hidden the social cost that the people have had to pay
in terms of privations and shortages of every kind. The market,
for which we have no reverence, is harmful to certain values; it
promotes individualism, not solidarity. We counteract all this
by reinforcing the patriotic and socialist consciousness that
characterizes our revolution.

For the Communist Party of Cuba, the building of socialism is

---

10. Transcript of the bimonthly meeting of the Ministry of Industry, December 5, 1964.

also based on the search for the specific characteristics of each region or country. In this, not in copying, lies the possibility of success. That is why we believe there is not one sole and exclusive road for the construction of this new society. We respect the experiences of everyone. We must study these experiences, in order to take from them those things applicable to each reality.

In our socialism, the axes of the dialectical development of Cuban society are constituted by the role of politics, ideology, and ethics, together with detailed attention to social needs, in line with our economic possibilities. This is quite different from the course followed in societies that are beaten down by injustice, stripped of human solidarity, overwhelmed by poverty, subjected to political corruption and ungovernability, and victimized by the brutal oppression of transnational capital.

If socialism is the science of example, Fidel has said, then an ethical standard guides attitudes toward the betterment of men and women in life and society. By insisting that moral values are an essential trench of revolutionary resistance, Che contributed, in ways few others have done, to this course that has been advanced by Fidel through his teachings, and by the party through its organizational and educational work.

Ernesto Che Guevara is the model of human betterment that Cubans aspire to. (There are those who want to eliminate, by force, the example this model exerts.) Che made a significant contribution by analyzing, studying, and interpreting our revolution with new, fresh, and original views, endowing it with thoughts and actions that enrich it.

The concept of the new man — the effort to make a reality of that concept — is already part of the impressive work of the revolution. It can be seen in the doctors, teachers, vanguard workers, and ordinary combatants; in the students, scientists, professionals, and intellectuals who are inspired by Che's work and emulate him daily with great efforts of sacrifice and heroism. They are the ones who believe that Che is still living among us — and they are right.

There is an idea that is as simple as it is impossible for the capitalist system to achieve — an idea that Cuban socialism has placed at its very center. That idea, consistent with what Martí taught us, is: "Preserve human dignity and transform it into the first law of society."

It gives us pride that today Cuba has a new people. In this society new men and women are being forged, not as an unrealizable ideal or something belonging exclusively to a distant future, but as an attainable ideal through revolutionary practice that transforms social consciousness.

Revolutionary unity has been a decisive factor in our ability to get to where we are today. Thanks to being united around their party and their historic leaders, the Cuban people have been able to confront, with admirable resistance, the conditions imposed by the disappearance of European socialism and the USSR, exacerbated by the most criminal and genocidal blockade.

Our unity is based on a political system with democratic principles of a genuinely socialist character, such as the consultation with our civil society and its organizations on the most important political, social, economic, and legal decisions of the state. This includes popular participation in government at all levels, and the election of candidates who are representatives of the people to the various levels of People's Power. Our party does not propose, elect, or remove those who are chosen. That is the job of the people. One example of this democracy is the elections held last Sunday, October 19, 1997, and their results.[11] Through these elections the people have given a clear

11. Elections to the municipal assemblies of People's Power, Cuba's local government bodies, were held October 19, with a second round October 26 in districts where no candidate received more than 50 percent of the vote. Municipal elections are held every two and a half years. A higher percentage of Cubans voted than in the previous municipal elections held in April 1995, and the percentage of blank or spoiled ballots was lower.

vote of support to our revolution, because the people are the central ingredient of this revolution.

Democracy is another element that defines and gives power to our socialism. Nothing explains better the essence of the principles on which our democracy is based than the ideas expressed by Fidel when he affirmed: "Democracy for me means that government, first of all, is intimately linked to the people, it emerges from the people, has the support of the people, and it is dedicated totally to work and struggle for the people and for the people's interests. Democracy to me implies defending all the rights of the citizens, among them the right to independence, liberty, national dignity, and honor. Democracy to me means fraternity among all, real equality among all, equal opportunities for all, for every human being who is born, for every intellect that exists."

Our enemies try to ignore this concept embodied in the Cuban revolution. At the same time, they want to impose on us the conventional and worn-out schemes of "representative democracy," which point to nothing more than a return to capitalism.

In search for a solution to the present crisis

Dear compañeros:

The political scene in many countries of the world is marked by executive, legislative, and repressive institutions that are discredited. It is marked by an increase in contradictions within parties and political currents, leading to their fragmentation. There is a growing mistrust in the electoral systems and processes, as well as an accelerated exhaustion of recently elected governments and an increase in abstentionism. There is a proliferation of corruption-related scandals. There is increased production of and trafficking in drugs. There is a worsening situation of crime and institutionalized violence, as well as the marginalization of broad social layers. There is the spread of demagogy as a means to capitalize on the frustration and desperation in the population. These are only some of the phenomena that lead to what has been called a "crisis of governability." This crisis is reflected in the rise of social and popular movements, as well as the unprecedented increase in opposition to corruption and fraud, in many cases without leadership from any political party.

Expressing the ruling elites' concern that the situation will worsen, initiatives proliferate with the goal of designing a model of social control able to neutralize the effects of the social and economic crisis. Some of these seek to maintain the neoliberal pattern of accumulation, while others try to find alternatives to that position within the capitalist system.

Increasingly, the transfer of sovereignty and decision making toward the centers of world power and their transnational bodies is creating a vacuum of power in the underdeveloped nation-states, and many others that are partially developed. Politics and its institutions are reduced to a largely homogenous pattern that increasingly eradicates the political identity of parties, while many organizations of the left feel constrained to work within "variables" and "norms" that permit only irrelevant differences with the framework established by capitalism.

State power, one of the objectives for which revolutionary struggles are fought, begins to be undervalued. That is why it is a priority to reassess the question of the struggle for power, as well as to assess the instruments and forms of political participation by the left in society. Revolutionary struggles in today's world will inevitably have an internationalist component, and change will be impossible without confronting the groups and institutions toward which decision making is being shifted today.

At the same time, the transition to intensive production, the concentration and contraction of capital, with a growing expulsion of wage labor and the social fragmentation and cultural and political segmentation brought about by the current process of changes in capitalism — all this is producing profound transformations in the social and class composition of our societies. These factors are changing the composition of the popular classes and social groups. They are altering some of the political arenas of the left, as well as its patterns of political work. There has not been an expansion of the regularly employed working class, but instead a growing process of people being pushed out of the workforce, frequently resulting in the creation of casual and marginal workers.

The progressive parties, like other political and economic institutions, are vulnerable to the effects of the system of international relations that is being imposed. This makes more complex the conditions necessary for succeeding in the political, economic, and social transformation that is essential for overcoming dependence and underdevelopment.

The left confronts today a qualitatively different situation, the product of the disappearance of so-called "actually existing socialism," the transformations of world capitalism, and changes taking place within the societies in which struggles unfold.

O̶NE OF THE MOST important questions in present-day struggles of the left is the *policy of alliances*, which is a condition for formulating responses to neoliberalism. It is up to each party and organization, however, to assess the bases for such alliances in their own countries and regions, depending on the characteristics and peculiarities of their realities.

In our opinion, an agreement of revolutionary forces with other sectors around short-, medium-, or long-term objectives should be a process in which the parties present their essential interests with crystal clarity. We don't consider it acceptable to renounce socialism or revolutionary positions in order to gain acceptance. Thus, what is primary and most important is to define the objectives and basis on which you can function in an alliance.

Unlike the never-ending "deals" of the traditional parties, an alliance in which revolutionary organizations participate should not be reduced to negotiations among national elites, leaders, and executives. It serves no purpose to propose agreements that weaken us, or help undermine the internal unity and political stability of the organizations. The support and understanding of the rank and file is essential for success; the incorporation of their views and interests is necessary and possible. There will be no solid alliances without the agreement and participation of popular sectors. The essence of any alliance that claims to have a left perspective is to build it from, by, and for the ranks.

It is only logical that reaching agreements necessarily implies negotiation, in which each party makes concessions on some points and prevails on others. But for revolutionaries, the one thing that is not negotiable is principles.

The course of giving in and giving up does not seem to be the right one, nor the one that would enable us to be respected in the framework of initiatives that might arise. Favoring alliances that rest on adaptation contributes to demobilization, endangering the results achieved and the very existence of revolutionary organizations. No political offer, no alliance is more important than conviction and firmness of principles.

If our immediate objective is to defeat neoliberalism, it is necessary to strive to incorporate or influence all those who oppose that model, not just some of them. Alliances among some groups, in order to exclude others heading in the same direction, simply reproduce in a different fashion the old sectarian traditions that render us so vulnerable in the face of imperialist domination.

The developing conflicts and contradictions of the system itself are engendering a great diversity of new social layers, while reshaping others. The system excludes them all, creating conditions and opportunities for a broad policy of alliances. This includes environmentalists and peasants, the landless and the roofless, fighters for health and social welfare, individuals organized against gender, religious, racial, and ethnic discrimination — in short, those who are not part of the prevailing political maneuvering. It would also be important to include a wide range of marginalized, excluded, and generally unorganized sectors, among whom lies the possibility and the necessity of creating a new, liberating universalism.

On the other hand, it should be noted that the unfolding of the system's contradictions, especially the tendency to concentrate and exclude, is changing the outlook of some sectors. Views that corresponded to the role of these social layers in earlier capitalist formations no longer do so. This is the case with part of the middle classes — the small and medium-sized businessmen, for whom the growing polarization closes off space to achieve their aspirations. It also includes groups of patriotic and nationalist military officers, as well as other affected layers, whom we would have to include in any proposal opposing neoliberalism.

At the Fourth Meeting of the São Paulo Forum, Comrade Fidel stated, "Defeating neoliberalism would create hope for the future, it would mean safeguarding the conditions to continue advancing, because the barrier to our progress will be capitalism and there will be no human progress if humanity does not set itself the task of transcending the frontiers of capitalism. This is a task for another time, but I wouldn't say it is the task of other generations. . . ." At the same time he stressed that defeating neoliberalism requires level-headedness and wisdom, because only "without extremism of any sort, in a wide-ranging manner, talking about uniting forces, making alliances which allow us to win the battle against today's enemy, neoliberalism, which is going to continue to create dreadful, unbearable social conditions," will it be possible to obtain victory.[12]

Companeras and companeros:

Just a few days ago we concluded the Fifth Congress of our party. It was a process started months ago at the rank-and-file level, in which the party leadership's basic theses were analyzed

---

12. Castro's speech of July 24, 1993, is published in its entirety in *Granma International*, August 18, 1993.

not just by party members, but by all our people. It has also been an example of democracy in our party, whose ranks nominated tens of thousands of candidates to be delegates to the congress, as well as nominees for the Central Committee.

The Congress concluded that the course adopted at the time of the Fourth Congress in 1991 was correct, that the revolution has known how to resist, that we are defending socialism and our independence, that we are preparing to conquer the economic development of socialism.

As we said in our congress, imperialist ideas are discredited and will not be able to win over anyone. The world they want to impose on us is not viable, it has no future. They can buy, they can corrupt, but they cannot win the hearts and minds of the peoples.

Despite the enormous difficulties our country is going through, in face of the economic war that U.S. imperialism has imposed on us and reinforces every day, we have confirmed that our economic recovery is on the march and is irreversible.

Confronted with the ideological offensive unleashed by capitalism — the idea that state participation in the economy must end — Cuban communists concluded that the most revolutionary thing we can do is to demonstrate that a socialist enterprise can function with maximum efficiency.

As our first secretary, Comrade Fidel, put it, the key task of the party in the coming years is to turn inefficiency into the exception, not the rule. Cuban communists proclaim that we will work to demonstrate in life, in reality, that socialism — with social justice as an inseparable element of its principles — equals efficiency. We will show that socialist society is the only viable option for peoples seeking genuine happiness.

Thank you very much.

Celebrating the Homecoming of Ernesto Che Guevara's Reinforcement Brigade to Cuba

ARTICLES FROM THE 30TH ANNIVERSARY CELEBRATION OF THE COMBAT WAGED IN BOLIVIA BY CHE AND HIS COMRADES

Reports on:
- International conference in Havana on "Socialism on the threshold of the 21st century"
- Twelve-part series "Che Guevara and the Cuban revolution"; articles and interviews by fellow revolutionists who knew and worked with Che
- Fifth congress of Communist Party of Cuba
- Cuban generals speak out

In English and Spanish $8.00

Pathfinder Was Born with the October Revolution

THREE REPORTS BY MARY-ALICE WATERS

- Transforming Pathfinder production and ourselves as we respond to growing workers' resistance (Toronto, April 1998)
- Pathfinder was born with the October Revolution (Havana, February 1998)
- Extending the arsenal of communist propaganda and reconquering the apparatus through revolutionary centralism (the "turtle" report, adopted by Socialist Workers Party convention, Chicago, June 1991)

An Education for Socialists booklet. $8.00

Available from Pathfinder Press, 410 West St., New York, NY 10014.

BASIC WORKS OF MARXISM

The Communist Manifesto
KARL MARX, FREDERICK ENGELS
Founding document of the modern working-class movement, published in 1848. Explains why communism is derived not from preconceived principles but from facts and proletarian movements springing from the actual class struggle. $3.95 Also in Spanish.

Imperialism: The Highest Stage of Capitalism
V.I. LENIN
"I trust that this pamphlet will help the reader to understand the fundamental economic question, that of the economic essence of imperialism," Lenin wrote in 1917. "For unless this is studied, it will be impossible to understand and appraise modern war and modern politics." $3.95

Collected Works of Karl Marx and Frederick Engels
The writings of the founders of the modern revolutionary working-class movement. Vols. 1–47 of 50-volume set are now available. Each volume contains notes and index. Progress Publishers, cloth only. Set (47 vols.), $1,185. Write or call for prices of individual volumes.

Collected Works of V.I. Lenin
The writings of the central leader of the Bolshevik Party, the October 1917 Russian revolution, the young Soviet workers and peasants republic, and the early Communist International. 45-volume set, plus 2-volume index. $500

THE SOCIALIST WORKERS PARTY IN WORLD WAR II
WRITINGS AND SPEECHES, 1940–43
James P. Cannon

Preparing communist workers in the United States to stand against the patriotic wave inside the workers movement supporting the imperialist slaughter and to campaign against wartime censorship, repression, and antiunion assaults. $22.95

THE JEWISH QUESTION
A MARXIST INTERPRETATION
Abram Leon

Traces the historical rationalizations of anti-Semitism to the fact that Jews, prior to the rise of industrial capitalism, were forced to become a "people-class" of merchants and moneylenders. Explains why the propertied rulers incite renewed Jew hatred today. $17.95

FASCISM: WHAT IT IS AND HOW TO FIGHT IT
Leon Trotsky

Writing in the heat of struggle against the rising fascist movement in Europe in the 1930s, Russian communist leader Leon Trotsky examines the origins and nature of fascism and advances, for the first time, a working-class strategy to combat and defeat it. $3.00

WHAT IS AMERICAN FASCISM?
James P. Cannon and Joseph Hansen

Analyzing examples earlier in the 20th century—Father Charles Coughlin, Jersey City mayor Frank Hague, and Sen. Joseph McCarthy—this collection looks at the features distinguishing fascist movements and demagogues in the U.S. from the 1930s to today. $8.00

WOMEN'S LIBERATION & SOCIALISM

Cosmetics, Fashions, and the Exploitation of Women

JOSEPH HANSEN, EVELYN REED, AND MARY-ALICE WATERS

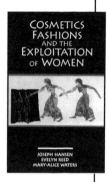

How big business promotes cosmetics to generate profits and perpetuate the inferior status of women. How the entry of millions of women into the workforce during and after World War II laid the basis for advances women have won through struggle over the last three decades. $12.95

Feminism and the Marxist Movement

MARY-ALICE WATERS

Since the founding of the modern workers movement 150 years ago, Marxists have championed the struggle for women's rights and explained the economic roots in class society of women's oppression. $3.00

Sexism and Science

EVELYN REED

Are human beings innately aggressive? Does biology condemn women to remain the "second sex"? Taking up such biases cloaked as the findings of science, Reed explains that the disciplines closest to human life—anthropology, biology, and sociology—are permeated with rationalizations for the oppression of women and the maintenance of the established capitalist order. $15.95

Communist Continuity and the Fight for Women's Liberation

DOCUMENTS OF THE SOCIALIST WORKERS PARTY 1971–86

How did the oppression of women begin? Who benefits? What social forces have the power to end women's second-class status? 3 volumes, edited with preface by Mary-Alice Waters. $30.00

U.S. IMPERIALISM
HAS LOST
THE COLD WAR

U.S. IMPERIALISM
HAS LOST THE COLD WAR

by Jack Barnes

The resolution "U.S. Imperialism Has Lost the Cold War" was discussed and adopted by delegates to the 35th national convention of the Socialist Workers Party in the United States, August 8-12, 1990. It was presented to convention delegates on behalf of the National Committee by SWP national secretary Jack Barnes, the principal drafter of the resolution. The second component of the resolution, "The Communist Strategy of Party Building Today," was presented by its drafter, Mary-Alice Waters, as part of her report on part IV of "U.S. Imperialism Has Lost the Cold War."

Coal miners on strike against Pittston Co. join in solidarity with striking Eastern Airlines workers at January 15, 1990, Martin Luther King Day celebration in Miami, Florida. "These fights have set an example for other unionists by putting up a banner of resistance, of the use of union power, of reaching out for unity and solidarity."

PART I

LABOR MOVEMENT REMAINS
AT CENTER STAGE OF U.S. POLITICS

A. Rank-and-file leadership spreads

1. A more than ten-year offensive by the employers has failed to drive the labor movement from the center stage of politics in the United States.

    a) The labor movement remains where it has been since the second half of the 1970s when it fought its way back to center stage, from which it had been driven nearly three decades earlier.

    b) Two developments signaled this shift for the working-class movement in the United States:

        (1) the 1977–78 coal strike by the United Mine Workers of America (UMWA), preceded by women breaking through into underground mining, and followed by the union's deepening involvement in the antinuclear, coal safe-energy movement[1]; and

---

1. In the longest nationwide coal strike in U.S. history, more than 180,000 miners in twenty-two states went out on strike for 110 days beginning December 6, 1977. UMWA miners were able to block efforts to cripple the union being pressed by the coal bosses and backed by the Democratic administration of James Carter.

In the early 1970s women broke down the barriers to being hired in the mines. In 1973 only 1 woman was hired out of 6,714 newly employed coal miners, but by 1979 the figure reached 555 women out of 4,856 hired (11.4 percent). With the subsequent reduction of the coal mining workforce, women have been laid off in disproportionate numbers; the percentage of women in the mines has declined from its high point of 4 percent in the late 1980s to 1 percent in 1996.

On March 28, 1981 — the second anniversary of the Three Mile Island nuclear reactor accident in Pennsylvania — some 15,000 unionists and

(2) the movement for democracy in the United Steelworkers of America (USWA) built around the Steelworkers Fight Back union election campaign.[2]

2. In the wake of the 1981–82 recession, labor's retreat under the blows of the employers' offensive that began at the end of the 1970s turned into an all-out rout of the unions.

a) The union officialdom's capitulation to the bosses turned into workers running away from a fight.

b) The membership went along with, and often voted for, not only cuts in wages, concessions on job safety, and speedup, but also multitiered wage scales and various outsourcing (subcontracting) and temporary-worker schemes that qualitatively deepened divisions in the work force and among union members.

c) Despite these heavy blows dealt to labor and the working class by the employers' offensive, and the resultant further weakening of the unions, the capitalists

(1) have not broken workers' resistance; and

(2) have not improved their competitive position vis-à-vis other capitalists sufficiently to be able to buy off a large layer of the working class.

3. The recent attempts by capitalists — especially those in weak competitive positions in their industries (Lorenzo/Eastern Airlines, Douglas/Pittston Coal, Currey/Greyhound bus lines) — to

---

other opponents of nuclear power marched in a labor-sponsored demonstration in Harrisburg, the state capital. The action was called by an October 1980 conference of the Labor Committee for Safe Energy and Full Employment, held in Pittsburgh. The United Mine Workers union took the lead in organizing that conference, which was attended by nearly 1,000 union members and others.

2. Steelworkers Fight Back was launched in 1975 under the leadership of United Steelworkers District 31 president Ed Sadlowski to oust the entrenched regime of USWA president I.W. Abel. A central issue in the campaign was the fight to extend union democracy, including the right of the membership to vote on contracts. The election was held February 8, 1977. According to the official results, Sadlowski received some 43 percent of the vote.

press the union movement harder and deepen the union-busting pattern of the early 1980s is meeting growing resistance.[3]

a) This resistance was first signaled, during the rout itself, by the decision of the coal operators to back off from another fight with the UMWA when the national contract expired in 1984 and to offer the miners a contract with no major takebacks and with wage increases.

(1) At that point, the UMWA alone among major industrial unions had been able to hold off concessions of the kind whose spreading cumulative effects marked the rout.

(2) This was a product of the fact that in the late 1960s and early 1970s the UMWA ranks had begun to confront the decline and degeneration of their union. Through a powerful movement for rank-and-file democracy, they confronted the entrenched, corrupt bureaucracy and carved out space for union democracy, using it to organize union power against the coal operators. On that basis they waged successful strike battles in 1977–78 and 1981.[4]

---

3. For more on the Eastern, Pittston, and Greyhound strikes and other labor struggles discussed in this section of the resolution, see *The Eastern Airlines Strike: Accomplishments of the Rank-and-File Machinists and Gains for the Labor Movement* by Ernie Mailhot, Judy Stranahan, and Jack Barnes (Pathfinder, 1991). Frank Lorenzo, Paul Douglas, and Fred Currey were the chief executive officers, respectively, of Eastern, Pittston, and Greyhound.

4. In the late 1960s UMWA coal miners began mobilizing in response to the Farmington, West Virginia, mine disaster, in which 78 workers were killed, and for government-funded health and disability benefits for victims of black lung disease, caused by inhalation of coal dust. In 1969 miners in southern West Virginia walked off the job to demand black lung protection, and 3,000 miners marched on the state capitol in Charleston. In December of that year Jock Yablonski, a supporter of these struggles challenging UMWA president Tony Boyle for the union presidency, was assassinated. In 1972 Boyle was defeated by the Miners for Democracy slate headed by Arnold Miller. Boyle was subsequently convicted and imprisoned for his role in the murders of Yablonski and his wife and daughter.

(3) Only this successful battle by the ranks to win enough union democracy to deploy union power against the mine owners explains the relative strength and combativity of the UMWA today. For other unions, that crossroads still lies ahead.

b) In late 1985 United Food and Commercial Workers (UFCW) members began to fight back against the intensifying speedup, unmatched brutalization, and second- and third-round wage cuts demanded by the meatpacking bosses.

(1) These battles became a focus of nationwide publicity with the 1985–86 Hormel strike in Minnesota, which had an impact on union fighters across North America.[5]

(2) A wave of strikes rolled across Midwest packinghouses in late 1986 and the first half of 1987, while during the same period striking cannery workers in Watsonville, California, were winning an important victory.

(3) In 1987–88 paperworkers in several regions of the United States waged a hard-fought sixteen-month strike; UMWA miners in western coal conducted a series of strikes, winning several of them; and the coal bosses again recoiled from a head-on fight with the UMWA for major concessions when the national contract came up in 1988.

(4) Although seldom able to hold off takeback contracts or prevent recruitment of permanent scab replacements, this resistance, beginning with the packinghouse battles in 1985–86, marked a break in the pattern of the rout.

c) In spring 1989 something new happened: machinists, ramp workers, and cleaners at Eastern Airlines, organized by the International Association of Machinists (IAM),

---

5. See *The 1985–86 Hormel Meat-Packers Strike in Austin, Minnesota* by Fred Halstead (Pathfinder, 1986).

launched the first *sustained nationwide strike* in the decade that was not rapidly checked if not defeated by the bosses.

d) Moreover, the Eastern battle quickly *overlapped and interlinked* with a new stage in resistance by the ranks of the UMWA.

  (1) The fight by the Pittston miners was embraced by the ranks of the entire union, who launched a wave of solidarity strikes in mid-1989 in an attempt to ensure that Pittston workers were not isolated and beaten in the same way that UMWA strikers had been defeated by the A.T. Massey company in 1985.[6]

  (2) The Pittston strike won growing nationwide support from Eastern strikers and other workers, as well as from miners and trade unionists from around the world, many of whom visited Camp Solidarity, the union's strike center in southwest Virginia.

  (3) The miners' fight, which forced Pittston Coal to settle in early 1990, set back the effort by the bosses to break the UMWA's resistance and turn the Massey defeat into a new pattern in the coalfields.[7]

  (4) The mutual solidarity of these ongoing fights by IAM and UMWA members against Eastern and Pittston, together with several other hard-fought strikes, served to reinforce each of the battles and stiffened the re-

---

6. The A.T. Massey Coal Company refused to sign the 1984 agreement between the UMWA and the Bituminous Coal Operators Association. In 1984–85 a strike by UMWA-organized miners against the contract imposed by the company was defeated and the union was broken in Massey mines.

7. In February 1990, the Pittston Coal Group signed a new contract with the UMWA covering more than 1,900 miners in Virginia, West Virginia, and Kentucky. Over the course of the eleven-month strike, some 40,000 UMWA members throughout the Eastern coalfields walked out in support of the action and more than 50,000 supporters visited Camp Solidarity.

sistance of other workers to employer attacks.

e) The labor battles that have broken out in 1989–90 have come largely in industries where

   (1) devastating conditions — second and third rounds of givebacks, major pressures on job safety, slashing of health coverage — push the workers to the wall;

   (2) employers in particularly weak competitive positions in their industries are driven to impose terms that the labor officialdom feels cannot be sold to the already hard-pressed ranks; and

   (3) there is a large element of lockout to the bosses' stance, threatening the existence of the union itself as the employers press their goal of hiring scabs as permanent replacement workers.

f) These are defensive battles by workers who have decided there is nothing left for them to do but fight. Their example has a nationwide impact.

   (1) These are desperate battles, in which workers begin with less chance of winning than relatively better-positioned workers striking for improved contract terms (e.g., the Eastern strike in comparison to the Boeing strike).[8]

   (2) For these reasons, the very act of fighting rapidly began to pose broader stakes for millions of other working people.

      (a) Growing layers of strikers in these battles said: "We're not just fighting for ourselves but for the entire labor movement."

      (b) Those who extended solidarity, whether from un-

---

8. Some 58,000 IAM members employed by Boeing at plants in Washington, Oregon, and Kansas went on strike in October 1989, at a time when the company enjoyed an enormous backlog of orders. After 48 days of the strike, Boeing signed an agreement for a 10 percent wage increase over three years, an additional 19 percent in annual bonuses, improved cost-of-living increases, and a reduction in forced overtime.

ions or elsewhere, increasingly said: "Your fight is a fight for all of us."

   (c) The example set for the ranks of other unions encourages them to go beyond solidarity to say: "Next time, we'll fight like you."

g) The Eastern strike in particular indicated how the paralysis of the union bureaucracy in face of the need to mobilize union power, even if only as a bargaining chip in response to employer intransigence, can open space for the ranks to press forward and for rank-and-file leadership to establish itself.

   (1) The IAM officialdom, like other bureaucracies in similar positions, resorted to tough-talking demagogy in the initial week or so of the strike. But their bluster collapsed as the government obtained injunctions against projected railroad solidarity actions and as Lorenzo called their bluff by entering the protection of bankruptcy court and, for all practical purposes, broke off negotiations.

     (a) Under such conditions, the officialdom had no clothes; it is structured for negotiations punctuated by threats, not for sustained combat.

     (b) The top levels of the bureaucracy are too distant from the ranks to lead combat, even as a means of pressure to advance their own limited ends. The big pockets of rot and corruption among local officials make a very large majority of them unfit for battle as well.

     (c) After several weeks of the strike, in order to advance their fight the ranks of the IAM pressed forward into this leadership vacuum.

   (2) Over time, a rank-and-file leadership was tested and began to be structured.

     (a) The initiatives of this rank-and-file leadership, including a few more struggle-minded local union officials, gave the membership a little taste of *us-*

ing union power and prevented the dissipation of the strikers' energy and determination.

(b) They also kept pressure on the officialdom to continue putting union resources into the fight and sanctioning requests for solidarity from the rest of the labor movement.

(3) The fact that the current union structures are unsuited to combat, even for limited battles to serve the bureaucracy's own ends, is a permanent objective problem that the officials cannot fundamentally alter.

(a) This explains why, as class-struggle pressure mounts, the bureaucracy must make use of more radicals and draw young fighters into the union apparatus in order to maintain control, thus diverting rank-and-file leaders from concentrating energy on the tactics that can most effectively advance the fight.

(b) At the same time, vanguard fighters, including communists, have had to contend more and more with efforts by antilabor "left" organizations such as the Workers League to disrupt their struggles and narrow the space for rank-and-file leadership to emerge.[9]

h) While the Eastern fight and stage of the miners' resistance represented by the Pittston battle have not charted a new strategic course for the labor movement, they have demonstrated how the ranks can find ways to overrun the

---

9. Between 1975 and 1995 the antilabor group called the Workers League (renamed the Socialist Equality Party in 1996) carried out a campaign of harassment and disruption targeting the Socialist Workers Party and numerous labor actions, including unionists involved in the Eastern and Pittston strikes, the 1987–88 strike against International Paper, and the 1985–86 Hormel packinghouse workers strike. See *A New Probe by the Workers League against the Communist Movement: Record of an Antilabor Outfit, from the Gelfand Harassment Case to the Campaign against Mark Curtis* (Pathfinder, 1995).

boundaries of the officialdom's trade union strategy and carve out tactical space to use union power to fight the bosses.

(1) These battles have unfolded before the minimal conditions have yet been met to organize the nucleus of a class-struggle left wing in the labor movement, in other words

   (a) before the unions are united enough to win substantial numbers of strikes;

   (b) before such fights are generalized throughout other industries and unions;

   (c) before other social and political struggles are of substantial enough size and scope to give an added impulse to union battles; and

   (d) prior to a broader radicalization that can help further transform the social and political consciousness of the rank-and-file leadership as they go through combat experiences.

(2) The ripening of these conditions will open the road for fighting workers to bust up the current rotten union structures that block them and chart an alternative strategic course of organizing the unions as a fighting social movement.

i) In the course of the current battles, strikers have been tested by their capacity to fight effectively within the narrow tactical limits they confront. Rank-and-file leaders emerged defined by determination, tactical savvy, consistency, and ability to reach out and broaden unity and solidarity.

(1) The rank-and-file leaders are recognized by other fighters on the basis of their ability over the course of the strike

   (a) to expand the effective tactical limits they originally inherited; and

   (b) to press toward greater use of union power while sidestepping fights with the officialdom that cannot be won under current conditions without the ranks losing more than could be gained.

(2) This way of functioning by the rank-and-file leadership is the *opposite* of oppositional groupings in the unions (or oppositional publications outside the unions) that direct their fire against selected union officeholders and seek to replace them in union posts, instead of organizing the ranks to use effective tactics that can bring union power to bear.

(3) Rank-and-file IAM leaders in the Eastern fight charted a course to maximize unity among striking employees.

   (a) They forged an alliance between the IAM strikers and the flight attendants organized by the Transport Workers Union (TWU) and pilots of the Air Line Pilots Association (ALPA), who walked out for the first several months of the strike.

   (b) The course of the rank-and-file leaders headed *away from* the orientation promoted by the officialdom of relying on the bankruptcy court, buyout schemes, and management shuffles to save "our" airline, and *toward* mobilizing the IAM ranks and through them reaching out for broader labor solidarity to strengthen *our* union.

   (c) As a result, striking IAM members were not diverted from their course by the first big breach in unity, the ALPA-led defection by the pilots and flight attendants, which culminated in November 1989. This was the biggest test in the strike. Passing it demonstrated a class consciousness and confidence on the part of the IAM strike militants and brought the battle to bring down Lorenzo — and to show that "Lorenzoism" cannot succeed — to a new and more determined stage in December 1989–January 1990.

(4) The analysis and course of action adopted by the SWP National Committee from the outset of the strike in

the spring of 1989 has converged in practice with conclusions drawn by growing layers of rank-and-file leaders from their experience in the fight.

(a) It was necessary to keep the fire focused on Lorenzo as chief executive officer of Eastern. "Stop Lorenzo" was not a slogan that could or should be bypassed. Only *through* "Stop Lorenzo" could the ranks wage the fight against Lorenzoism.

(b) The role of the bankruptcy court is to prevent the dissipation of social capital. As more and more rank-and-file leaders came to recognize, the court would act as necessary to preserve the capital represented by Eastern Airlines. It would protect Lorenzo against the unions and Eastern's creditors until the results of his proposed course threatened the very existence of hunks of social capital. Reliance on action by the judge or courts, to whom Lorenzo's actions could be appealed, offered no way forward for the fight to use union power.

(c) Strikers had to be prepared for the growing probability that the ALPA strike-support action would break prior to Lorenzo. Growing numbers in the IAM ranks came to see this as inevitable based on their experience with the pilots and ALPA officials as the battle stretched out.

(d) The strikers had to build their strength and momentum by reinforcing airline workers' unity *and* reaching beyond it, expanding solidarity in the broader union movement. They especially had to win support from other IAM members who were being pressed to perform struck work, as well as workers engaged in battles, such as the Pittston miners and other UMWA members. They had to press beyond the borders of the United States to receptive workers around the world.

(e) By pressing along this course in a determined way — "doing more of the same" — it would be possible to strengthen the rank-and-file fighters of the IAM, continue using union power to nail Lorenzo, and, as has now happened, bring the fight to a new, as yet unresolved, level. It would be possible to face off Lorenzoism with its slave-labor contracts and scab havens, in order to prepare for the most difficult battle — to maintain the union and the spirit of its fighting cadres, not Eastern Airlines with or without Lorenzo.

j) By waging hard-fought battles, the Eastern, Pittston, and other workers (e.g., the Communications Workers of America strike against NYNEX telephone, the District 1199 hospital workers strike in New York) have already placed new limits on the Lorenzo pattern of repeated givebacks and "the scabs all stay and you're out of a job" union busting (Continental Airlines, International Paper, etc.). The attempt by Pittston CEO Douglas to generalize the Massey pattern in the coalfields has been pushed back.

(1) These fights have set an example for other unionists by putting up a banner of resistance, of the use of union power, of reaching out for unity and solidarity.

(a) They have blazed a trail to be emulated by other workers of not cowing before the growing refrain of the bosses (not always a bluff): "Either deal on my terms or the company goes under. Take it or leave it."

(b) The workers at Eastern and Pittston fought anyway, and the entire union movement is being strengthened as a result.

(2) Under these conditions, the outcome of strikes is measured by how much more the workers win by *fighting*, not by how much the bureaucracy's misleadership blocks them from achieving (e.g., Pittston).

(a) The stronger the fight, the more the gap between what was won and what could have been won is narrowed.

(b) The strike registers an advance if it was fought in such a way as to encourage other workers and trade unionists to emulate the fight.[10]

B. Response of the labor bureaucracy to the continuing employer offensive

1. The class-collaborationist course of the AFL-CIO officialdom has deepened, focusing in more than ever on how to keep "our" company and "our" industry "well managed" and profitable.

a) Increasingly the policies pursued by the bureaucracy have been aimed at becoming junior partners of the bosses, somehow getting a share in the prerogatives of capital.

b) This takes the form of schemes hatched by the officialdom for the unions themselves to sink pension funds and other resources of the membership into stocks and bonds, to negotiate Employee Stock Ownership Programs, and to become principals in buyouts of the company.

c) The bureaucracy increasingly seeks ways to ensure that it has a say over selecting "good" management, and that union officials be given spots on boards of directors and creditors' committees.

---

10. The twenty-two-month-long strike by Machinists against Eastern Airlines ended in January 1991 when the company went out of business, some eight months after this resolution was published. "Finally, after almost two years on the picket line, the strikers at Eastern forced the once-mighty airline to admit defeat, close its doors, and put its properties on the auction block," explained the authors of Pathfinder's *The Eastern Airlines Strike* in their preface to the book. "Thanks to the tenacity of the Eastern strikers, union busting has been dealt a blow. The Machinists' struggle sent a message to other working people that it is better to stand up and fight for your rights than to passively accept the bosses' dictates."

d) A greater percentage than ever of union treasuries is being spent not only on lawyers and consultants, but for the "services" of financial advisers, investment banking counselors, and takeover specialists. This has become a further drain on union resources, added to the long-standing expenditures on Washington lobbyists and "political action committees" for "friendly" Democratic and Republican candidates.

e) If successful, the officialdom's course imposes on the ranks the risks of holding debt and equity (the logic of which is the union's "interest" in "cost-cutting" concessions, wages and benefits pegged to profits, etc.), while the prerogatives of ownership remain in fact in the hands of capital.

2. This course of ever more deeply identifying the interests of labor with those of capital — of trying to make the union and the board of directors converge — further undermines the use of union power, reinforcing the class-collaborationist policies that have increasingly weakened the labor movement over half a century.

a) Contracts are negotiated with termination dates pushed further and further into the future. Contracts are longer and ever more complicated legal documents that serve as operations manuals for management, rather than a brief, clear guide to workers codifying what they have won at a given point in their ongoing battle with the bosses.

b) The differential in pay and job conditions widens among workers doing the same jobs side by side. This is the result of multitier wage scales and agreements that permit a growing percentage of employees to be part-time and temporary workers with no union protection, or workers with second-class status within the unions.[11]

---

11. Since 1968 the percentage of part-time workers in the U.S. labor force has risen from 14 percent to nearly 20 percent; the median wage of part-time workers was $6.01 in 1994 versus $9.36 for full-time workers. Even more significant has been the growth of so-called temporary work-

c) Instead of using the power of the labor movement to lead a social and political fight for federally funded social programs to meet the health and pension needs of the entire working class, the bureaucracy continues to deepen reliance on negotiating company-by-company plans for which workers are pressed to pay an increasingly greater share.[12]

d) The officialdom continues to subordinate the unions to capitalist, usually Democratic Party, politicians.

(1) As the framework of bourgeois politics shifted to the right in the 1980s, the AFL-CIO bureaucracy's support for its "friends" did not waver.

(2) Despite the labor officialdom's respectful attentions, the Democratic-controlled Senate and House of Representatives pay less heed to the bureaucracy's wish list of labor and social legislation than ever before.

(3) Even in bourgeois terms, the unions have less political clout than any time since the rise of the CIO.

e) The fruit of this evolution is that CIO unions function less like *industrial unions* — even in a limited trade union sense — than ever before in their history.

---

ers, who accounted for more than 10 percent of the expansion in employment in the mid-1990s, up from an average of 4 percent in the 1980s and 2 percent in the 1970s. The goal of the ruling families in expanding "temporary" employment is to hold down wages and speed up production by creating a growing section of the working class that has no union protection and can be hired and fired on a day's notice.

12. According to the U.S. Department of Labor, the percentage of full-time workers employed by large or midsize companies who are covered by employer-sponsored health plans fell from more than 95 percent in 1983 to 80 percent ten years later. Over that same period, the percentage of these workers paying a portion of the costs of these plans directly out of wages rose from 54 percent to 76 percent, and the average monthly amount of such contributions more than doubled. The percentage of retired employees covered by a health plan of a former employer fell from 44 percent in 1988 to 33 percent in 1993. In 1996 some 42 million residents of the United States — 17 percent of the population — had no health insurance of any kind; 48 percent of employed workers with incomes below the official poverty line are uninsured.

(1) Growing acceptance of multitiered wage structures, contract labor with no union protection, and similar schemes heads back in the direction of the inequalities and divisions — and reinforces among a layer of workers the aristocratic, antidemocratic, and reactionary social attitudes — that are characteristic of craft unionism.

(2) Instead of leading campaigns to organize the growing number of nonunion industrial workplaces, the officialdom has carried out mergers with unions in entirely different sectors of the work force, or else sought to incorporate layers of professionals, prison guards, and others outside the working class, thus further undermining the unions' industrial character.[13]

(3) The gap between the character of CIO and AFL unions is narrower today than at any time not only since the industrial unions were forged in battles during the late 1930s, but even since the mid-1950s when the CIO merged with the AFL and the ballyhooed promises of organizing the unorganized were promptly forgotten.

------

13. The United Auto Workers union officialdom, for example, has affiliated the National Writers Union, which describes itself as "the trade union for freelance writers of all genres," as well as the National Organization of Legal Service Workers, an organization of attorneys and others employed by federally funded legal services programs in the United States. The American Federation of State, County and Municipal Employees has organized prison guards into a unit called AFSCME Corrections United, which publishes a pamphlet euphemistically entitled *Managing a Prison Disturbance*. AFSCME president Gerald McEntee and secretary-treasurer William Lucy preface this anti-working-class manual with the following words: "To keep the community safe, and to keep their families clothed, fed and sheltered, [prison] employees work with criminals in a volatile environment, often with inadequate resources. . . . It is our greatest hope that this manual never has to be put to the test, but our experience in Attica, Santa Fe, Lucasville, Southport, Camp Hill and elsewhere has taught us that we must always be prepared."

(4) One example of the consequences of this evolution is the recent success of the company-minded Aircraft Mechanics Fraternal Association (AMFA) in splitting mechanics at Trump Shuttle at La Guardia Airport from the IAM local, and the current raiding operation against the IAM at Northwest, United, and other airlines. AMFA bureaucrats push to their "logical" conclusion the divisions among workers agreed to by union officials over the past decade, seeking to convince "skilled" mechanics that they will be better off outside a union that also includes workers who are "just" ramp workers and cleaners. AMFA arguments cannot be countered effectively by the current elected officials of the IAM.[14]

3. The Trumka leadership of the UMWA is converging with the AFL-CIO officialdom and its tactical course.

a) Trumka is tightening the screws on the UMWA ranks east and west of the Mississippi to alter long-standing class-struggle principles that reflect the use of the union's power to defend miners' interests against the coal operators (e.g., no contract, no work; no victimizations; the unconditional right to read and vote on all contracts; and national, not selective, coal strikes).

b) This course is expressed in and accelerated by Trumka's deepening integration within the top AFL-CIO officialdom.[15]

---

14. In March 1998 AMFA succeeded in a union-busting raid at Alaska Airlines, capturing the votes of a majority of mechanics and cleaners previously organized by the IAM. Ramp workers and customer service workers at Alaska remain in the IAM. AMFA also has company-recognized units of mechanics at Northwest Airlink and United Express, and continues its so-far unsuccessful union-busting operations at Northwest Airlines and United.

15. Richard Trumka was president of the UMWA from 1982 to 1995, when he was elected secretary-treasurer of the AFL-CIO on the slate headed by John Sweeney, formerly president of the Service Employees

    c) While the union is being eroded by the officialdom's course, the gains in the strength of the UMWA from the Miners for Democracy fight and miners' resistance in the 1970s and 1980s have not been reversed.

    d) Most important, the scope, determination, and imagination of the Pittston battle demonstrate that the UMWA membership has a rank-and-file leadership that can be renewed and transformed by new forces in explosive struggles. It remains broad, capable, and experienced enough to block the defeat at A.T. Massey from being generalized. It remains strong enough to push in the other direction, that of using the UMWA's power to strengthen the union vis-à-vis the unremitting offensive of coal boss after coal boss and, in doing so, to reach out and affect the labor movement in the United States and abroad.

C. New space that can be taken, held, and used by the revolutionary workers movement

1. The labor struggles that opened in 1989 with the Eastern and Pittston strikes, throwing up new rank-and-file leaderships and strengthening existing ones, create new responsibilities and opportunities that communists must organize to meet and use to the fullest.

    a) As we participate in these struggles, workers who are communists combine two tasks.

        (1) We function as effective unionists as part of the fighting rank and file and its emerging leadership, gaining combat experience and deepening our integration as blood and bone of the working-class resistance.

        (2) We talk socialism with fellow fighters, expanding the permanent readership and influence of the communist press, books, and pamphlets. We reach out with our election campaigns, forums, and other party activities.

International Union (SEIU). The UMWA reaffiliated with the AFL-CIO in October 1989.

b) These two aspects of communist work in the unions diverge during retreats of the labor movement; they increasingly converge in the course of intensified labor struggles, as opportunities for mass work grow.

    (1) The growing involvement of communist workers as part of a rank-and-file cadre in these struggles — a cadre becoming more and more effective within the relationship of forces that cannot be altered in the short run — pushes us farther away from taking union posts.

        (a) The crippling burden of such posts on militants becomes more obvious, both from the standpoint of advancing union power and building the communist movement.

        (b) At the same time, the officialdom needs more than ever to absorb radicalizing militants into the existing union structures to maintain their credibility and their stability.

    (2) At some point in the evolution and deepening of labor struggles, the cumulative impact of the ranks' growing use of union power can lead to a qualitative leap that begins shattering existing structures of the labor movement (e.g., late 1934 in Teamsters Local 574 in Minneapolis).[16]

        (a) There is no way of knowing beforehand how such a shattering will come about. It will be the product of a combination of factors in the class strug-

---

16. The story of the class-struggle leadership of Teamsters Local 574, and of the 1934 strikes that built an industrial union movement in Minneapolis, is told in *Teamster Rebellion* by Farrell Dobbs (Pathfinder, 1972). Dobbs was a central leader of those battles and of the strikes and organizing drives that grew out of them in the mid- and late 1930s, transforming the Teamsters union throughout much of the Midwest into a fighting social movement. Those later battles are recounted by Dobbs, who subsequently served as national secretary of the Socialist Workers Party, in the books *Teamster Power, Teamster Politics,* and *Teamster Bureaucracy.*

gle — greater numbers and overlapping of labor battles; the involvement of a growing percentage of both union and unorganized workers; reinforcement from struggles outside the unions (fights for Black rights and women's rights, exploding farmers' battles, mounting opposition to U.S. military aggression, etc.) that impel greater numbers of union fighters toward thinking socially and acting politically.

(b) Only in such a situation can opportunities open up for communists to be part of a developing class-struggle left wing in the unions. Motion toward independent labor political action will coincide not only with a big expansion of opportunities for socialist propaganda but also with recruitment of workers to the revolutionary proletarian party.

(3) How well the communist movement will take advantage of the opportunities in those kinds of class battles that lie ahead depends above all on our prior political and organizational preparation — beginning in today's struggles.

2. The Eastern strike is the first labor battle in which cadres of the Socialist Workers Party have been direct participants and also organized a common fight with worker-bolsheviks in our world movement to build international solidarity.

a) Our participation in the Eastern and Pittston battles not only provided special class-struggle experience to comrades who are IAM members at Eastern and UMWA coal miners, it involved the entire cadre of our movement.

(1) The industries and unions in which these battles broke out, and thus the party industrial fractions that were most directly involved, were determined by forces outside our control; this will continue to be the case.

(a) The cumulative results of the experiences and practical work of all ten national fractions since their beginning in the turn provided the indispensable preparation for what we have confronted and accomplished over the past year.[17]

(b) For well over a decade we have fought to place the union resistance in the coal industry, and ourselves as part of that resistance, at the center of conquering the turn; this was key in preparing the party to participate in these union struggles.

(c) Many of the lessons from these experiences are recorded in reports and resolutions in *The Changing Face of U.S. Politics*; the political resolution and the trade union report by Joel Britton adopted by the 1985 party convention; and other reports and articles contained in party bulletins over the past decade.[18]

(d) In the coming battles cadres in each of the fractions, as well as the party as a whole, will gain increasing experience in class combat. The party will be led in these battles by the comrades who are in the midst of the fight, and through these experiences in communist political leadership the party will become more effective in leading all mass work.

(2) Members of every branch and every industrial fraction organized solidarity with the IAM and UMWA

---

17. In the latter half of the 1970s, the Socialist Workers Party carried out a turn to the industrial unions, organizing to get the overwhelming majority of its cadres into jobs where they could carry out political activity among unionized industrial workers. This work is structured through party industrial union fractions. In 1990 the SWP had fractions in ten industrial unions, including the United Mine Workers of America.

18. The 1985 resolution, "The Revolutionary Perspective and Leninist Continuity in the United States," is published in issue no. 4 of *New International*. The 1985 trade union report by Joel Britton can be found in *Background to "The Changing Face of U.S. Politics" and "U.S. Imperialism Has Lost the Cold War"* (Pathfinder, 1998).

struggles through our unions. We brought co-workers, friends of the party, active supporters, Young Socialist Alliance members, and workers from other countries with us to Eastern picket lines, Camp Solidarity, Greyhound strike pickets, and rallies to support striking NYNEX workers, New York City hospital workers, garment workers at the Domsey plant in Brooklyn, and New York *Daily News* workers.

(3) Both the Eastern and Pittston struggles were an acid test of the fact that we face no barriers to sales of subscriptions and single issues of the *Militant* and *Perspectiva Mundial*; to sales of Pathfinder books and pamphlets and copies of *New International* to fighting workers; or to integrating the entire range of campaigns and united-front activity the party is involved in into our work as part of the union movement. Evidence of this fact from the past year includes:

(a) the results of our coalfield subscription teams, and sales of our press, Pathfinder books and pamphlets, and issues of *New International* to striking IAM Eastern workers and to other unionists, on and off the job;

(b) The meetings we helped organize for visiting Cuban revolutionists with Eastern strikers, UMWA coal miners, Watsonville fighters, many other unionists, farm workers, and farmers;[19]

---

19. In April and May, 1990, Pathfinder Press organized a U.S. speaking tour for Cuban economist Carlos Tablada, author of *Che Guevara: Economics and Politics in the Transition to Socialism* (Pathfinder, 1989). Tablada spoke at public meetings and on college campuses in more than twenty-five cities and towns. During the tour, he met with Eastern strike leaders, several of whom spoke on platforms with him. Tablada also met with some twenty Teamsters-organized cannery workers in Watsonville, California; more than forty union textile workers at a factory cafeteria meeting in Lawrence, Massachusetts; and members of several other unions. A few months earlier, in October and November 1989, Cuban painter Aldo

(c) the involvement of Eastern and Pittston fighters in anti-apartheid solidarity actions; and

(d) the growing numbers of workers who from their own experience in struggle understand the stakes both in fighting the Mark Curtis frame-up[20] and turning back Workers League disruption of the working-class movement.

b) Through our participation in these struggles shoulder to shoulder with other fighters, we have brought broader layers of workers around the party as friends who respect us, search out our views, subscribe to the *Militant*, buy Pathfinder literature, and attend various party-sponsored events and meetings or protest actions we are building.

(1) We need to pay careful attention to winning new members from these fighters whenever possible.

(2) We also recognize the objective limits on the pace of

Soler toured the United States, sponsored by the Pathfinder Mural Project. Soler had come to the United States to paint the portraits of Fidel Castro and Karl Marx on the six-story mural on the Pathfinder Building in New York City (pictured on the cover of this issue). Along with making presentations at art galleries, on college campuses, and elsewhere, Soler also spoke to a meeting organized by the United Farm Workers union in Washington State, visited striking coal miners on the picket lines in southern West Virginia, and met with leaders of the farm movement in Iowa.

20. In March 1988 Mark Curtis, a socialist and member of the United Food and Commercial Workers Union working at the Swift packinghouse in Des Moines, Iowa, was framed up on rape and burglary charges. Curtis was arrested and brutally beaten by Des Moines cops only a few hours after he had left a meeting to defend sixteen Mexican workers and one Salvadoran worker at Swift who had been pulled out of the plant during a raid by federal Immigration and Naturalization Service cops and threatened with deportation. In September 1988 Curtis was convicted and sentenced to twenty-five years in prison. He was released from prison on parole in June 1996, seven and a half years later — substantially longer than average in Iowa for individuals convicted on similar charges. For an account of the frame-up and the international campaign to free Curtis, see *A Packinghouse Worker's Fight for Justice: The Mark Curtis Story* by Naomi Craine (Pathfinder, 1996).

recruitment to the communist movement at this stage in the class struggle; we develop friends and supporters in the unions much faster than party members right now. In a period of deepening labor radicalization, the party's influence in the unions will lead to direct recruitment of workers in growing numbers.

(3) We have learned that serious educational work must be organized in collaboration with each new member in order to help her or him acquire a solid foundation and understanding of the historical conquests of the international workers movement.

(4) We have also learned that just as our cadres in the unions are a fraction of the working class and rank-and-file leadership, we are at the same time a fraction of fighting workers who *need* to read the *Militant* each week.

    (a) The *Militant* provides the broader social, political, and world news and analysis that our class needs to see itself as part of the international working class and to advance along our historic line of march. It is the only way to keep up with what is going on in the labor movement, a precondition for effective union work.

    (b) Union work that does not lead to an expanding readership of the *Militant* and *Perspectiva Mundial* among workers, as well as increased circulation of the *New International* and Pathfinder books and pamphlets, is not communist union work.

3. Our experiences in the labor struggles that began in 1989, like other aspects of party activity, have been marked not only by the period of intensifying class battles into which we are heading, but also by the *semisectarian existence* out of which we have been emerging throughout the twelve years of the party's turn to industry. The errors and weaknesses of our participation in the Eastern and Pittston battles are marked by this fact.

  a) In the name of throwing ourselves fully into the latest

stages of the Eastern battle, and without being fully conscious of what we were doing, we committed two ultraleft sectarian errors. These errors reflected a mistaken assessment that our weight within a union battle today can be decisive in determining the outcome, and thus produced strains and distortions on the valuable weight and energies we were exerting.

(1) We retreated from the kind of confident, nationwide communist propaganda effort built around *Militant* subscription work that was both possible and important to advancing the working-class fightback.

    (a) In fact, selling more *Militant* subscriptions to striking IAM members is one indispensable way that the cadres of a communist organization can use political leverage to advance the strike, not a diversion from doing everything we can to help win it.

    (b) Most importantly, the *Militant* provides the weekly axis through which working-class fighters can be led toward communism, and communist workers can remain politically sharp as they read, sell, *and discuss* the paper with co-fighters.

(2) In a number of branches we overcentralized our Eastern strike support work, substituting ad hoc structures for upgrading strike work through the local fractions.

    (a) This hindered us from deploying and retooling the local fractions as the bodies to lead this trade union work (with executive committees responsible for the day-to-day strike support work of the branch as a whole).

    (b) Inaccurate analogies drawn from the Eastern Strike Work Steering Committee's overall nationwide responsibility for our fraction of IAM members and others assigned to strike-support work contributed to this error.

b) Our errors in the Pittston battle were twofold

    (1) First, during the opening months we were slow in fully recognizing and acting on the interconnected character of Eastern and Pittston solidarity work in the labor movement. We tended to view an orientation to the Pittston battle as a diversion from Eastern solidarity work, instead of as a complementary effort that brought more strength to both struggles.

    (2) Second, in early 1990, when Trumka announced a proposed settlement was pending, we correctly responded as fighting workers, from within the strike, knowing that vanguard fighters had been fired, heavy fines had not been lifted, and key contract provisions remained unsettled. But when this talk of a settlement occurred — at a point when we were getting in stride in organizing Eastern strikers and other workers to go to Solidarity City — we engaged in wishful thinking that the membership might vote down the pact and continue the strike. As a result, we were slow in recognizing the character and importance of the victory won by the UMWA ranks.

c) Despite these errors, which we caught and took steps to correct, there are two errors that the SWP *did not* make and, as a party of worker-bolsheviks, could not make.

    (1) We did not make the error of standing aside from the thick of these battles. We recognized their world importance and not only threw ourselves into them but drew in our North American and international movement. We focused on the stakes in these fights, not the limits. We set no preconditions (e.g., union democracy, or shutting down production) to joining in these battles, shouldering large responsibilities in the process, and becoming the indispensable international weekly source of accurate news about them.

    (2) We did not make the error of orienting toward individuals in the union officialdom, rather than keeping

our eyes on the fighting ranks who *are* the union.

d) What a party of worker-bolsheviks was able to accomplish and learn as part of these labor struggles is particularly striking given the fact that

(1) only two of our ten industrial union fractions were directly involved;

(2) none of our UMWA members were on strike against Pittston;

(3) half of our branches are in areas with no direct, week-to-week reflection of these fights; and

(4) we have fewer than a dozen IAM Eastern strikers, and even fewer working UMWA miners.

e) What we have accomplished and are accomplishing shows the kind of communist work that can be done only by organizations that have conquered or are conquering the turn to industry.

(1) It is practical proof of the leverage that our industrial union fractions and their individual members have *as part of* a revolutionary centralist proletarian party.

(2) It shows that sharing responsibilities over time with fighting workers — getting to know, discuss with, and learning to trust each other — increases confidence and openness to collaboration in future struggles.

(3) It demonstrates the indispensability of functioning not just as a national organization, but as part of a world communist movement with its components all involved in working-class life through industrial union fractions.

(4) It shows how a revolutionary workers party draws strength, renews itself, and reenergizes itself as part of any advances of our class; and how that sets us on a course to repoliticize our movement after nearly a decade of objective conditions pushing toward depoliticization.

f) In the course of these battles, the cadre of the SWP has been transformed.

(1) Our accomplishments as part of these fights, like no other experience since the turn to industry, put the party on a new footing for the first wave of bigger class battles in the decade to come — battles that we cannot predict, and that we will not initiate.

(2) But whenever and however the next struggles come, we will move into them more rapidly, more confidently, and more prepared as a fraction of the fighting vanguard of our class — with more worker-bolsheviks pushing ahead, taking initiatives, leading their party deeper into action — because of what we have conquered through being an integral part of the Eastern and Pittston battles of 1989 and 1990.[21]

---

21. Participation in these labor battles was decisive in preparing the cadres of the Socialist Workers Party for the next big test they faced, which began as this resolution was being adopted at the party convention in August 1990. That same month, Washington opened the war drive in the Arab-Persian Gulf that culminated at the beginning of 1991 in the six-week bombardment and 100-hour invasion of Iraq during which at least 150,000 Iraqis were slaughtered. For an assessment of the results of that assault, and of the working-class campaign against imperialism and war carried out by the cadres of the SWP and its co-thinkers in other countries, see "The Opening Guns of World War III: Washington's Assault on Iraq" by Jack Barnes in issue no. 7 of *New International*.

Teamsters rally in Jersey City, New Jersey, during August 1997 United
Parcel Service (UPS) strike, which ended in the first union victory in a
major nationwide labor struggle in the United States for nearly a decade.
"The outcome of a strike registers an advance if it was fought in such a
way as to encourage other workers and trade unionists to emulate the
fight."

Unionists employed by Bremer Vulkan in west German city of Bremen (above) and east German city of Stralsund occupied shipyards in 1996 to stop shutdowns and layoffs. "Steps toward yoking together the imperialist and workers states of Germany set the German bourgeoisie on a more direct collision course with the working class of the East as well as the West, while facilitating united action of the working class in Germany."

PART II

U.S. IMPERIALISM HAS
LOST THE COLD WAR

**A. The offensive of the imperialist ruling classes in the 1980s —
marked by the Reagan/Thatcher course — has ended in failure**

1. During the 1980s the capitalist offensive in the imperialist countries did deal major blows to the labor movement, blows with devastating consequences for broad layers of working people.

2. This offensive, however, accomplished neither of the goals necessary to lay the basis for a sustained period of capitalist expansion and mounting social and political stability, preconditions to reversing the increasing probability of a world economic and social crisis:

    a) The capitalist rulers failed to reverse the tendency of the rate of profit to decline.

    b) They proved unable to break the resistance of the working class to the degree necessary to fundamentally alter the relationship of forces between labor and capital.

3. The imperialist rulers' effort to stabilize a solid middle-class base also failed.

    a) Large numbers of professionals and other petty-bourgeois layers prospered while the capitalist rulers carried out the antilabor offensive.

    b) By the end of the 1980s, however, tax increases, rising interest and mortgage rates, and growing economic instability hit broad sections of the middle class as well as workers and working farmers in the imperialist countries.[1]

---

1. A decade later, interest rates in the United States, the United Kingdom, and most other imperialist countries had fallen sharply from levels in the 1980s, when mortgage rates were often in double digits. The

4. Aggressive "free market" capitalism à la Reagan and Thatcher was given its best shot in the 1980s, but the capitalists could not achieve their goals.

5. The decisive class battles between the imperialist ruling classes and the workers are not behind us but lie ahead.

B. The economic and social contradictions of U.S. imperialism have sharpened

1. The greatest economic danger to imperialism is the growing potential for a breakdown of the international capitalist banking system, and the worldwide depression and social crisis this would inevitably open.

2. The various elements of the world capitalist crisis, any of which alone or in combination could precipitate such an international banking crisis, have worsened over the short period since the adoption in August 1988 of the Socialist Workers Party's political resolution, "What the 1987 Stock Market Crash Foretold."[2]

    a) The weakening of the savings and loan system in the United States has accelerated.

        (1) Washington's bipartisan plans to bail out the failing savings and loan network at an estimated cost of up to $500 billion signals the capitalists' decision to try to socialize the mounting losses of the banking system and stem a broader banking crisis.[3]

        (2) The acute crisis of the savings and loans represents

---

deflationary conditions of world capitalism that developed in the 1990s spurred rising middle-class insecurity, however, as real household income declined for all but the best-off families, rates of failure of small businesses remained at historically high levels, and big capital "downsized" many mid- and lower-level supervisory and managerial personnel.

2. That resolution is printed in issue no. 10 of *New International.*

3. The U.S. Treasury paid out nearly $200 billion between the late 1980s and December 1995, closing failed savings and loan institutions and paying off depositors. An estimated $200 billion more will be paid out to wealthy holders of thirty-year government bonds issued to finance the bailout.

only the tip of the iceberg of the financial strains on insurance companies, large stock and bond brokers, semigovernmental mortgage and loan agencies, and on the stability of real estate and land prices. Most important are the mounting pressures on the commercial banks transmitted through all these agencies.

b) The Third World debt remains massive, with no chance of being paid off by even the strongest semicolonial countries (e.g., Mexico, Brazil, Argentina).

   (1) Whatever minor competitive gains stronger imperialist banks have registered in the last year or so by writing down a portion of their enormous Third World debt, the capitalists are still no closer either to a solution or to a medium-term stabilization of the debtor countries.

   (2) In Argentina — and lately in Brazil — the drastic deflationary policies imposed by capitalist governments in face of the debt crisis are creating the worst depression conditions since the 1930s.

   (3) Some one-fifth of the world's population, and a much larger percentage of those living in semicolonial countries, suffer devastation from diseases such as tuberculosis, malaria, and AIDS, as well as the effects of famine and permanent malnutrition. Social conditions such as these have worsened over the past decade, above all in sub-Saharan Africa but throughout the Third World with few exceptions.[4]

---

4. According to a 1998 World Bank report, nearly one-third of the population of the Third World, plus Eastern Europe and the former USSR, live in poverty, and the percentage "is rising rapidly in Europe and Central Asia, and continuing to rise in Latin America and Sub-Saharan Africa." Only in East Asia has poverty been declining, says the World Bank, "and the financial crisis in East Asia will slow the pace of poverty reduction there." In fact, the Asian financial crisis threatens to turn into an economic depression with devastating results. In the year following erup-

   (4) The probability of a default undermining the entire world financial system is greater than at any time since the explosion of the Third World debt crisis in the early 1980s. Social upheavals in debt-ridden countries against the devastating consequences of austerity and the drain of wealth to imperialist banks are more likely.[5]

c) The debt-driven "junkification" that has marked U.S. capitalism's expansion since the 1981–82 recession is peaking.

   (1) The size of the corporate debt balloon in the United States as a percentage of corporate profits or of the gross national product is greater than at any time since the Great Depression of the 1930s.

   (2) The limits of the sustainability of the paper-driven expansion are evidenced by the slump beginning in 1989 in the market for junk bonds; the declining number and dollar size of leveraged buyouts; and the

---

tion of the crisis in mid-1997, for example, the percentage of the population of Indonesia (the world's fourth-largest country) living beneath the official poverty level jumped from 11.3 percent to 40 percent.

5. At the end of 1996 the Third World foreign debt stood at some $2.25 trillion according to World Bank figures, up from $1.3 trillion in the late 1980s. Total foreign debt in Latin America rose more than 155 percent to $657 billion between 1980 and the end of 1996. Imperialist banks pressed short-term loans on governments and corporations in Asia at an accelerating rate in the 1990s, precipitating the "Asian Crisis" that opened in mid-1997. By the end of 1997 the external debt of South Korea stood at more than $150 billion; Indonesia at $140 billion; Thailand at $95 billion; and the Philippines at $40 billion.

"The size of Japan's bad debts" — estimated at nearly $1 trillion in July 1998 — "may be the most important statistic in the Asian financial crisis," admitted David Sanger in the July 30, 1998, issue of the *New York Times*. "Since the crisis struck, Japanese banks have become so beleaguered that their lending at home and elsewhere in Asia has all but halted. . . . This has contributed to a scarcity of credit that has worsened the recession — in some places the depression — that stretches from South Korea to Indonesia."

continuing instability of the stock, bond, and commodities markets.[6]

(3) Capitalist investment in capacity-expanding plant and equipment continues to stagnate, remaining — as it has throughout the 1980s — at the lowest ebb in the post–World War II period.[7]

(4) U.S. capitalism is more vulnerable than at the time of the 1987 stock market crash to the shock of a recession, an explosion of inflation and interest rates, or other partial crises, bringing on a banking collapse.

d) In 1986 U.S. capitalism experienced a sharp economic downturn that was equivalent in its effects to a recession.

---

6. During the post–Gulf War capitalist boomlet, corporate debt in the United States declined for several years but began climbing again in the latter 1990s. Trading in high-profit, high-risk corporate bonds — so-called junk bonds — reached a record level of nearly $100 billion in the first half of 1998. This was almost five times the amount floated each year between 1986 and 1989, when Michael Milken, Wall Street's junk bond pioneer, was imprisoned for leaving well-heeled clients with stacks of worthless, defaulted bonds. Announcements of debt-financed corporate mergers, which also fell in the early 1990s, reached a new peak of $973 billion in the first half of 1998 — more than the record twelve-month total the year before.

7. This trend continued in the 1990s despite talk in the big-business press about an "investment boom." The total stock of industrial plant and equipment in the United States has grown at an annual rate of 2 percent since 1980, compared to an annual rate of 3.9 percent over the previous three decades. Investment as a share of national income has also fallen in the imperialist countries as a whole since 1980.

"There can be little doubt about the option that corporate America has chosen in the 1990s: downsizing has triumphed over rebuilding," wrote Stephen Roach, chief economist for the Wall Street investment house, Morgan Stanley, in November 1996. "Downsizing means making do with less — realizing efficiencies by pruning both labor and capital. . . . Historically, periods of accelerating productivity have been associated with *increased* employment." Roach reports that computer hardware accounted for 57 percent of the growth in capital spending from 1994 to 1997. But the vast majority of such spending goes to replace obsolete equipment, not expand capacity.

(1) Substantial enough amounts of capital were devalued to
   (a) lay the ground for renewed, even if slow, economic growth; and
   (b) postpone the next downturn in the U.S. economy for roughly another half decade.
(2) The next recession will take place under the cumulative effects of a new set of destabilizing economic conditions: worsening banking crisis; largest-ever debt balloon; continuing stock and bond market instability; renewed vulnerability of working farmers; and stagnant capital investment.
(3) Because of the weight of the U.S. economy in the world and the increasingly integrated character of world capitalism, such a downturn can trigger major recessions in other imperialist countries and have a further devastating impact on the majority of semicolonial countries. It will accelerate the already intensifying competition and protectionist conflicts among the major imperialist powers.[8]

3. The above elements of the capitalist crisis are all manifestations of the continuing tendency for the rate of profit to decline.

a) This remains the dominant tendency, despite the employers' success over the 1980s in lengthening the average workweek for the first time in half a century.

b) Limits on the rulers' willingness to grant either economic or social concessions to the working class are stiffening. The capacity of individual capitalists to look ahead is be-

---

8. The U.S. capitalist economy sank into recession between July 1990 and March 1991. The first half decade of the subsequent expansion was marked by the slowest growth of any business cycle recovery since World War II. The median real wage of workers fell during each of those five years — the first time in U.S. history this had happened during an upturn. Only in 1997 did real wages begin modest growth, although they remain well below their level a quarter century ago in 1973.

coming foreshortened, as each one presses to generate the greatest possible short-run revenues in hopes of staying afloat and beating out the competition — regardless of the consequences in terms of indebtedness, declining expenditures on research and development, and financially motivated mergers with no production- or marketing-related advantages.[9]

C. Shifts in post–World War II imperialist alignments and intensifying capitalist competition

1. Shifts in the post–World War II international alignment of class forces have been and continue to be marked above all by alterations in the degree and character of Washington's economic, political, and military dominance within the imperialist system.

2. The preparations for the organization of a fourth Reich have once again placed Germany at the center of European and Atlantic politics and signal a fundamental change in international relations among the imperialist powers.

   a) The accelerating intertwining of the monetary and economic prospects, political alignments, and class struggle in the imperialist Federal Republic of Germany (FRG) and the workers state, the German Democratic Republic (GDR), marks the biggest shift in interimperialist rela-

---

9. Between 1992 and 1998, profits rose as a percentage of the U.S. national income, although this percentage remained well below the norm for the post–World War II period. This uptick came largely as a result of further extension of the workweek and intensified cost-cutting by the employing class, not expansion of productive capacity or a rapid increase in sales revenues. "The 1990s have clearly been an era of slow sales growth," reported a front-page article in the April 13, 1998, *Wall Street Journal.* "[T]he weak sales environment triggered moves that led to the strong profit performance of the 1990s. Says James Paulsen, chief investment officer at the investment-management unit of Norwest Corp., in Minneapolis, the 1990s executive became a 'contractionary-minded capitalist' who slashed payrolls, added computers, minimized inventory, stopped building factories, and eliminated middle management."

tions and conflicts in Europe and the Atlantic Alliance. It also has a greater impact than any other single development on the deepening economic and political crises in the Eastern and Central European workers states and their relations with the Soviet Union.

b) These changes reflect first and foremost the relative strengthening of German finance capital within the imperialist system.[10]

(1) The industrial and trading power of German finance capital is the source of the strengthening mark and growing weight of the German central bank in capitalist Europe and beyond.[11]

---

10. The Berlin Wall fell on November 9, 1989, in face of growing popular mobilizations across the German Democratic Republic against the regime. In August 1990 the East German parliament voted to reunify under the terms of the FRG's constitution. But formal reunification — which took place on October 3, 1990 — did not register "a relative strengthening of German finance capital within the imperialist system." In fact, the single biggest shift in world politics since this resolution was written in 1990 has been the relative weakening of the German bourgeoisie both economically and politically in capitalist Europe, especially vis-à-vis its imperialist rival in France. While the resolution accurately points to the sharp economic and social contradictions posed for German imperialism by its effort to swallow and absorb the workers state in the east, it fails to draw the only conclusion consistent with these facts — that is, anticipation of the rapid and debilitating consequences for Germany's capitalist rulers of this effort to unify two states with antagonistic social relations.

11. Bonn has transferred some $100 billion a year to eastern Germany since that time, roughly 5 percent of western Germany's annual GDP, and 40 percent of the GDP of the former GDR. Most of these funds have been spent on jobless benefits and other social payments, not capital investment. The German government has shut down much industry in the east, resulting in official unemployment that topped 20 percent in early 1998 (and substantially higher if low-paying government make-work plans are not counted). Reflecting the strains on German capital and deflationary pressures across Europe, unemployment in western Germany reached its highest levels since the early 1930s in 1997–98.

German capital is also much more vulnerable than its imperialist rivals to the economic effects of the deepening crisis in Russia. German banks in mid-1998 were owed $30.5 billion by the government and other insti-

(2) The capitalist rulers of the FRG are moving inexorably to bring their world political and military power more in line with this strengthening economic position relative to U.S. imperialism and European capitalist rivals.

c) The accelerating rapidity of steps toward the FRG's economic and monetary union with the GDR further undermines prospects for: 1) the growing integration and homogenization of the member capitalist nations of the European Community (EC) as 1992 approaches; and 2) the dampening of labor and working-class struggles in West Germany, the linchpin of capitalist Europe.[12]

(1) The even greater economic, political, and military dominance of German imperialism vis-à-vis its European rivals (in and out of the EC) will sharply exacerbate the disequilibrium, conflicts, and contradictions that stand in the way of any harmonious course toward an integrated capitalist Europe.

(2) The pre–World War II reality of a Central Europe dominated by German finance capital is also being pursued, as the rulers of the FRG seek to complement their position in capitalist Europe by also estab-

---

tutions in Russia — more than four times the outstanding Russian loans of U.S. banks, and more than 40 percent of all Russia's debt to foreign banks. Some 14 percent of the capital of German banks is exposed to loans to Russia.

12. Bonn's decline since 1990 vis-à-vis Paris and London spoiled plans by German capital to exploit the strength of the mark in order to dominate a strong European currency by the end of the decade, simultaneously placing Germany's stamp more forcefully on foreign and military affairs across Europe. The "euro," scheduled to begin being used to denominate stock, bond, and banking transactions across eleven European countries on January 1, 1999, will be a weaker and more unstable currency than the mark, which has itself become much weaker since 1990. Actual "euro" notes are to replace marks, French francs, and other national currencies in circulation in 2002. The rulers of the United Kingdom, as well as Denmark and Sweden, have opted for now to retain their national currencies.

lishing an edge in economic relations with the governments of the European workers states.

(3) Steps toward yoking together the imperialist and workers states of Germany in economic union set the German bourgeoisie on a more direct collision course with the working class of the East as well as the West, while facilitating united action of the working class in Germany.

d) Britain's capitalist rulers are less able to lean on a "special relationship" with Washington as a counterbalance to the growing dominance of Germany in Europe and the continuing decline of British imperialism.

(1) The pound has fallen victim to Thatcher's nearly decade-long pretense that the foundations of British capitalism are stronger than they are. The pound will now inevitably become increasingly pegged to the German mark rather than the U.S. dollar.

(2) The strength of British capitalism and support for Thatcherism continue to be eroded by the highest inflation and interest rates in capitalist Europe, combined with growing resistance to employer and government attacks, notably to increasingly regressive and onerous taxation.

(3) The 1982 Malvinas War, far from showing that British imperialism remains a world power, proved the opposite. The war against Argentina could not have been sustained, let alone won, by Britain without decisive intelligence and logistical support made possible by Washington's decision to put U.S. air and naval power at London's service for the duration of the conflict.[13]

---

13. Given the relative weakening of German imperialism since 1990, and the approaching replacement of the mark by the euro, the rulers of the United Kingdom have pressed the "special relationship" with Washington with renewed vigor to bolster their position vis-à-vis rival powers on the European continent. In particular, the Tory government of John Major

3. Interimperialist competition (both in trade and the export of capital) continues to sharpen, increasing protectionist pressures and related world political conflicts and tensions.

   a) The European Community is seeking to end all internal barriers to trade, labor, and capital movements by 1992 and present a common front against other imperialist rivals. In response, the United States and Canada have taken steps to create a similar bloc.[14] The Australian and New Zealand ruling classes have formed their own "free trade zone" as well.

      (1) This growing protectionism, by further closing markets to the semicolonial countries, reinforces their economic devastation.

      (2) It will also kick back into explosive divisions within the imperialist trading blocs themselves under the pressure of any sharp economic crisis.

   b) Mounting interimperialist rivalry and its trade-war consequences can be dramatically illustrated by the U.S. rulers' escalating assault on their Japanese imperialist rivals.

      (1) Washington's protectionist assault takes place in the context of the 1990 collapse of Japan's superinflated stock market; the fall in the value of the yen measured against the mark and the dollar; the instability of sky-high real estate prices; and the effects of inflated prices of food and other necessities on the

---

acted as Washington's most solid ally militarily and politically during the 1990–91 Gulf War, and the Labour Party government of Anthony Blair as the White House's most reliable backer during its renewed war moves against Iraq in late 1997 and early 1998.

14. The U.S. and Canadian imperialist rulers, together with the Mexican bourgeoisie, launched the North American Free Trade Agreement (NAFTA) on January 1, 1994. It was preceded by a trade pact between Washington and Ottawa signed in January 1988. For a discussion of NAFTA, especially its place in intensifying the superexploitation of the peasants and workers of semicolonial Mexico, see "Imperialism's March toward Fascism and War" by Jack Barnes in *New International* no. 10, pp. 269–76.

extreme class skewing of income distribution. Japanese capitalism is more vulnerable to partial economic crises and world economic fluctuations than it was during the 1980s.[15]

(2) At the same time, Japanese finance capital continues to buy up factories throughout East Asia and Southeast Asia at a rapidly accelerating rate, and to offer stiffer competition to U.S. imperialism for domination over markets in the Asia and Pacific region.

(3) Protectionist assaults against Japanese capital by its imperialist rivals have racist, anti-Asian overtones that the U.S. rulers play on, aided by the trade union bureaucracy, in particular, as well as by bourgeois and petty-bourgeois misleaders among the oppressed nationalities.

(4) Japanese imperialism continues to build up its military forces (it maintains the largest military budget of any imperialist power other than Washington). At the same time, it has no nuclear arsenal or short-term prospects for one, and thus remains subordinate to U.S. strategic air and naval power in the Pacific.[16]

c) Economic and social instability, and prospects for intensifying class struggle, are increasing throughout the imperialist world.

(1) Across capitalist Europe, unemployment since the

---

15. Japanese capitalism has been in a deflationary crisis throughout the 1990s. The Tokyo stock market collapsed from 40,000 at the end of 1989 to below 14,000 in August and September 1998. In 1989 Japanese shares in dollar terms accounted for 45 percent of total world stock market prices; by mid-1998 the figure had fallen to about 10 percent. Land values in Tokyo in mid-1997 were roughly one-fifth their level at the opening of the decade. Unemployment is at its highest post–World War II levels.

16. The countries with the world's top seven military budgets as of 1996 are the United States ($265 billion); Russia ($48 billion); Japan ($45 billion); France ($38 billion); the United Kingdom ($33 billion); Germany ($32 billion); and China ($32 billion).

1982 recession has hovered at the highest levels in the post–World War II period, as economic growth rates decelerate.[17]

(2) The viability of the "Swedish model" as an "alternative to capitalism" is being increasingly called into question as economic crisis and class conflict become more visible in this imperialist country.

    (a) Economic growth in Sweden has stagnated, inflation remains high, and taxation levels are felt to be more and more onerous by broad layers of the population.

    (b) This is spurring increased resistance in the working class to demands by the capitalist government and employing class, despite Sweden's relatively low unemployment rate and relatively high social wage.[18]

    (c) With a European Community increasingly dominated by German finance capital, Sweden's rulers — who remain outside the EC — will face sharply intensifying capitalist competition.

(3) Despite the blows directed by Canada's rulers against the national rights of the Quebecois in the early 1980s, they have been unable to significantly reverse any of the major gains won by Quebec since World War II.

    (a) Since late 1986 the rulers' probes have been met by a number of substantial actions in defense of French-language rights.

---

17. As of April 1998 the unemployment rate for the European Union had been above 10 percent since the opening months of 1993.

18. Joblessness in Sweden shot up from 3 percent at the opening of the 1990s to 14 percent in early 1994, and remained at historically high rates around 8 percent in early 1998. Both Social Democratic and Conservative governments have taken aim at jobless benefits, pensions, and other social gains of the working class. Class polarization has heightened in Sweden as well, with mounting rightist attacks on immigrants' rights and civil liberties.

    (b) The new rise of support for Quebec's independence signals a new phase in the fight for national self-determination there.

    (c) This fight will be increasingly intertwined with the struggles of working people across Canada to defend their class interests in face of the deepening capitalist economic and social crisis.[19]

(4) New Zealand is the only imperialist country that never came out of the 1982 world recession.

    (a) Amid deep and persisting economic stagnation throughout the 1980s, the New Zealand capitalists have intensified their antilabor offensive, which by the latter half of the decade turned into a rout of the labor movement.

    (b) The economic and social consequences for the working class have been particularly devastating on the Maori population and Pacific Island immigrants.

    (c) Tens of thousands of New Zealand workers have been forced over the past decade to emigrate to Australia in search of jobs and a living wage.[20]

---

19. Tens of thousands of Quebecois working people and youth joined in rallies and took to the streets in 1995 in support of a "yes" vote on a Quebec sovereignty referendum. Expressing growing proindependence views, one of the most popular chants was, "We want a country!" The "yes" position received more than 49 percent of the ballots cast, and 60 percent of those cast by members of the oppressed Quebecois nationality. A similar referendum fifteen years earlier received a 42 percent "yes" vote, including 46 percent of the ballots cast by Quebecois.

20. The upturn in the capitalist business cycle in New Zealand that began in 1992 (and was slowing by 1998) did not reverse the onslaught against the working class. New Zealand's capitalist rulers launched an assault on collective bargaining and other union rights; slashed unemployment benefits and spending on health care and education; and drove wages down and hours up. Unemployment, near zero by government figures for most of the 1970s, reached 11 percent by the end of 1991 and remained above 6 percent throughout the upturn. An April 1996 study revealed that one-fifth of the New Zealand population was living below the

(5) Over the past two decades tens of millions of workers and peasants from the oppressed countries of Africa, Asia, the Pacific, the Caribbean, and Central and South America have migrated to the imperialist countries. This historic wave is the largest since the massive, pre–World War I immigration into the United States, primarily from Europe.

(a) This process will continue as the laws of capital work to create pools of workers who can be superexploited through poverty wages and long hours, and who can be forced to accept monstrous working conditions and speedup.

(b) Immigrant workers face systematic racist and chauvinist attacks and language discrimination, as the capitalist rulers seek to keep them as a pariah pool of cheap labor with the status of "aliens," "foreigners," "guests," or "illegals," while fostering and maintaining divisions among working people.

(c) As a result of these new waves of immigration, the working class in the imperialist countries is more multinational than ever before. While "national" working-class traditions are less and less meaningful, the working class in imperialist countries is more and more directly connected to the struggles and experiences of workers and farmers elsewhere, as people from around the world work and fight side by side.

(d) This changing composition and scope of knowledge strengthens the working-class movement in the imperialist countries. Over time, immigrant workers gain confidence and become more assertive, leading the capitalist class to underestimate

official poverty line for a family of three, and that the incidence of poverty was two and a half times higher for Maoris and three and a half times higher for Pacific Island immigrants.

their combat potential (the growing weight of Spanish-speaking, Asian, and other immigrant workers in the U.S. meat-packing industry is a good example). As the class struggle sharpens, this process will result in the emergence of stronger proletarian leadership.

4. The deepening capitalist economic and social crisis in the 1990s will place the democratic rights and political space of working people under increasing pressure.

a) Bourgeois-democratic regimes exist today in every major imperialist country. With the onset of intensifying social crisis, however, these countries will not escape sharp tendencies toward Bonapartist political rule, such as those that marked much of capitalist Europe during the 1920s and 1930s.[21]

b) The imperialist ruling classes will use all the means that the relationship of class forces allows, legal and extralegal, in order to defend their property rights and class privileges in the face of mounting working-class resistance.

(1) There will be increased use of the cops and courts against the labor movement, farm activists, fighters against racist discrimination, and those involved in progressive social struggles. There will be repeated efforts by the rulers to narrow the limits on political space for the oppressed and exploited to organize and resist (e.g., censorship, frame-ups, attacks on criminal justice protections and prisoners' rights, increased use of capital punishment).

(2) Deepening class polarization will at the same time spawn rightist, racist, and antilabor outfits in various guises. They will probe the use of more open violence against unionists, rank-and-file fighters, and political

---

21. See "Imperialism's March toward Fascism and War" by Jack Barnes in *New International* no. 10, as well as *Capitalism's World Disorder: Working-Class Politics in the 21st Century* by Jack Barnes (Pathfinder, 1998).

activists, including those among them who are cadres of communist organizations.

(3) As Bonapartist trends arise, the labor bureaucracy will collaborate with the bosses in an attempt to tie the unions more closely with the capitalist state as instruments to police and control the working class.

c) Although there will be no simple growing over from today's conditions to Bonapartism, the mounting economic and social pressures in the imperialist countries are already leading to sharpening class polarization, including its expression in increased resistance by oppressed nationalities to racist and chauvinist discrimination and violence.

D. U.S. imperialism has lost the Cold War

1. The "Cold War" was the term used to describe the strategic military course forced upon U.S. imperialism and its allies in face of the limitations imposed by the international balance of class forces coming out of World War II. These limitations made impossible for the foreseeable future the use of massive armed forces to accomplish Washington's strategic goal — overturning the Soviet Union and Eastern European workers states and reestablishing capitalism there.

a) During the period just after World War II, Washington was blocked from pursuing this goal by the refusal of the GIs to go back to war, this time against former allies, the Soviet Union and the workers and peasants of China. Faced with a popular "Bring Us Home!" movement organized by the soldiers themselves, the imperialist rulers were politically forced to live up to their promises to demobilize the bulk of their armed forces.[22]

b) The U.S.-organized imperialist assault on Korea in 1950, which tested the "back door" military approach to the Soviet Union, failed in its objective to overturn the Dem-

---

22. See "1945: When U.S. Troops Said 'No!'" by Mary-Alice Waters in *New International* no. 7.

ocratic People's Republic of Korea, as the war ended in a stalemate at the thirty-eighth parallel.

(1) The consequences of the aggression against Korea speeded the overturn of capitalist property and the consolidation of a workers state in neighboring China. Massive numbers of Chinese worker and peasant volunteers poured across the Yalu River to fight together with the Korean people to turn back the imperialist invading forces.

(2) The imperialists concluded that the political price they would pay throughout Asia for unleashing nuclear weapons for a second time in the region precluded their use in the Korean conflict. The difficulties of maintaining a politically unpopular land war in Asia against a workers state foreshadowed the U.S. defeat in Vietnam some two decades later.

(3) The war left a divided Korea, denied its national unification after more than half a century of occupation by Tokyo and Washington. This remains the most important and explosive unresolved national division imposed by the victors of World War II.

c) By the latter half of the 1950s, the USSR's development of nuclear weapons and space technology convinced the imperialists that the risks of massive destruction not only of capitalist Europe but also the United States were too great to consider a direct assault against the Soviet and Eastern European workers states. Since the end of the 1960s, the Soviet Union has had rough parity with U.S. imperialism in nuclear weaponry and delivery systems (parity not in the sense of equal numbers of warheads and missiles, but the capacity of both governments to inflict devastating damage against each other — Mutual Assured Destruction, or MAD, in Pentagon lingo).[23]

---

23. Despite John F. Kennedy's demagogy during his 1960 U.S. presidential campaign against Richard Nixon, alleging a "missile gap" that gave

2. Given these realities, Washington was restricted during the Cold War to using its military power to attempt to contain any extension of the revolutionary overturn of imperialist domination and capitalist property relations. Its strategic effort to weaken the Soviet and Eastern European workers states became one of applying pressure on the bureaucratic castes to police the working class, squelch all political initiatives, and keep working people isolated from the struggles of workers and peasants around the world, with all the depoliticizing and demoralizing consequences that flow from such a separation.

a) For imperialism this was an unavoidable interlude, preparing for the day when the workers states would be sufficiently weakened by Stalinist policies that demoralized the working class to make possible their destruction in a direct imperialist assault.

b) Instead, what has culminated in 1989 and 1990 is an accelerating and irreversible crisis of the Stalinist parties and parasitic petty-bourgeois castes on which they are based, whose counterrevolutionary policies have been weakening the degenerated or deformed workers states for decades.

(1) The workers states and their proletarian property foundations have proven stronger than the castes.

(2) Although brutalized and depoliticized, the working class in the workers states has demonstrated its ability — even within the limits of bourgeois trade union consciousness — to resist the economic and social

---

the USSR a military advantage over Washington, the truth was the opposite. In 1962 the U.S. government had some 5,000 nuclear warheads and 500 intercontinental missiles, while the Soviet Union had 300 or fewer nuclear warheads and only a few dozen missiles. The Soviet government stated that it reached parity with Washington in the number of missile launchers in 1971, although Moscow continued to have many fewer warheads. Currently Washington has more than 7,100 nuclear warheads on intercontinental ballistic missiles, submarine launchers, and bombers; Russia has some 6,200 warheads.

consequences of the deepening parasitism and bureaucratism of the governing castes.

(a) This resistance, beginning with the Polish workers' uprising in 1980, has triggered the crises that are now ravaging the regimes across Eastern and Central Europe and in the Soviet Union.

(b) The workers of these countries will resist the consequences of moving toward capitalist restoration even more fiercely.

(3) These events confirm the continuing truth of the prognosis advanced by communists in the 1930s. As succinctly put by Trotsky: "As a conscious political force the bureaucracy has betrayed the revolution. But a victorious revolution is fortunately not only a program and a banner, not only political institutions, but also a system of social relations. To betray it is not enough. You have to overthrow it. The October revolution has been betrayed by the ruling stratum, but not yet overthrown."[24]

3. With the betrayers — who have been the biggest obstacle to strengthening the workers states — either crumbling or on the defensive, and with prospects of a military assault against the Soviet Union and Eastern European less feasible than ever before, imperialism still confronts the same historic battle, but from a weakened position. Instead of waging a "Cold War" against the petty-bourgeois regimes of the bureaucratic caste, *imperialism will have to directly take on and try to defeat the working class in order to overthrow the workers states and reestablish capitalism in Eastern and Central Europe and the Soviet Union.*

a) The continued relative economic and political weakening of U.S. imperialism, combined with the deepening crisis of the regime in the Soviet Union, lessens the direct impact of their bilateral relations on world politics and reduces their control over struggles.

---

24. Leon Trotsky, *The Revolution Betrayed: What Is the Soviet Union and Where Is It Going?* (Pathfinder, 1972), pp. 227.

(1) Given the strategic nuclear stalemate between the U.S. and Soviet governments, there is no likelihood of a U.S.-USSR nuclear war; the portions of the globe covered by this U.S.-Soviet "nuclear umbrella," however, will continue to diminish. Fewer political conflicts or struggles than ever before pose the direct prospect of nuclear showdown between the U.S. and Soviet governments.

(2) The crumbling of the Warsaw Pact military alliance under these conditions sharply accelerates the disintegration of the reactionary NATO military alliance, which was already under growing strains from intensifying interimperialist competition and shifting alignments among the rival national capitalist classes.

b) This breakdown of a world relationship of forces marked by the standoff of two nuclear-armed military blocs means greater political instability in the imperialist countries, the workers states, and worldwide.

(1) The disintegration of the Stalinist regimes opens greater political space for organization and struggle by the working classes in Eastern and Central Europe and within the Soviet Union, as they fight back against the devastating consequences of increasing reliance on capitalist methods and encroachments on the conquests of the workers states.

(2) Struggles by workers in capitalist Europe and the Eastern and Central European workers states will mutually affect and influence each other more than any time in over four decades. The relatively impenetrable wall that has previously blocked these interconnections is breaking down with the disintegration of the NATO and Warsaw Pact alliances and the accelerating course toward the unification of Germany.[25]

25. The U.S. rulers began reconstructing NATO in the 1990s on the corpses of the Yugoslav peoples, acting simultaneously to tighten Wash-

(3) Moreover, these struggles will be seen over time less as a fight by workers in Western Europe against capitalist exploitation and a separate fight by workers in Eastern Europe against an entrenched bureaucratic caste. Instead, they will be increasingly recognized as an intertwined fight by workers throughout Europe and worldwide against the dehumanizing and earth-destroying system of exploitation and oppression of the imperialist ruling classes and their reflections through various transmissions belts, in particular

    (a) the labor officialdoms and social democratic, Stalinist, and other petty-bourgeois misleaderships in capitalist Europe; and

    (b) the petty-bourgeois regimes, political parties, un-

---

ington's military encirclement of the workers states in Russia and other former Soviet republics and to reinforce U.S. dominance over rival capitalist powers in the Atlantic alliance. In the early 1990s the U.S. government sabotaged one initiative after another by Paris, Bonn, and London to act as power brokers in the war-ravaged Yugoslav workers state; each hoped to gain military and economic leverage against Washington and against one another. As failures mounted for the European occupation force in Bosnia, operating under a United Nations flag, and as diplomatic efforts foundered, Washington successfully pressed for U.S.-led NATO air strikes and naval and ground shelling against Serbian forces, conducting more than 3,000 such assaults between February 1994 and September 1995. In late 1995, in the wake of this sustained bombardment, the U.S. rulers brought representatives of the Serbian, Croatian, and Bosnian forces to Wright-Patterson Air Force Base in Dayton, Ohio, for talks that authorized Washington to spearhead an occupation army in Bosnia of some 60,000 NATO troops, including 20,000 from the United States. As of August 1998, the U.S.-organized occupation force, initially scheduled to depart in late 1996, remained in Bosnia with no settled departure date.

During the same January 1994 NATO summit at which the U.S. administration won approval for air strikes in Yugoslavia, president William Clinton initiated the proposal to expand NATO eastward closer to the borders of the Russian workers state. The July 1997 NATO summit meeting set spring 1999 as the date to admit Poland, the Czech Republic, and Hungary as the "first wave" of new member states.

ion officialdoms, and other institutions staffed primarily by middle-class social layers emanating from the disintegrating castes in the deformed and degenerated workers states.

c) Washington has also suffered a historic blow to its capacity to use its strategic nuclear arsenal as leverage vis-à-vis its strongest imperialist rivals to slow the political consequences of its relative economic decline.

   (1) The sharply decreasing significance of the U.S. nuclear umbrella in face of the decline of the Warsaw Pact gives Washington less clout than ever before against its rival imperialist ruling classes, in particular against German finance capital.

   (2) The U.S. rulers, however, will continue to use their overall nuclear and conventional military dominance to exercise political power within the imperialist system greater than their economic might would otherwise allow.

   (3) Whatever new trade and investment opportunities open up between the imperialist powers and the governments of the workers states, these will remain far too small to reverse the consequences of intensifying interimperialist competition and the tendency of the rate of profit to decline.

4. Washington-Moscow "summitry" has less impact on the course of world politics than any time since the Yalta and Potsdam conferences attempted to divide up stable "spheres of influence" at the close of World War II.

a) Washington is less able than ever to speak, negotiate, and act as the undisputed leader of a world imperialist alliance, and Moscow is no longer able to speak for the Warsaw Pact, or even for growing parts of the "Union" of Soviet Socialist Republics.[26]

---

26. The Soviet Union was formally dissolved in December 1991 in the aftermath of an abortive August coup to overthrow Soviet president Mik-

b) Thus, summitry is more and more narrowed to negotiations over

    (1) reductions in arms and troops stationed abroad, which both the U.S. rulers and the Soviet caste need to achieve for their own domestic economic and political reasons; and

    (2) nuclear arms "limitations," which both Washington and Moscow will continue to use as public relations cover for ongoing modernization and miniaturization of their strategic nuclear arsenals.

c) The petty-bourgeois caste in the USSR has less to offer imperialism. It is less able than ever before to deliver on "peaceful coexistence" deals.

    (1) It continues to seek a stable relationship with imperialism, but this goal remains illusory. So long as the property foundations of the workers state exist, no long-term stability is possible between U.S. imperialism and the Soviet Union. Nor will there be any relief from the class struggles that will continue to rip both countries.

    (2) The Soviet government will continue to chart its foreign policy in relation to Cuba and various national liberation movements on the basis of diplomatic expediency and economic needs, not internationalist principle. It will continue to try to muscle revolution-

---

hail Gorbachev. Gorbachev resigned as general secretary of the Communist Party immediately following the coup and organized the dissolution of its Central Committee. He later resigned as president of the Soviet Union less than an hour prior to its disbanding December 25. Boris Yeltsin succeeded Gorbachev as head of state. The Russian government (and those of other former republics of the USSR) is largely staffed by personnel from the former regime. Moscow no longer seeks to justify its legitimacy, however, by claiming to represent the continuity of the Bolshevik-led October 1917 revolution. The crystallized social castes of the Stalinist regimes — held together by material interest in perpetuating their own privileged consumption of the social surplus — have shattered into countless shards, each seeking to maximize their own well-being.

ary movements to fall in step with its diplomatic dealings with imperialism.

(3) It is not in the state interests of the caste in the USSR (either diplomatically or economically), however, to impose massive reductions in trade with Cuba, nor to break ties with national liberation organizations such as the African National Congress and others.[27]

d) The fact that a U.S.-Soviet nuclear war is less probable than ever should not be confused with a lessening danger of the use of nuclear weapons.

(1) The more governments that possess nuclear arsenals (Israel, India, and Pakistan have been added over the past two decades, and more are on the way), and the more class, national, and state conflicts intensify the world over, the greater the dangers that one of these capitalist regimes will resort to the use of nuclear weapons in the face of extreme pressure.

----

27. In January 1990 the Soviet government announced plans to begin trading with Cuba (and other workers states) in hard currency and at world market prices. Since the early 1960s the USSR had purchased Cuban sugar, citrus fruits, and other exports at prices above those on the world market, and had sold Cuba oil, industrial goods, and wheat and other agricultural products at prices below those on the capitalist market. Cuba's five-year economic agreement with the Soviet Union expired at the end of 1990, and the long-standing preferential prices were phased out over the following year. Even after the collapse of the Soviet Union at the close of 1991, trade continued between Cuba and the new regime in Russia, but the sudden unfavorable shift in terms made it impossible for the Cuban government to import petroleum and other products from Russia at anything close to the level of previous years.

Since some 85 percent of Cuba's trade had been with the Soviet Union and Eastern European workers states, this rupture in trading patterns — together with the effects of deepening world capitalist deflation and an intensified U.S. trade embargo — precipitated the difficult economic conditions in the 1990s that Cubans refer to as the Special Period. By 1996, through the efforts of Cuban working people, the decline in industrial and agricultural production had bottomed out, and shortages of food and other essentials, though still severe, had begun to be eased.

(2) Moreover, while the imperialist nuclear powers have shown their political unreadiness since Hiroshima and Nagasaki to use nuclear weapons (having rejected using them in Korea, Vietnam, and against Cuba), they continue to foment "proxy wars" in which allies may eventually be prodded into a nuclear assault.

(3) Only socialist revolutions in the imperialist countries can bring the danger of a world nuclear conflagration to an end once and for all.

(4) It is possible the U.S. imperialist ruling class might lash out with nuclear weapons at an advanced stage in the world socialist revolution, when the exploiters are backed into a corner.

    (a) The only way to forestall that possibility, however, is to build a revolutionary working-class movement powerful enough to overthrow the U.S. capitalist rulers and disarm them.

    (b) That requires a course toward building a proletarian communist party as part of a world communist movement.

(5) The dynamics set in motion by the events of 1989–90 open the prospects for a new wave of protest movements in country after country across Europe that will fight for the elimination of the production or basing of nuclear weapons. These prospects are particularly important in Germany. Such struggles limit the imperialists' political capacity to use nuclear blackmail in their foreign policy dealings and create greater space for struggle and class politics both in Europe and worldwide.

e) The lessening probability of U.S.-Soviet military conflict in the immediate future does not mean peace for the semicolonial world.

(1) Washington is less and less able to effectively justify U.S. military aggression by reference to the Cold War and "Soviet threat."

(2) Imperialism, however, will use other pretexts — from "drugs," to "terrorism," to cold-blooded provocations — to continue to probe the limits to the use of its massive military power to crush worker and peasant struggles and national liberation movements.

(3) There will be no détente with toilers anywhere in the world who are fighting for national liberation and socialism. There will be no relief for the millions of children the imperialists are starving, for the millions of peasants and workers they are exploiting and oppressing unto death; no relief from the massive ecological destruction wreaked by the workings of their law of value.

E. Changing place of U.S. military power

1. Military power, both tactical and strategic, remains U.S. imperialism's most important instrument of diplomacy and foreign policy.

a) Washington is the only imperialist government for which this holds true today, and that fact continues to give it greater dominance in the world imperialist system than the relative economic and political strength of U.S. capital alone would allow.

b) In the 1980s Washington has militarily upgraded its arming and financing of bourgeois "proxy" regimes for policing the world (from Israel, its imperialist junior partner, to Pakistan, El Salvador, and others).

c) Despite increasing economic and political pressures, it has maintained a massive worldwide network of military bases (from Iceland to Germany in Europe, to Hawaii, the Philippines, Panama, Puerto Rico, Japan, South Korea, etc.) and a strategic naval presence throughout the world's seas.

d) It has armed rightist movements against regimes it opposes in semicolonial countries (including the Nicaraguan contras, the Pol Pot alliance in Cambodia, UNITA in Angola, Afghan rightists).

e) It carried out brutal air assaults against Libya in 1986 and used its naval armada against Iran during the 1980-88 Iran-Iraq war.[28]

f) It used F-4 jet fighters from Clark Air Base in the Philippines to prop up the government of Corazon Aquino against a December 1989 coup attempt by opponents in the armed forces.[29]

g) It provided decisive logistical, supply, and intelligence assistance to London in its 1982 war to prevent Argentina from reestablishing sovereignty over the Malvinas Islands,

---

28. On April 15, 1986, a U.S. aerial strike force bombed the Libyan cities of Tripoli and Benghazi, killing or wounding dozens of people. Several bombers targeted the living quarters of Libyan leader Mu'ammar al-Gadhafi, killing his daughter and wounding other family members. The Thatcher government aided the Reagan administration, permitting eighteen bombers to take off from bases in the United Kingdom.

In September 1980 the government of Iraq launched what became an eight-year-long war against Iran, hoping to contain the impact of the 1979 Iranian revolution on toilers throughout the region and to seize oilfields and port facilities. Hundreds of thousands of soldiers and civilians lost their lives on both sides. Behind a thin veil of neutrality, Washington, London, and Paris provided military supplies to Iraq during the war in order to weaken and if possible destroy the revolution in Iran. The U.S. government dispatched an armada of more than two dozen warships to the Arab-Persian Gulf in 1987. U.S. forces fired on the Iranian ship, the *Iran Ajr*, in September 1987, killing five seamen. And in July 1988 a U.S. Navy crew in the Arab-Persian Gulf shot down an Iranian airliner, killing all 290 passengers and crew aboard.

In a January 1995 sworn affidavit, former White House National Security Council official Howard Teicher acknowledged that "President Reagan decided that the United States could not afford to allow Iraq to lose the war to Iran" and that "CIA Director [William] Casey personally spearheaded the effort to ensure that Iraq had sufficient military weapons, ammunition and vehicles to avoid losing the Iran-Iraq War."

29. In face of broad popular opposition to maintaining U.S. military bases on Philippine soil, that country's senate in 1991 rejected a pact negotiated by Washington and the Aquino government to extend the lease on Clark Air Base and Subic Bay Naval Base for another ten years. The U.S. government withdrew from Clark Air Base in November 1991 and from Subic Bay in November 1992.

which remain a colony of the British crown.

h) It has furnished helicopter gunships with U.S. pilots to Peru, where — in the name of the "war against drugs" — they have been used in combat against antigovernment guerrillas, and has announced agreement with the Peruvian government to establish a $35 million Green Beret counterinsurgency base camp there, equipped with twenty attack jets.

i) It has carried out direct U.S. military invasions of Grenada in 1983 and Panama in 1989.

j) Even as it has sharply cut back nuclear war maneuvers aimed at the Warsaw Pact, Washington continues large-scale strategic air and sea maneuvers targeting Cuba, whose national territory it occupies at Guantánamo, and — in conjunction with the U.S. client regime in Seoul — targeting the Democratic People's Republic of Korea.

2. Since its defeat in Vietnam in the mid-1970s, Washington has politically rejected trying to sustain a protracted war involving large numbers of U.S. troops.

a) The U.S. government's decisions to invade Grenada and Panama were based on judgments that U.S. forces could count on little resistance, assuring victory in a matter of days, not months, thus with very few casualties.

(1) Victory in each case was handed to U.S. imperialism on a silver platter. The political cost to the U.S. rulers was so minimal that the aggression never produced large or ongoing protest actions even in the United States, Latin America, or the Caribbean.

(2) In Grenada, the counterrevolutionary coup by the Stalinist faction led by Bernard Coard, culminating in the murder of Maurice Bishop and other revolutionists, destroyed the revolutionary workers and farmers government and undermined the basis for popular resistance to the U.S. aggression.

(3) In Panama, sustained resistance to the U.S. invasion was blocked by the capitulation of General Manuel

Noriega, reflecting the corruption and political character of the bourgeois military regime.

   (4) In both Grenada and Panama, large numbers of civilian deaths and injuries resulted from cold-blooded tactical decisions by Washington to minimize U.S. casualties.[30]

b) "Low intensity warfare" is not an effective new U.S. military "strategy" reflecting a strengthening of U.S. imperialism.

   (1) To the contrary, it is a description of what Washington is reduced to when it is not politically strong enough to employ "high intensity warfare," the direct use of its military might. It is a manifestation of the political limits on Washington's use of its military power, reflecting the relative weakening of U.S. imperialism.

   (2) With pressures building toward mounting workers' and peasants' struggles and anti-imperialist explosions throughout the semicolonial world, Washington will at some point judge that it has no choice but to commit massive U.S. infantry forces to fight a war (it made a calculated bet along these lines in Panama).

   (3) Following such a commitment of U.S. forces, a deepening social crisis will open in the United States, and open rapidly in comparison to the Vietnam War. Opposition to such a sustained ground war abroad will come faster, and more explosively, with working-class and union involvement from the start.

3. In Nicaragua the FSLN-led Sandinista army scored a military victory over the contras by the latter half of 1987. U.S. "low intensity warfare" was defeated.

---

30. See "The Second Assassination of Maurice Bishop" by Steve Clark, in *New International* no. 6, and *Panama: The Truth About the U.S. Invasion* by Cindy Jaquith, Don Rojas, Nils Castro, and Fidel Castro (Pathfinder, 1990).

a) The dominant FSLN leadership, however, proved incapable of building on that victory to chart a communist course for the tested fighters among the workers and peasants to propel the revolution forward.

(1) Each military victory by the workers and peasants was consolidated not by deepening a course toward extending the land reform, strengthening workers' control in the factories, and advancing and broadening the working-class fight on the Atlantic Coast and in Nicaragua as a whole. Instead, FSLN leaders deepened class collaboration, turned their face to the "patriotic" capitalists and landlords, and subordinated the interests of the exploited toilers to the maintenance of this alliance.

(2) FSLN leaders rejected a course toward building a mass communist party based on vanguard workers, peasants, and soldiers. In doing so, they dissipated the energies and abilities of the force in Nicaragua capable of taking the revolution forward toward establishing a workers state based on a firm worker-peasant alliance.[31]

b) The capacity of the Nicaraguan toilers to resist and turn back the destruction of the revolution was never tested, because they were not organized, mobilized, and led to do so at a point in the revolution that could have made a decisive difference.

(1) The workers and farmers government had rotted away before the retreat of the revolution was registered in the FSLN's defeat in the February 25, 1990, parliamentary elections and the establishment of a bourgeois coalition regime.

(2) The dominant FSLN leadership is playing an irreplaceable role in initial efforts to consolidate the new

---

31. See issue no. 9 of *New International* on "The Rise and Fall of the Nicaraguan Revolution."

government, including taking responsibility for the deployment and control of the armed forces.[32]

(3) Important conquests of the revolution are not yet lost, however. The defense of a number of concrete gains will be decided in struggle. Out of the coming confrontations, new leadership of the workers and peasants will emerge and seek tactics that can advance their class interests.

4. In Afghanistan, substantial U.S. aid to counterrevolutionary forces for more than a decade has failed to overturn the government.

a) The pullout of Soviet troops in 1989, instead of weakening the government's defense against the U.S.-backed rightist armies, undermined the ability of these reactionary forces to continue mobilizing broad support around "national unity" against the Soviet invaders.

b) Today, the government of Afghanistan is further away from, not closer to, being toppled, than during the period of the Soviet occupation.[33]

5. In southern Africa U.S. "low intensity warfare," in the form of aid to the UNITA counterrevolutionary forces, failed in Washington's nearly fifteen-year-long effort to overturn the Angolan government, which was aided at its request by volunteers from the Revolutionary Armed Forces of Cuba.

---

32. FSLN commander Humberto Ortega remained chief of staff of the Nicaraguan army until February 1995.

33. The new Afghan government brought to power in an April 1978 revolutionary uprising carried out some popular measures in response to mass pressure. The brutal administrative methods and murderous infighting of the Stalinist People's Democratic Party of Afghanistan (PDPA), however, culminated in December 1978 in Soviet military intervention to back one of the warring factions. Rightist forces armed and trained by Washington grew rapidly in the aftermath of Moscow's assault on Afghan sovereignty. The morale of Soviet troops — fighting a war unpopular at home — disintegrated, and the Soviet government had to withdraw the last of its forces in February 1989. The discredited regime Moscow left behind fell to a coalition of rightist forces in April 1992.

a) The attempt to compensate for the inability to use U.S. forces by relying on the military might of a junior imperialist power, South Africa, was defeated decisively at Cuito Cuanavale by a combined force of Angolan troops, Cuban volunteers, and fighters from SWAPO (the South-West Africa People's Organisation of Namibia). This victory, combined with the deepening resistance of the South African people, shifted the relationship of forces throughout southern Africa.[34]

(1) More than a decade of South African aggression against Angola was brought to an end, and the military and political position of the UNITA counterrevolutionaries has been further weakened.

(2) The way was opened for Namibia to win its independence from South African colonial rule.

(3) The consequences of these shifts within South Africa itself are the cause of the decision by the apartheid regime of Fredrik W. de Klerk in February 1990 to

---

34. The battle of Cuito Cuanavale was fought in early 1988. Cuban forces had first been sent to Angola in 1975 at the request of its newly independent government to help turn back a South African invasion. The apartheid regime — which operated in collusion with CIA-armed Angolan rightists in UNITA — was pushed back in 1975–76 but launched repeated invasions over the subsequent thirteen years. During that period more than 300,000 Cuban volunteers fought in Angola; 2,000 were killed.

In the wake of the victory at Cuito Cuanavale, the white supremacist regime in South Africa was forced to withdraw its forces from Angola and to enter negotiations with the Cuban and Angolan governments that culminated in Pretoria granting independence to Namibia in early 1990. SWAPO won a decisive majority in elections for Namibia's newly independent government. The final Cuban troops departed from Angola in May 1991. African National Congress leader Nelson Mandela said in 1991 that Cuba's role in defeating the apartheid army constituted "a turning point in the struggle to free the continent and our country from the scourge of apartheid." See Nelson Mandela and Fidel Castro, *How Far We Slaves Have Come! South Africa and Cuba in Today's World* (Pathfinder, 1991), p. 20.

unban the African National Congress, release Nelson Mandela and other long-standing ANC leaders from prison, and permit the return to the country of many exiled leaders of the anti-apartheid movement.

b) A new stage in the battle for a democratic, nonracial South Africa has now opened. Decisive to the historic progress being made has been the political vision, tone, and lead given by Nelson Mandela in his public speeches since his release.

(1) New space for political action by working people is being carved out. Real politics, involving toilers in their tens of millions, has begun.

(a) The largest mobilizations in the history of the apartheid system have spread throughout South Africa, not only in the most populous cities and townships but also — to the greatest degree ever — in the rural "homelands" (the "legal" residence of the majority of Black South Africans).

(b) Strikes and other working-class actions are exploding beyond the bounds of any existing trade union structures and leaderships.

(2) Grounded in the perspectives of the Freedom Charter, and focusing on the demand for the election of a constituent assembly based on one person, one vote, the Mandela-led ANC has sought in the opening months of 1990 to use and expand the space that is being conquered in South Africa to broaden the revolutionary mobilization of the masses aimed at shattering the apartheid system.

(a) The ANC has begun the fight to win the leadership of a political alliance that speaks for the great majority of South Africans, not only for their interests. It has uncompromisingly advanced its program for building the movement on a nonracial basis. In the process, the ANC is seeking to strengthen and restructure itself in a manner commensurate with its historic tasks.

(b) The ANC has reached out in a new way to mobilize the dispossessed in the "homelands" to destroy the Bantustan system as part of the battle to overcome divisions created by the apartheid state. This has opened the road to bring the rural toilers into the revolutionary struggle and into the ANC to a greater degree than ever before, thus confronting one of the biggest weaknesses that the apartheid regime has taken advantage of over the years.

(c) The ANC has launched initiatives to end the fratricidal violence in Natal and unite the oppressed in the struggle against apartheid. It has placed Chief Mongosuthu Buthelezi's collaborationist Inkatha movement on the defensive politically, while disassociating itself from those who would use the banner of the ANC to justify factional thuggery as a substitute for work to win a majority based on political conviction.

(d) The ANC has called on governments throughout the world to hold firm on sanctions against the apartheid regime, maintaining Pretoria's isolation as an international outlaw.

(e) The ANC has used the leverage of the mounting struggle to force the de Klerk regime to open negotiations, and has put together a representative delegation (broader than the current ANC) to participate in the talks. The ANC is seeking to use the negotiations to demand broader political space (freedom for all political prisoners, ending the state of emergency), in order to have the time and the opening to organize the kind of forces and leadership necessary to advance the struggle for a united, nonracial democratic republic.

(3) That the apartheid system is a crime against humanity

is an idea that has been embraced by workers, farmers, and progressive-minded people around the world; it has become a material force in world politics.

(a) The new stage of struggle in South Africa is exacerbating divisions among and within the imperialist ruling classes over how to respond to the apartheid regime, creating new opportunities to mobilize world opinion in action to support the revolutionary democratic struggle led by the ANC.

(b) A victory that brings down apartheid would sound a call that would politically revive the working-class movement in much of the world, including in the imperialist countries.[35]

6. There is no prospect for imperialist-imposed stability in the Middle East. Civil war continues to rage in Lebanon, and the two-and-a-half year long "intifada" by Palestinians in Gaza and on the West Bank has reconfirmed the inevitability of a continuing fight for a democratic and secular Palestine.

a) The power of the Palestinian struggle in the face of Israeli repression and expansionism has fundamentally changed world public opinion.

(1) Today a large majority of the world's people, including in the imperialist countries, are in favor of recognition of the Palestine Liberation Organization and the right of the Palestinian people to an independent state.

(2) At the same time, the imperialist governments and growing numbers of the regimes in the deformed workers states are working to guarantee the maintenance of an Israeli colonial-settler state in some ver-

---

35. In face of ANC-led mass mobilizations and strikes, the apartheid regime was forced to the negotiating table and finally agreed to the first-ever one-person, one-vote elections, which took place in April 1994. The ANC won a decisive majority in those elections and Nelson Mandela was elected president. See "The Coming Revolution in South Africa" by Jack Barnes in *New International* no. 5, and *Nelson Mandela Speaks: Forging a Democratic, Nonracial South Africa* (Pathfinder, 1993).

sion of the pre-1967 boundaries.[36]

b) Israeli capitalism's dependence on Palestinian labor is strengthening the working-class and farmer base of the movement for national self-determination. The deepening world capitalist crisis will spark growing battles by both Palestinian and Jewish workers and farmers against the Israeli exploiting class, helping to break down divisions between them and open up prospects for a working-class-led revolutionary democratic leadership of the struggle.

7. A Havana-Washington axis of conflict will be at the center of world politics in the 1990s. It is the most direct manifestation of the international conflict between imperialism and the dictatorship of the proletariat.

a) The communist vanguard in Cuba is determined not only to defend the revolution, but not to budge from its internationalist course in support of the world struggle for national liberation and socialism.

b) U.S. imperialism will continue to seek ways to maintain and intensify pressure on revolutionary Cuba. No military victory by U.S. imperialism in Cuba is possible, however, because of the revolutionary political course of the

---

36. In the wake of the 1987–92 Palestinian uprising (the *intifada*) in the Israeli-occupied West Bank and Gaza Strip, the PLO signed a series of agreements with Tel Aviv in late 1993 and the first half of 1994. The so-called Oslo accords established limited Palestinian self-administration over certain areas of the West Bank and Gaza, with the Israeli government retaining overall sovereignty, control of all borders, and veto power over questions of land and water usage. In January 1996 elections were held for president and a legislative assembly of the Palestinian Authority, which functions as the municipal administration for some two-thirds of Gaza and one-third of the West Bank. Yasir Arafat was elected president. Palestinian workers and youth have organized continuing resistance to the dispossession of their homeland by the State of Israel, including rebellions against continued settler colonization of occupied territory and protests against army and police repression. Ongoing negotiations between the Israeli government and the PLO leadership broke down in early 1997 when Tel Aviv began building a new settlement in occupied East Jerusalem.

leadership, mobilizing an armed population.

(1) The defense of the Cuban revolution has been strengthened since 1980 by the launching of the Territorial Troop Militia, the implementation of a strategy of defense called the "war of the entire people," repeated mass anti-imperialist mobilizations (beginning with the 1980 "marches of the fighting people"), the victory in Africa over the apartheid regime and U.S.-backed UNITA forces, and the opening and deepening of the rectification process.[37]

(2) In Cuba, unlike Grenada, there will be no betrayal of the revolution; no cowardice of a governmental and military command structure as in Panama; no subordination of the workers and farmers to an alliance with capitalists and landlords and reliance on bourgeois parliamentarism as in Nicaragua; no use of the armed forces and interior ministry against the people, as happened in Eastern Europe and is happening in the Soviet Union today.

(3) A U.S. "conquest" of Cuba could only come through invasion and prolonged war at an almost inconceivable cost in lives and resources. It could only be a Pyrrhic victory for Washington.

c) "Low-intensity warfare" is a description of what U.S. imperial-

----

37. The rectification process in Cuba between 1986 and the beginning of the 1990s marked a turn away from increasing reliance on the system of economic management and planning used in one variant or another throughout the Soviet Union and Eastern Europe. Policies copied from those countries had become more and more dominant in Cuba throughout the 1970s and early 1980s. At its height, rectification took on the character of a growing social movement led by Cuba's most conscious and disciplined working people. See the section on "The Communist Party of Cuba" at the opening of Part IV of this resolution, as well as "Cuba's Rectification Process: Two Speeches by Fidel Castro" in *New International* no. 6; issue no. 8 of *New International* on "Che Guevara, Cuba, and the Road to Socialism"; and *Che Guevara and the fight for Socialism Today* by Mary-Alice Waters (Pathfinder, 1992).

ism has done to Cuba for thirty-one years because of Washington's political incapacity to use direct military power against the Cuban revolution. That was settled by the failure of U.S.-organized invasion and infiltration attempts in 1961–62, not by Cuba's supposed protection under the nuclear umbrella of the Soviet Union, which was never a fact.

d) To maintain its unrelenting pressure against Cuba, Washington has used an economic embargo, occupation of the Guantánamo Naval Base, constant provocations, assassination attempts, encouragement of counterrevolutionary terror, and attempted isolation of Cuba in the Americas and worldwide.

e) The failure of Washington's "low-intensity war" against Cuba has depended above all on the capacities of the communist leadership; its ability to mobilize and lead the workers and farmers to defend their interests; its integrity and self-confidence; and its ability to recognize and correct errors.

  (1) The continued advance and deepening of the rectification process will be decisive in this regard.

  (2) Washington's difficulty in mounting effective assaults in the face of Cuba's communist leadership has been recently demonstrated by

    (a) the political and physical courage of the unarmed crew on the commercial freighter *Hermann*, a small group of Cubans who were picked at random by U.S. imperialism for an armed assault;[38] and

---

38. On January 31, 1990, only a few weeks after the invasion of Panama, the U.S. Coast Guard shelled the Cuban merchant ship *Hermann*. The ship, leased from Panama and carrying chrome to Mexico, was sailing in international waters in the Gulf of Mexico at the time of the attack. It had been ordered to stop and allow U.S. forces to board, under the pretext of a search for drugs. When the crew flatly refused and continued sailing, U.S. forces open fire, aiming nearly 500 rounds at the vessel over a period of an hour and 45 minutes. Crew members had no guns but gathered on deck with machetes, screwdrivers, kitchen knives, and axes to defend the ship if the Coast Guard acted on their threat to board. The

(b) the fiasco of TV Martí, which Cuba has not only blocked technologically, but also — and more importantly — over which it has won the battle for world public opinion, even in the United States.

(3) The axis of Washington's political offensive will continue to revolve around the "human rights" propaganda campaign against the Cuban government.

F. Imperialism enters the 1990s in a weakened position

1. Despite the blows dealt to the working class and farmers in the imperialist countries in the 1980s, and the defeats for toilers in the semicolonial world (the Malvinas, Grenada, Burkina Faso,[39] Panama, Nicaragua and the resultant weakening of the position of the Salvadoran rebels), the greatest blows were taken by imperialism itself.

a) The imperialist ruling classes were unable to reverse the tendency of the rate of profit to decline or to smash the capacity of the working class and labor movement to resist capitalist assaults on their rights, living standards, and job conditions.

b) U.S. imperialism lost the Cold War. It has failed to establish conditions for stable capitalist property relations in any of the workers states and will now confront a new and more confident actor in the international class struggle, the working classes of Eastern and Central Europe and the Soviet Union.

U.S. forces halted the assault when the *Hermann* reached Mexican waters later that morning. A crowd of 100,000 gathered in Havana outside the U.S. Interests Section later that day to give the returning crew a heroes' welcome.

39. In October 1987 the popular revolutionary government in the West African country of Burkina Faso was overthrown in a military coup. Thomas Sankara, the central leader of the revolutionary government established four years earlier in 1983, was assassinated. See *Thomas Sankara Speaks: The Burkina Faso Revolution 1983–87* (Pathfinder, 1988).

c) The oppressed countries of Africa, the Americas, and Asia are in the throes of a worsening and irresolvable economic and social crisis, creating the conditions for growing revolutionary struggles by workers and peasants. Cuba and the struggle in South Africa are beacons pointing to a way forward that has not and cannot be erased.

d) Washington's capacity to advance imperialist interests through summit deals with the Soviet government is at low ebb. At the same time, the U.S. government continues to confront big political obstacles at home and abroad to the use of its massive military might in a sustained war.

2. Intensifying interimperialist competition and the deepening instability and vulnerability of the international capitalist system converge with the prospects for a world depression and social crisis in the 1990s.

Russian coal miners walk off the job during 1996 strike demanding payment of back wages. "The restoration of capitalism is impossible short of defeating the working class in bloody, counterrevolutionary battles."

PART III

WORLD CAPITALISM HAS SUFFERED A HISTORIC DEFEAT IN EASTERN EUROPE AND THE SOVIET UNION

**A. The construction of socialism is
a revolutionary political task of the working class**

1. It is the conscious organization of the production and distribution of goods and services so as to advance the transformation of working people into new human beings, into socialist men and women, as they organize to transform their social relations and conditions of life and work.

2. The tasks shouldered by the working class in this stage of its historic line of march, as it strives to overcome scarcity through progressively raising the productivity of labor, are

a) To reduce the scope of bourgeois norms of distribution, which are inherited from the capitalist mode of production and continue to exist during the opening of the historic transition to socialism, taking steps to progressively narrow economic and social inequalities from the outset;

b) To shift the balance in productive activity from wage labor — inherited from capitalist social relations and maintained in the opening of the transition period — toward voluntary labor freely given for common social advancement — which will progressively become the foundation of work under socialism;

c) To raise the educational and skill level of working people; increase the proportion of administrative tasks of production and distribution conquered by the working class as opposed to being reserved to a specialized layer of administrative personnel (tasks such as organization of the work process and discipline, quality control, financial accounting, inventory and stock controls, etc.); narrow the social division of labor by assuring that more and more scientific tasks, separated from but necessary to production, are carried out by workers themselves; and reduce wage differentials;

d) To strengthen the worker-peasant alliance and narrow the social differentiation between city and countryside, promoting the growing voluntary cooperative labor of urban and rural working people in producing and processing food and fiber and in preventing destruction of the environment;

e) To progressively reduce the deeply entrenched social inequalities inherited from capitalism that are rooted in the oppression of women, racist discrimination, and national oppression, including immediate measures to end all forms of official and de facto discrimination in employment, education, housing, and other arenas of social and political life;

f) To increase the conscious, organized political control by working people over economic and social planning and management, recognizing that reliance on mechanisms and blind laws reinforces commodity fetishism and bourgeois ideology, reversing rather than advancing progress toward socialism; and

g) To make proletarian internationalism the most fundamental guide for political activity and priorities; to guide the workers state as one component of a federation of soviet states in becoming, the expansion of which is necessary not only in order to reach socialism but also to counter bureaucratization and corruption within any single workers state.[1]

---

1. The soviets (the Russian word for "councils") were bodies of delegates elected by soldiers, peasants, and workers in factories and other workplaces at the opening of the revolutionary uprising in Russia in February

3. Proletarian internationalism is essential if workers and farmers are to consolidate the foundations of a workers state and on that basis advance toward socialism.

   a) The construction of socialism can take place only as part of the fight to bring new revolutionary victories worldwide, as part of fighting to extend the socialist revolution while pushing back the world imperialist system of exploitation and domination.

   b) The alternative perspective of "socialism in one country," advanced originally by the Stalinist faction in the USSR, is reactionary, a variant of the "national" socialism that has been and remains at the heart of all class collaborationism.

   c) A proletarian internationalist course requires active solidarity with all battles against national oppression, imperialist subjugation, and capitalist exploitation, as well as active efforts to aid revolutionists around the world in becoming communists in the course of their struggles.

4. The advance toward socialism requires organized communist leadership of the working class.

   a) Building socialism is a more difficult task than the revolutionary conquest of power from the bourgeoisie, requiring more political consciousness and greater proletarian discipline.

   b) The communist party and its leadership must renew and deepen their working-class composition by conscious steps to proletarianize the party. They must always be incorporating broader layers and new generations of vanguard workers and peasants, taking special measures to draw in oppressed nationalities, women, and fighters with experience in internationalist missions. The entire party membership must be involved in leading voluntary social labor.

5. Nationalized property in a workers state, established by ex-

---

1917. The soviets became the fundamental state institutions of the workers and peasants government that came to power under Bolshevik leadership following the victorious October 1917 insurrection.

propriating the bourgeoisie, has no *automatic* bias toward socialism.

   a) The expropriation of capitalist property in industry, banking, and wholesale trade, a state monopoly of foreign trade, and a planned economy are necessary, but they are not sufficient conditions for the toilers to build socialism.

      (1) These revolutionary conquests of the workers and farmers break the domination of production and exchange by the form of the law of value that becomes dominant under capitalism: the establishment of prices of production through the competition of large capitals, determining an average industrial rate of profit.

         (a) Prices of production regulate the social allocation of labor, raw materials, and production goods.

         (b) They guarantee the reproduction of bourgeois social relations and distribution of income.

      (2) Wealth appears under capitalism as the accumulation of commodities, regardless of their origin, and regardless of their contribution to the needs and interests of the great majority of humanity, the workers and farmers. Their value is registered through exchange, through the market.

      (3) Private property in the means of production and exchange blocks the possibility of conscious planning of social and economic priorities by working people.

   b) The construction of socialism is not an engineering task of administering state property and planning, regardless of how committed and socialist-minded the administrators might be.

      (1) The conquest of state property is necessary to open the door to workers taking the productive mechanism of society into their own hands and beginning on that basis to reorganize and transform social labor, in the process transforming themselves. But the conquest of state property does not then guarantee this advance.

      (2) The advance toward socialism depends on a commu-

nist political course of the working class and its nonexploiting allies — the course advocated by Fidel Castro
and Ernesto Che Guevara; originally explained by Karl
Marx and Frederick Engels; followed by the Bolshevik
Party under the leadership of V.I. Lenin in the early
years of the first Soviet republic and first four congresses of the Communist International; and continued by the communist opposition led by Leon Trotsky.

c) A workers state is a transitional society, not a form of socialism.

   (1) The establishment of a workers state opens the *transition* from capitalism to socialism as part of the *world*
   struggle against imperialist and capitalist exploitation
   and oppression.

   (2) A workers state can go forward toward socialism, or
   backward toward laying the social basis for capitalist
   counterrevolution. The capacity to advance toward
   socialism depends on communist leadership of the
   working-class movement, deepening politicization of
   an increasingly working-class vanguard leading the
   transition, and advances in the world revolution.

   (3) During the transition period in a workers state the
   class struggle becomes more restricted, but it continues as long as the law of value continues to operate
   and the world market continues to exist. As a result,
   anti-working-class prejudices, in all forms and manifestations, continue to be generated and must be
   consciously combated.

d) To approach the construction of socialism in any other
way fosters the development of bloated and privileged
petty-bourgeois social layers and their relatively rapid
consolidation into a counterrevolutionary parasitic caste.

6. The foundations of a workers state, of the dictatorship of the
proletariat, are state property, a monopoly of foreign trade,
and economic planning, established through the expropriation of the bourgeoisie. On these foundations, the working

class can organize more rapid economic and social development and create new social relations of production.

    a) To advance toward socialism on the foundation of these conquests following the October 1917 revolution in Russia required

        (1) the consolidation and extension of the worker-peasant alliance; and

        (2) the construction and proletarianization of a mass communist party.

    b) These two conquests were destroyed by the successful political counterrevolution carried out against the working class during the late 1920s and early 1930s by the petty-bourgeois social caste organized by the Stalinist apparatus.

    c) The state-property foundations of the proletarian dictatorship survived, however, precluding

        (1) the peaceful evolution of the Soviet workers state into capitalism or its absorption by finance capital into the world imperialist system; and

        (2) peaceful coexistence between imperialism and the workers state, regardless of the class-collaborationist course of the bureaucratic caste.

7. The bloated bureaucracy that over time becomes the self-expanding petty-bourgeois caste is able to maintain its social position and privileges not because it is historically necessary — it is not a new class — but because it is able to rely on the Bonapartist regime's massive apparatus of repression, above all its secret police.

    a) The origin and social necessity of the specialized administrative apparatus — out of which the bureaucracy grew — lay in the lack of experience of the Soviet working class in managing the economy and administering the state.

    b) The origin of the repressive police component of this apparatus lies in the scarcity facing the victorious Bolshevik revolution (sharply exacerbated by the famine and devastation from years of civil war and imperialist aggression) and the ensuing struggle for the basic necessities of human existence.[2]

(1) Just as lines for consumer goods were policed, so distribution was administered to ensure that the bureaucracy never had to do without; the resultant police apparatus developed as the fundamental pillar of bureaucratic rule.

    (a) The apparatus gained further opportunity for plunder by assuming the role of defender of the "nation" in response to hostile pressure from the imperialist rulers.

    (b) Through the organization of "distribution" and "defense" by the police and officer corps, the regime assumed a Bonapartist character. That is, the apparatus — appearing to stand above an atomized society divided between the working masses (whose interests lie in state property) and the crisis-wracked petty-bourgeois caste of administrators, officials, and professionals with their bourgeois outlook and values — emerged as the guarantor of the parasitic consumption, relative perks, and privileges of the bureaucratic caste.

    (c) The Bonapartist regime is also needed to arbitrate between the endlessly warring wings of the unstable and decomposing caste.

(2) The power and privileges of the caste are maintained

---

2. By mid-1918 the landlords and capitalists of the old tsarist empire had launched a civil war against the Bolshevik-led workers and peasants republic. The governments of fourteen countries — including the imperialist rulers of the United Kingdom, France, Japan, and the United States — dispatched invading forces to help drive the toilers from power. By the end of 1920 the Red Army had defeated the counterrevolution and its international allies. The war took a terrible toll, however. Millions of workers and peasants — many of the vanguard fighters — were killed or died from famine and disease. Industrial and agricultural production was devastated.

through police methods, escalated by the Bonapartist regime to systematic mass murder when needed. These methods rolled back the use of democratic rights and political space by the toilers and their allies to levels below those conquered in struggle by workers and farmers in many bourgeois states.

(3) This evolution of the bureaucratic caste comes into sharper and sharper conflict with any possibility to draw the producers into an indispensable directing role in the development of a planned economy.

c) A Bonapartist regime is the *only* form of rule possible for the bureaucratic caste.

8. The caste is petty bourgeois in its social character and bourgeois in its attitudes and aspirations.

a) It is not a privileged section of the working class (although it absorbs a layer from the working class), but a social stratum with interests alien to those of the workers and peasants.

b) This petty-bourgeois caste — not small nonexploiting property holders — is the transmission belt into the workers states of imperialist pressures and bourgeois values: contempt for workers; racism, national chauvinism, anti-Semitism; reactionary views on women and family; fear of unfettered scientific experimentation and international debate; philistinism at best and bureaucratic terrorism at worst in relation to the arts and artistic creation; anti-internationalism; and even anticommunism.

c) The growth of such a petty-bourgeois layer deepens class divisions and social differentiation in the workers states.

(1) The petty-bourgeois caste is a massive social layer (numbering tens of millions in the Soviet Union) that consumes a large proportion of the national income.

(2) The members of the caste are not capitalists; that is, they are not property owners accumulating money as capital.

(3) While the caste cannot pass on property, its core

comes to comprise a hereditary stratum, the *nomen-klatura*, that does pass along its prerogatives and privileged standard of living to sons and daughters.

(4) The most fundamental social conditions of workers and peasants increasingly diverge from those of the privileged caste, for example

   a) food, housing, transportation, medical services, child care, literacy, access to higher education, recreation;

   (b) infant and maternal mortality rates and life expectancy;

   (c) differential and discriminatory access to safe, effective, nonbrutal contraceptive methods that protect a woman's right to privacy in sexual matters (e.g., multiple abortions as the only available method of birth control for millions of working women in the Soviet Union; the subordination of a woman's right to choose to shifting "population policies" of the caste, as in Romania); and

   (d) differential exposure to the results of environmental devastation.

(5) The most extreme degree of social and economic differentiation in the Union of Soviet Socialist Republics is between the European republics, especially Russia, and the republics peopled by various oppressed nationalities, especially those in Central Asia (Kazakhstan, Uzbekistan, Tadzhikistan) and the Transcaucasus (Azerbaijan, Armenia, Georgia).

B. The fight for national self-determination: the only road toward a world without borders

1. In bringing to power and consolidating a workers and peasants regime, the socialist revolution opens the beginning of the end of the centuries-old history of national oppression, divisions, and enmities.

   a) The fight against national oppression is always intertwined with radical agrarian reform to liberate the rural toilers from

(1) precapitalist forms of exploitation, by expropriating the landlord classes and abolishing all forms of feudal and semifeudal rents, including compulsory labor duties; and

(2) capitalist exploitation under the rents and mortgages system, by nationalizing the land, guaranteeing the right of peasants to till the soil, and ensuring them adequate means to do so (low-interest credit, seed, fertilizers, tools, and cooperative production and marketing facilities).

b) The advance toward socialism is possible only on the basis of guaranteeing the right of national self-determination to all oppressed nations and nationalities, as well as forging a voluntary federation of workers and farmers republics.

(1) The socialist revolution sounds the bell of "nation time" for oppressed nations and nationalities.

(2) This course was advanced by the Bolshevik leadership under Lenin's guidance following the October 1917 revolution.

(a) As the October victory in Russia gave an impulse to revolutionary uprisings elsewhere throughout the old tsarist empire, the communist leadership began to forge a voluntary federation of the various republics organized on the basis of soviet power — both where the dictatorship of the proletariat had been established (as in Russia and the Ukraine), as well as where it could not yet be established but revolutionary workers and peasants governments had come to power (as in most of the Central Asian and Transcaucasian republics).

(b) Lenin insisted on a *Union* of Soviet Socialist Republics, not a new "Soviet" nationality with patriotism used as cover for maintenance and expansion of Great Russian chauvinism and bourgeois nationalism; not a new "socialist nation-state" suppressing minority nationalities; and not a federation limiting itself to formal equality, but one that took affirmative action to develop the economies and culture of the oppressed nations in order to close the historical gap in social and economic conditions between them and the formerly oppressor Russian nation.

(c) National self-determination, like other democratic rights, is subordinate to defense of the workers state in face of counterrevolutionary assault and imperialist aggression. The denial of national rights, however, weakens rather than strengthens the defense of a workers state. The Soviet republic's policy on national self-determination and its revolutionary agrarian reform were key to mobilizing the peasantry and the victims of tsarist national oppression behind the workers' struggle during the civil war against the combined military forces of imperialism and the domestic landlords and capitalists.

(d) Defense of the workers state itself is subordinate to initiatives by the revolutionary leadership of the state to advance the world struggle for national liberation and socialism (e.g., the transfer of crack Cuban troops and equipment to Angola to win the battle of Cuito Cuanavale; preparations to aid the FMLN, Panama).

(3) The Communist International adopted the Bolsheviks' course on the right to self-determination as the foundation of communist policy on the national question.[3]

---

3. See Lenin's report and theses on the national and colonial question in *Workers of the World and Oppressed Peoples, Unite! Proceedings of the Second Congress, 1920*, vol. 1, pp. 211–16, 283–90, part of the Pathfinder series, The Communist International in Lenin's Time.

2. The Bolsheviks' policy on national self-determination and voluntary federation began to be reversed in the early 1920s by the political course of the emerging bureaucratic caste, led by Stalin. In 1922 Lenin opened a political battle against this counterrevolution, but Stalin's reactionary policies prevailed following Lenin's death.[4]

a) Stalin's course was intensified and institutionalized with the consolidation of the caste's counterrevolution in the early 1930s. The "Union of Soviet Socialist Republics" reemerged in fact as a prison house of nations inherited from tsarism and imperialism.

   (1) The USSR was no longer a voluntary federation, but a "Soviet" super-state.

   (2) The resurgence and domination of Great Russian nationalism within this "Soviet" state obliterated proletarian internationalism.

b) In the wake of World War II, the regimes imposed on the newly established workers states in Eastern and Central Europe served as agencies for the national oppression of these countries by the caste in the Soviet Union. The USSR's invasions of Hungary in 1956 and of Czechoslovakia in 1968 were gross violations of national sovereignty and weakened all the workers states involved.

c) The invasion of Afghanistan by Soviet troops at the end of 1979 violated national sovereignty and set back the struggle against imperialist-backed counterrevolution there.

d) Far from ending national oppression and narrowing national divisions, Moscow's policies — from Stalin through Mikhail Gorbachev — have reinforced oppression and exacerbated divisions. Each additional year that national aspirations have been suppressed by murderous force, the more explosive the inevitable uprisings for self-determination and independence have become.

---

4. See *Lenin's Final Fight, Speeches and Writings 1922–23* (Pathfinder, 1995).

e) Once Stalinism had transformed the Soviet Union into the opposite of a voluntary federation of workers and peasants republics, its break-up, its disintegration from within, was inevitable. This became a precondition to a new advance of the worldwide struggle for national liberation and socialism.[5]

f) The Soviet bureaucracy's oppression of the Eastern and Central European workers states, including through the use of police repression and military force, began to be shattered in 1989. That too is a precondition to a new advance of the world revolution.

3. Communists and other revolutionists unconditionally support the right to national self-determination.

a) Mass struggles for national rights in the oppressed republics of the USSR, regardless of their initial leadership, reflect not imperialist-inspired counterrevolution, but the aspirations and interests of workers and farmers.

b) Given the break in communist continuity in the Soviet Union and European workers states, national struggles there will not begin with revolutionary proletarian leadership; they are today taking place under petty-bourgeois leadership.

c) Only through the fight for and conquest of the right to national self-determination can space open to develop communist leadership of the toilers in the oppressed nations; to open the road once again toward a voluntary union of soviet republics; and to forge links with antiimperialist and anticapitalist struggles worldwide.

4. In the contemporary revolutionary movement, the African

---

5. By the end of 1990 the former Soviet republics had declared their sovereignty, but Moscow only recognized these declarations in the aftermath of the abortive August 1991 coup attempt. By December 1991 all had declared themselves independent. Following the dissolution of the Soviet Union, twelve of the former fifteen republics — all except Estonia, Latvia, and Lithuania — formed the Commonwealth of Independent States, a loose and weak regional confederation.

National Congress has charted a revolutionary course on the national question.

   a) The ANC's goal, laid out in the Freedom Charter and publicly advanced with a broad historic sweep by Nelson Mandela, is not to replace apartheid with rule by a new majority nationality (i.e., the ANC does not espouse the goal of "Black majority rule"). Instead, the ANC fights for a democratic, nonracial South African republic through national liberation, self-determination, and the forging of a South African nation.

   b) This course of the ANC heads away not only from Stalinism but also from the limitations of petty-bourgeois nationalism, which is itself bred in reaction to Stalinist, workerist, and liberal misleaderships of the anti-apartheid and workers' movements. The ANC's revolutionary democratic policy is sharply differentiated not only from the collaborationist nationalist course of Mangosuthu Buthelezi's Inkatha movement but also from the narrow petty-bourgeois nationalist perspectives of the Pan-Africanist Congress (PAC) and groups such as the Azanian People's Organisation (AZAPO).

5. Despite the initial reactionary and disastrous course followed by the leadership of the Sandinista National Liberation Front on the Atlantic Coast, the Autonomy Process initiated in December 1984 represented an important step toward combating racism and national oppression of the indigenous peoples and Blacks in Nicaragua.

   a) On that basis, a Nicaraguan nation began to be forged for the first time, on a voluntary basis and with respect for national rights, opening the possibility of building a worker-peasant alliance that truly extended from the Pacific to Atlantic coasts.

   b) The potential of the Autonomy Process to advance and strengthen the revolution was cut short, as the FSLN leadership began to pursue economic and social policies that eroded the foundations of the workers and farmers government on the Atlantic Coast and the rest of Nicaragua.[6]

6. "Workers and oppressed peoples of the world, unite!" was the slogan raised by Lenin to summarize the international communist policy of unconditional support for national liberation struggles against imperialist oppression.

a) The regimes in the Soviet Union, Eastern Europe, and China have reversed this policy of political solidarity and material assistance to the fight for national liberation, subordinating these struggles to the national diplomatic interests of the castes and their unending search for stable relations with imperialism.

b) Unlike the imperialist ruling classes, the castes do not directly exploit Third World nations through the export of capital. But the castes are complicit with imperialist exploitation through the benefits they reap from unequal trade at prices determined by the world market.

c) The Communist Party of Cuba is the first mass communist leadership of a workers state since the Bolsheviks to carry out a proletarian internationalist approach to the fight for national liberation from imperialist oppression and exploitation.

(1) Following a course explained most clearly by Che Guevara on behalf of the revolutionary government in a February 1965 speech to the Afro-Asian Conference in Algiers, Cuban communists advocate a conscious policy by the more industrially developed workers states to close the gap in economic and social conditions with less developed workers states, workers and farmers governments, and regimes in the Third World arising from popular revolutionary struggles.[7]

---

6. For further discussion of the Autonomy Process in Nicaragua, see "Defend Revolutionary Nicaragua: The Eroding Foundations of the Workers and Farmers Government," pp. 203–5, in issue no. 9 of *New International*.

7. Guevara's speech, presented to representatives of 63 African and Asian governments and 19 national liberation organizations, is available in *Che*

(a) They demand that trade with such governments *not* be based on prices of production reflected in the world market, which embody and perpetuate the exploitative transfer of labor time from oppressed nations to imperialist countries. Instead, trade should take into account the widely differing levels of labor productivity among these nations in order to foster development aimed at more equitable relations.

(b) They propose that the more economically advanced workers states provide direct aid to foster the industrialization and economic and social development of countries that face a legacy of imperialist plunder.

(2) The Cuban government and Communist Party have applied this policy in their fight for preferential trade and pricing policies for Mongolia, Vietnam, and Cuba within the Council for Mutual Economic Assistance (CMEA or Comecon) trading bloc.[8]

(a) The Cuban government and party have advocated that similar CMEA policies be applied toward Grenada, Nicaragua, Angola, and other governments established through victorious popular revolutions or under fire from imperialism.

(b) To the degree allowed by its own limited resources, Cuba itself sends internationalist volunteers and

---

Guevara and the Cuban Revolution: Writings and Speeches of Ernesto Che Guevara (Pathfinder, 1987).

8. The CMEA was founded in 1949 at Moscow's initiative with the stated purpose of coordinating trade and investment policies of the Soviet and Eastern European workers states. In subsequent years Mongolia (1962), Cuba (1972), and Vietnam (1978) joined the council. Yugoslavia was not a member but participated in some CMEA bodies. Albania withdrew in 1961. North Korea and China were never CMEA members or associates. The CMEA announced in January 1990 that it would begin functioning on the basis of world market prices payable in hard currency, and officially dissolved eighteen months later, in June 1991.

provides unstinting help to advance the social and economic development of such countries.

(c) In advancing these policies, communists in Cuba link them to the call for united action to demand that imperialism cancel the Third World debt, to the call for a New International Economic Order that establishes trade and barter arrangements that cease transferring the fruits of labor from oppressed nations to industrially advanced ones, and to the call for greater social and economic justice in Third World countries themselves.

C. Stalinist ideological rationalizations

1. The caste is unable to openly justify either its vast privileges and growing social inequalities or its political expropriation and repression of the working class. Thus, from the time of Stalin, the caste has had to present ideological rationalizations for its domination, repression, and privilege.

a) These do not constitute theory, nor even the ideology of a historic ruling class, but pragmatic and often shifting mystifications and pretexts for the anti-working-class course of the caste.

b) These rationalizations constitute a new revisionism, which communists in the 1930s labeled the "second wave of Menshevism."[9]

---

9. The Mensheviks were a class-collaborationist party in Russia, affiliated to the Socialist International, that broke with the Marxist program and revolutionary organizational principles of the Bolsheviks in the opening years of the twentieth century. During World War I, the Mensheviks opposed the Bolsheviks' course of using the war crisis to advance the revolutionary overthrow of the tsarist regime, and some influential Mensheviks openly backed the war policies of the landlord-capitalist government and called for the victory of the Russian army and those of its imperialist allies. The Mensheviks actively opposed the October 1917 Bolshevik-led revolution and joined in the counterrevolutionary assault on the workers and peasants republic during the 1918–20 civil war.

2. In an effort to justify the gutting of soviet democracy, the caste in the Soviet Union retained the term "soviets" but emptied those bodies of their revolutionary and class content, thus transforming them from organs of political rule by the working class and its toiling allies into instruments to entrench the power and privileges of the bureaucratic caste.

a) That was a central purpose of the 1936 Soviet constitution — and all subsequent amendments to it — that promulgated the claim that socialism had already been established, and thus no classes, class divisions, or class struggles any longer existed in the USSR.

b) The truth is the opposite. The bourgeoisie has been expropriated, but class and social differentiation and conflict remain

(1) the development of the hereditary nomenklatura within the state and party apparatus;

(2) burgeoning layers of privileged petty-bourgeois professionals and intelligentsia;

(3) vast differences between city and countryside, as well as between Russia and the other republics;

(4) oppressor and oppressed nations and nationalities;

(5) social and economic inequality of the sexes, perpetuated by policies that unnecessarily maintain women's domestic responsibilities and workload; and

(6) better- and worse-off layers of workers and peasants everywhere.

c) Behind the pretense of a classless society, the Soviet constitution fills the forms of soviet democracy with an empty and fraudulent bourgeois parliamentary democracy "of the whole people."

(1) This was a cover for tightening Bonapartist rule by the caste.

(2) Since the end of the 1920s, the caste has ruled through the secret police and the apparatus of the degenerated Communist Party, when necessary using terror and murderous repression on a mass scale

heretofore unknown in human history.

(3) Due to the weakening of the Stalinist regime over the decades, Gorbachev is implementing new methods to place Bonapartist rule on different foundations

   (a) establishment of his position as president of the USSR, with the strongest-ever executive powers codified and institutionalized in law;

   (b) downgrading the party apparatus and position of "general secretary" of the party; and

   (c) replacement of many of the powers of the party Politburo by those of the president's handpicked cabinet.[10]

3. Stalinists falsely declare the "single party system" and the banning of political tendencies and factions to be Leninist organizational principles.

a) This is not consistent with the history of the first years of the Soviet republic under Bolshevik leadership. It is a rationalization born after the victory of the Stalin faction.

   (1) The *permanent* ban on factions and tendencies is rationalized on the basis of the decision of the Tenth Congress of the Soviet Communist Party in 1920. But the ban on factionalism was explicitly adopted by the Bolsheviks at that time as a temporary measure in face of the extreme conditions at the end of the Civil War, when both the worker-peasant alliance and Communist Party leadership of the working class were threatened, and open insurrection was breaking out in parts of the Soviet republic.

      (a) Its aim was to stop the factionalism that was tearing apart the party in the face of these pressures.

---

10. Gorbachev was elected general secretary of the Communist Party in 1985. In 1988 he engineered changes in the Soviet constitution strengthening the post of president, previously a largely ornamental state position held by lesser-known figures. Gorbachev was elected president in 1989, retaining his position as party general secretary.

(b) In Lenin's time the temporary ban on factions never barred, nor stopped, internal oral and written discussion and organized debate within the leadership and membership of the Soviet Communist Party.

(2) By 1921 the Bolsheviks were the only remaining party in the soviets of workers', peasants', and soldiers' deputies that had not gone over to open counterrevolution and been banned on that basis. A "single party system" was never presented as a principle of proletarian power, however, by Lenin, the Soviet Communist Party, or the Comintern under Lenin's leadership.

b) Cynically drawing fraudulent "generalizations" from the history of the Soviet republic in Lenin's time, the Stalinists stand revolutionary centralist principles on their head.

(1) Any organized tendency of thought in the party, any call for discussion and clarification, is deemed "factional," "divisive," an "aid to the class enemy," and thus banned.

(2) Any party other than the Soviet CP is declared counterrevolutionary by definition, and the political monopoly of the Stalinized Communist Party is enshrined in the state constitution.

(3) Classes have allegedly been eliminated, socialism established, and the class struggle — except through imperialist subversion — ended. Thus,

(a) Communist and revolutionary opponents of the regime are branded as "Trotskyite wreckers," "fifth columnists," "imperialist agents," or all three, and persecuted, imprisoned, and murdered;

(b) Any struggles by working people against the unbearable consequences of the regime are deemed expressions of imperialist counterrevolution;

(c) "Slandering the Soviet state" is declared a felony

under the criminal code;[11]

(d) Censorship and the falsification of history are institutionalized in every aspect of social, political, and cultural life; and

(e) Workers and peasants are driven out of politics, as every effort they make to take initiatives, discuss the road forward, or correct errors is met with hostility and repression by the apparatus. The working class eventually becomes more depoliticized and socially atomized than it was even under tsarism.

(4) Contrary to the rationalizations of the caste, its policies do not advance the defense of the workers states against imperialism.

(a) These policies destroy class solidarity and political self-confidence among the toilers, promoting fear and thus weakening the defense of the conquests of the October revolution.

(b) Their sole purpose is to maintain the state and party apparatuses as instruments to promote the interests of the caste.

4. As a "scientific" rationalization for increasing social inequality, the Stalinists present bourgeois norms of income distribution as "socialist norms of distribution" that should be maintained.

a) They claim to have established a "classless society," while at the same time declaring that reliance on the law of value not only persists but in fact *develops* under socialism.

b) This "discovery" was codified in Stalin's 1952 pamphlet *Economic Problems of Socialism in the USSR* and has served ever since as the basis of economic manuals and "theories of the transition to socialism."

c) In fighting together with Fidel Castro to apply a commu-

---

11. "Slander of the Soviet state or social system" was illegal under Article 190-1 of the criminal code.

nist course during the opening years of the Cuban revolution, Che Guevara polemicized against this distortion of Marxism, this attempt to make the building of socialism a task of administrators basing themselves on blind laws and mechanisms, instead of it being a political and revolutionary task of the working class based on advancing consciousness and political action.[12]

5. This package of shifting, pragmatic ideological justifications for the practices of a privileged social caste is the cumulative expression of decades of the corruption of communism and Marxism in the name of communism and Marxism.

    a) Stalinist ideology disorients and miseducates revolutionary fighters.

        (1) The caste has used its state power, massive resources, and repressive apparatus to establish falsifications of history and theory as the "orthodox Marxist-Leninist" canon.

        (2) It has monopolized the production and distribution of textbooks, manuals, journals, and the establishment of cadre schools, research institutes, etc. These have been the primary source of "Marxist education" not only in the Soviet Union, Eastern Europe, China, and by pro-Moscow parties worldwide, but also in Cuba, Grenada, and by many national liberation organizations throughout the colonial and semicolonial world.

    b) The presentation of the social reality under bureaucratic misrule by the caste as "actually existing socialism" is an expression of the corruption among Stalinist parties and other "friends of the Soviet Union" who are attracted to

---

12. See the articles by Guevara in Part II of Pathfinder's *Che Guevara and the Cuban Revolution*, as well as his two articles, "On the Concept of Value" and "The Meaning of Socialist Planning" in *New International* no. 8. See also "The Politics of Economics: Che Guevara and Marxist Continuity" by Steve Clark and Jack Barnes and related articles in that same issue of *New International*, as well as *Che Guevara: Economics and Politics in the Transition to Socialism* by Carlos Tablada (Pathfinder, 1989).

power — and to its privileges and perks — not to internationalist and communist principles.

c) As a result, communism in the minds of millions of working people in the workers states and worldwide has become identified not as the generalization of the workers' line of march toward liberation, but as the ideological rationalization for the hated policies and privileges of an oppressor caste. Everything is turned into its opposite.

  (1) "Proletarian internationalism" has been twisted into what best serves the caste interests of the Soviet government, including invasions of other workers states, not the worldwide fight for national liberation and socialism, which includes defense of the workers state.

  (2) "Voluntary work" has been transformed from labor freely given to advance collective social needs into compulsory unpaid overtime work to further fill the trough from which the bureaucracy fattens itself.

  (3) "Revolutionary centralism" has been converted from a weapon of self-confident, critically minded, educated, and disciplined cadres of proletarian parties into bureaucratic monolithism to enforce submission to the counterrevolutionary course of the officialdom of petty-bourgeois parties.

  (4) Marx, Engels, and Lenin have been transformed into icons memorialized in statues, busts, and decorations (even a display mummy, in the case of Lenin) to legitimize, glorify, and mystify the power usurped by the caste. They are "read" by way of manuals, never studied as a whole without "interpretation." Workers eventually come to identify the founders and giants of Marxism as sharing responsibility for the oppression of the toilers.

    (a) The blow to communism was in the erection of such idols by the caste, not their destruction as hated symbols of tyranny by toilers in Eastern and Central Europe.

    (b) Workers and farmers in the workers states will

find the road to Marx, Engels, and Lenin not by way of Stalinist manuals or "critical" Gorbachevian rereadings of history, but through revolutionary struggle at home and worldwide, out of which communist leadership emerges and is tested in class combat.

d) When Gorbachev and others who speak as leaders of "Communist Parties" take their distance from Marx, Engels, Lenin, and communism, when they openly reject the class struggle as the motor of historical development and the dictatorship of the proletariat as its necessary end, this is a positive development for the world revolution.

(1) It opens the road for vanguard fighters and revolutionists to bust through obstacles and obfuscations thrown up by the decades of misrule and find a way to link up with the continuity of communism.

(2) It begins to open up space for discussion and debate; to disentangle decades of lies, confusion, and falsification.

6. Behind the smoke screen of ideological rationalizations lies the reality of the caste's international murder machine.

a) Among the targets of Stalinist thuggery and gangsterism have been the millions of workers and peasants and hundreds of thousands of revolutionists who were murdered in the Soviet Union; the small nuclei of communists such as the SWP and those in other countries who continued to fight together to advance the interests of the international working class (a number of whom were assassinated, including Trotsky); the large number of revolutionary-minded workers and peasants assassinated during the Spanish civil war because of their opposition to the betrayal of that revolution by Moscow and its supporters; and many others.

b) These murderous methods continue to this day (e.g., Pol Pot's slaughter of millions in Cambodia, the Coard faction's assassination of Maurice Bishop and other revolutionists in Grenada, the murder of Commander Ana María by supporters of Salvador Cayetano Carpio in the

FMLN of El Salvador, the methods of the Sendero Luminoso leadership in Peru).

  c) The Stalinist movement is less able to get away with using such methods in today's world.

    (1) What has changed is the relationship of class forces, which makes such methods impossible on any scale comparable to the 1930s and 1940s.

    (2) What has not changed is the character of Stalinism and its practitioners, who, if their backs are to the wall, will use these methods to the degree they can get away with it.[13]

D. The castes' bureaucratic planning and management in the workers states inevitably degenerate toward a system worse than capitalism

1. Despite relatively rapid initial industrialization and urbanization in a deformed and degenerated workers state — the more rural the economy at the outset, the longer this period can be — the rate of labor productivity growth peaks and decelerates toward economic stagnation and irreversible crisis.

  a) This is a law of development of these states, demonstrated by the experience of both the Soviet Union and Eastern Europe.[14]

---

13. After the fall of the Gorbachev regime in the Soviet Union at the end of 1991, the already weakened Stalinist movement disintegrated as a force in world politics. With the enfeeblement, splits, or sometimes outright collapse of Stalinist parties, the class-collaborationist, Popular Front glue that held together "the left" — including social democrats, liberals, and petty-bourgeois radicals of varied stripes — came unstuck. This makes it more difficult today for petty-bourgeois currents to throw up factional obstacles to prevent revolutionists from working together, or from participating in broader action coalitions and united fronts. It ends the decades-long period during which the big majority of revolutionary-minded workers and youth attracted to communist ideas ended up being won to *a counterfeit* of communism that politically destroyed them as revolutionists.

14. The average annual rate of economic growth in the Soviet Union, for

b) Not only will these regimes never catch up with the most industrially advanced capitalist countries, i.e., the imperialist countries, in labor productivity and living standards, they will continue to fall further and further behind.

2. Even under Stalinist domination, these workers states were capable for several decades of promoting industrialization and urbanization of countries that were relatively backward economically.

a) This growth was accomplished largely by means of employing nationalized property, centralized planning, and the monopoly of foreign trade resulting from the expropriation of the bourgeoisie to accomplish in a shorter period of time what the bourgeoisie achieved historically through what Marx referred to as the "so-called primitive accumulation of capital"

(1) the transfer of surplus labor power from countryside to city for factory and construction work;

(2) holding the living standards of the peasantry and agricultural modernization to the minimum in order to finance industrialization (in Germany and Czechoslovakia, the caste was able to build on an already developed industrial base inherited from capitalism);

(3) construction of a basic infrastructure of electrification, transportation, and communication; and

(4) opening of new lands to cultivation, mining, and forestry.

b) Using such methods, these regimes were able to promote relatively rapid growth of industrial output.

(1) With no capitalist business cycle (the domination of prices of production set through the competition of industrial capitals having been broken by expropriation of the bourgeoisie), the Soviet Union continued

---

example, peaked at roughly 6 percent in the 1950s and steadily slowed to the point of an absolute decline by 1989, just before the Stalinist regime collapsed.

to expand industrial output throughout the Great Depression of the 1930s.

(2) This fact gave rise to another rationalization of the course of the Soviet bureaucracy: "Stalin industrialized a backward country and turned it into the world's number two industrial power. Without that course, even with its regrettable excesses, the Soviet Union could not have survived the German imperialist onslaught during World War II."

c) Even during this period of extensive growth, however, bureaucratic planning and management methods were a brake on development. They destroyed rather than encouraged working-class initiative. They set back the development of communist attitudes toward work.

(1) Moreover, this period was marked by the brutal forced collectivization of the peasantry, which permanently blocked the modernization of agriculture. Forced collectivization shattered the worker-peasant alliance, which can be based only on the increasing — and of necessity, voluntary — participation of workers and exploited peasants in economic and political decision making.

(2) Without deepening communist consciousness, growing workers' control and management, and a strengthening worker-peasant alliance, there is no way to reorganize labor, modernize production in industry and agriculture, and produce quality goods in the transition from capitalism to socialism.

(3) Such a course, however, is anathema to the layers of managers and technocrats in the caste, since it threatens the monopoly of power and social division of labor on which their privileges are based.

d) The narrow limits of bureaucratic planning were already clear by the end of 1930s with slowing growth in the USSR, but the regime of the caste got a new lease on life from the Soviet Union's victory over imperialist aggression in World War II and the character of the more primitive economic tasks posed by postwar reconstruction. The onset of the crisis of the Stalinist regimes was announced once again under Khrushchev at the beginning of the 1960s and has worsened in accelerated bursts since that time. This crisis is irreversible.

(1) The "market reforms" and agricultural reorganizations under Khrushchev and in the early years of the Brezhnev period, while resulting in temporary gains in this or that sector, not only failed to reverse the general decline but ended up accelerating the crisis with devastating consequences for the living conditions of working people.

(2) Under Gorbachev's *perestroika* policies, economic and social conditions have already gotten and will continue to get worse overall, not better.

   (a) Perestroika is not a plan or a program: it is the pragmatic response by a section of the caste to the crisis of bureaucratic rule.

   (b) What is striking is not how radical perestroika is, but how constrained the government has been in face of the workers' response. After three years, the regime has implemented none of the central measures proposed by the "perestroika planners."[15]

----

15. Since the early years of the Russian revolution, working people had paid low rents and low prices for bread and other necessities, and were guaranteed jobs — conquests successive Stalinist regimes had not sought to fundamentally reverse in hopes of fending off challenges to their domination. In June 1987 Gorbachev initiated the call for "perestroika," the Russian word for *restructuring*. "A radical reform of pricing is the most important part of the economic overhaul," he said. As of 1990, however, Gorbachev — in face of anticipated working-class unrest, as well as the first strikes by miners and other workers and substantial street protests in many years — had pulled back from planned price hikes and layoffs in state enterprises. "Your cries of alarm are reaching us," Gorbachev told workers during a factory visit in April 1990. In April 1991, when the regime finally announced a plan to raise the price of food and other neces-

(3) The "market reforms" and related schemes in the Eastern and Central European workers states have the same pragmatic character, and are constrained by the same ingrained social values and expectations in the working class and among other toilers.

(4) Such a crisis is equally inevitable in China and Vietnam, but is currently less acute despite their much lower level of economic development and living standards. Because of the weight of agriculture and the large size of the rural population in these countries, the methods that fostered the initial urbanization and industrialization of other deformed and degenerated workers states have not yet been exhausted.

3. Stalinism is not a distorted, very bad form of socialism or communism; it is their counterrevolutionary negation. The deepening crisis in the Soviet and Eastern European workers states shows the dangers of

a) confusing Stalinism with communism;

b) crediting the gains of the dictatorship of the proletariat to its betrayers; or

c) confusing what are in fact the inevitable results of decades of sabotage by the growing parasitic layers and their Bonapartist regimes with the irreplaceable economic foundations of the workers states.

E. Regimes of permanent crisis in deformed workers states

1. By the end of the 1930s the evolution of the Soviet workers state under domination by the caste, and of Stalinist policy in the Soviet Union and worldwide, had

a) Guaranteed the outbreak of the second world imperialist slaughter through organizing a series of devastating de-

---

sities, Gorbachev at the same time deployed joint army-police patrols in more than 400 cities and called for a ban on strikes and demonstrations. The price hikes were finally implemented by Russian president Boris Yeltsin in January 1992, following Gorbachev's resignation.

feats of workers and farmers, in particular

(1) the factional and thuggish course of the Stalin-led Comintern and Communist Party in Germany toward the ranks of the Social Democratic Party — a course that under the ultraleft cover of combating "social fascism" actually paved the way for fascism's triumph in 1933 by blocking any chance for a working-class united front to organize armed resistance;

(2) the Comintern's advocacy and support of the class-collaborationist Popular Front government in France (1936–38), which demobilized the wave of factory occupations and other mass working-class struggles during those years and set the stage for capitalist Bonapartism and the crushing defeat of the labor movement;

(3) the division of the revolutionary working-class forces during the Spanish civil war and murder of antifascist workers and youth, which opened the road to Franco's coming to power in early 1939; and

(4) the August 1939 Stalin-Hitler pact, in the aftermath of which Moscow organized the slaughter of Polish and German communists and revolutionary-minded workers. This action politically disoriented vanguard workers who still looked to the Soviet Union, thus paving the way for the German imperialist invasion of the USSR in June 1941;

b) Put a question mark over the survival of the conquests of the October revolution due to

(1) the devastating consequences of forced collectivization;

(2) the reversal of Leninist policies on the national question;

(3) mounting state terror against workers and peasants (including millions directly murdered);

(4) bloody purge trials, including of the top Soviet army officer corps, on the eve of the German imperialist invasion of the Soviet Union;

c) Dispersed, demoralized, corrupted, and murdered enough of the workers' vanguard worldwide to block the development of mass revolutionary parties under communist leadership. As a result, by the outbreak of World War II, aside from the nuclei of proletarian revolutionists in a number of countries who said "no" to the reversal of Leninism and survived despite Stalin's assassins, there was not a single communist current worthy of the name anywhere in the world.

2. Given the new complexities to the line of march of the working class with the degeneration of the first workers state and the Communist International, the communist nuclei that survived outside the USSR recognized the need to generalize the lessons of these new historical developments, incorporating them into the continuity of Marxist theory in order to guide revolutionary activity.[16]

a) Stalinism is counterrevolutionary through and through. It does not contain an iota of revolutionary or proletarian content.

b) The regime dominated by the petty-bourgeois caste functions in a contradictory way.

(1) The caste seeks by its own methods and for its own reasons to defend the workers state, which is the source from which it derives its material privileges.

(2) But the caste's counterrevolutionary methods gravely weaken the workers state and guarantee a regime of crisis.

c) The Stalinist counterrevolution betrays and rots out the workers state, but cannot overthrow it.

(1) In order to open the road to reimposing stable capitalist relations of production, imperialism must carry out a successful armed counterrevolution to overthrow the foundations of state property root and branch.

(2) Sections of the bureaucracy itself resist the overturn

---

16. See *The Revolution Betrayed* and *In Defense of Marxism* by Leon Trotsky for the most thorough and systematic presentation of these theoretical conquests. Both are published by Pathfinder.

of nationalized property relations.

   (a) While they ape bourgeois life styles and promote bourgeois values, members of the caste cannot be sure which of them, if any, will become the owners if state property is replaced by capitalist property.

   (b) Most importantly, they anticipate and fear massive workers' resistance to the social consequences of steps toward capitalist restoration.

(3) The working class is the only reliable defender of the workers state, the conquests of October, and the only source of their regeneration.

   (a) It will take mighty battles with the working class to reimpose the dominance of stable capitalist property relations, dismantle the state monopoly of foreign trade, and end centralized planning.

   (b) Such battles will be prepared as workers move to resist growing unemployment, accelerated inflation, cuts in the social wage, and deepening social inequality. These are the inevitable consequences of the castes' expanded reliance on capitalist methods and increasing integration of the workers states into the crisis-ridden world economy with its business cycles and depressions.

   (c) These economic and social consequences will manifest themselves in the workers states well before the battle over reestablishment of the supremacy of capitalist prices of production is joined and decided.

   (d) The restoration of capitalism is impossible short of defeating the working class in bloody, counter-revolutionary battles.[17]

17. Far from evolving toward stable capitalist social relations, the regimes in Russia and elsewhere in the former Soviet Union and across Eastern and Central Europe have been gripped by economic and social crisis since 1990. Production plunged for eight consecutive years in these

d) The prognoses implied by this scientific analysis of Stalinism and the class dynamics of the deformed and degenerated workers states have now been thoroughly tested by history. In 1990 we can reaffirm that our strategic and programmatic conquests have been confirmed and enriched by recent experiences of the world workers' movement.

3. In the aftermath of World War II anticapitalist revolutions resulted in the establishment of new workers states.

a) The prognosis of the Socialist Workers Party and its international co-thinkers going into World War II was the following:

(1) Without the extension of the revolution in the course of the war and its aftermath, the Soviet workers state

---

countries — at a rate of more than 20 percent a year in some cases. Only in 1997 was there once again modest, if uneven, net economic growth (1.7 percent) for the region as a whole. Nonetheless, at the end of 1997 output was still roughly 50 percent of its 1990 level in Russia and other former republics of the USSR. Capital investment in Russia has fallen by 90 percent over that period, and livestock herds have declined by 75 percent. And reverberations from the crisis in Asia shook the region in the first half of 1998.

Almost half the population in Russia live below the poverty line (defined as income below $120 a month), and a third of the population across the region as whole — 120 million people — barely scrape by on less than $4 a day, according to a 1997 United Nations report. Average life expectancy in Russia for men plummeted from 64 years in 1990 to 57 in 1995 and from 74 to 72 years for women. Since 1985 the birth rate in Russia almost halved, resulting in a population decline of nearly a million a year. A similar if less drastic decline in health and life expectancy has occurred in eastern Germany, Azerbaijan, Bulgaria, Latvia, and Romania.

Joblessness in Russia, by understated official figures, doubled to almost 10 percent as of mid-1998; unemployment was officially over 10 percent in Bulgaria, Hungary, Poland, and the Slovak republic, among others. And some 40 percent of workers in Russia have gone weeks or months without pay — with wage arrears standing at $11 billion in mid-1998 — leading to a wave of strikes beginning in mid-1998 by miners, rail workers, oilfield workers, and others.

would not survive the onslaught of imperialism; and

(2) Any extension of the revolution and successful defense of the workers state would sweep aside the caste in a revolutionary upsurge, reestablish communist leadership in the Soviet Union, and open the door to a revived revolutionary International.

b) Revolutionary crises and an extension of the socialist revolution did occur in the wake of the war, but in a more complex and contradictory way than communists had anticipated.

(1) Despite the counterrevolutionary course of the Stalinist regime, the workers and peasants of the Soviet Union successfully defended the workers state and turned back the German imperialist onslaught. They did so at great cost of lives and material sacrifice.

(2) Despite triumphing over its imperialist rivals in the war, Washington was prevented from using U.S. troops to launch any new military action against the Soviet Union or to block revolutionary blows against capitalism in Eastern Europe and China. During the latter half of the war itself there was a resurgence of battles by UMWA coal miners and other workers against the patriotic no-strike pledge and wage freeze, as well as struggles against racist discrimination in the war industries, that

(a) drew on reserves from the labor battles in the 1930s that built the CIO as a social movement;

(b) erupted in a postwar strike wave that continued through 1946 and into early 1947; and

(c) provided the impulse that gave rise by the mid-1950s to the mass proletarian struggle against Jim Crow and for Black civil rights.

(3) By the end of the 1940s and first half of the 1950s, capitalist property relations had been overturned in Yugoslavia, elsewhere in Eastern and Central Europe, North Korea, China, and then North Vietnam. These

transformations occurred under the domination of Stalinist, not revolutionary, leadership.

(4) The weakening of imperialism and failure to overturn the Soviet workers state impelled national liberation and independence struggles throughout Asia, Africa, and the Americas to a new stage.

(5) Stalinist and social democratic misleaderships, whose domination of the working-class movement in post–World War II Europe was the result of the historic defeats of the previous two decades, blocked the possibility for socialist victories that existed in France, Italy, and elsewhere in imperialist Western Europe at that time. This gave the capitalist rulers the breathing space needed to overcome the conditions that would have permitted small communist nuclei there to grow into mass revolutionary workers' parties.

c) As a result of this outcome of the war, the crisis of the Soviet caste, and of the newly emerging castes in Eastern Europe, was postponed. Moreover, the Stalinists temporarily restored some of their political credibility by standing at the head of several worker and peasant revolutions (Yugoslavia, Albania, China, Vietnam) and all of the newly emerging workers states.

d) Communists retained our political conviction that the survival of the Soviet workers state, the extension of proletarian property relations, and the advance of the colonial revolution would weaken Stalinism's hold and open new prospects for the emergence of revolutionary leadership.

(1) Communists rejected alternative prognoses for the Soviet Union implied by the analysis of various petty-bourgeois currents in the working-class movement

(a) that the survival of the Soviet workers state vindicated the Stalinist course, even if deeply flawed; that the USSR would surpass the economic growth and increase in labor productivity of the imperialist centers and continue to advance to-

ward socialism; and that in the process the bureaucratic regime would reform itself; or

(b) that the Soviet Union was not a degenerated
workers state with a Bonapartist regime of crisis,
but was marked by a new mode of production
and a new ruling class (whether such a social
formation was characterized as state capitalism,
bureaucratic collectivism, or some new historic
form of totalitarianism).

(2) Communists also rejected related alternative prognoses about the historic prospects of world Stalinism
and the renewal of communist leadership

(a) that the victories of the Yugoslav and Chinese revolutions under Stalinist-led parties would establish
the pattern for the rest of the century; that Stalinism would follow a revolutionary course, albeit
with serious deformations and weaknesses; or

(b) that Stalinism's postwar second wind would make
it strong enough to block revolutionary leaderships and prevent further advances for the socialist revolution and the development of communist
leadership.

(3) These questions were resolved in 1959–61 with the
victory of the Cuban revolution under a revolutionary
leadership that, bypassing the Popular Socialist Party
(the old CP in Cuba), had

(a) overthrown the U.S.-backed Batista dictatorship;

(b) won the leadership of the masses;

(c) established a workers and farmers government;

(d) carried through a thoroughgoing democratic
revolution and agrarian reform;

(e) gone on to expropriate Yankee and domestic
capitalists, explicitly opening the socialist revolution in the Americas as it decisively defeated the
U.S.-sponsored and -organized invasion at the
Bay of Pigs;

(f) built the Revolutionary Armed Forces;

(g) deepened a proletarian course in both its domestic and foreign policies; and

(h) pressed toward revolutionary unity and the forging of a mass communist workers' party.

4. The Stalinist counterrevolution broke communist continuity in the deformed and degenerated workers states.

a) By World War II the communist organization in the Soviet Union had become so decimated as to preclude its revival, even under the impact of postwar revolutionary victories in Yugoslavia and elsewhere.

b) The communist consciousness that survived in the Soviet Union among the generation that made the October revolution had eroded over the decades.

c) In more recent decades, communist continuity in the Soviet Union even among individuals has been broken.

d) There is no communist, no Marxist, no proletarian political vanguard in the Soviet Union, Eastern Europe, or China today.

e) New communist parties in these deformed and degenerated workers states can and will be forged, but only through deepening class-struggle experience and as part of a broader advance of the world revolution.

5. Given this reality, political revolution is not on the immediate agenda in the Soviet Union and other deformed and degenerated workers states, nor has it been for at least three decades.

a) Under such conditions, it became inevitable

(1) that these regimes would not be overthrown in a communist-led political revolution, but would first have to be torn apart by the popular masses in the face of a profound crisis, as is now happening; and

(2) that only then could the possibility of political life open up, out of which forging a communist leadership could be accomplished.

b) Cuba is the only workers state where it today remains possible to combat bureaucratic abuses, tendencies, and crimes and to halt the consolidation of a privileged social caste through politically revolutionary means. This is true

(1) because a communist leadership exists in Cuba; and

(2) because that leadership is part of a broad layer of workers and peasants who are consciously communist and proletarian internationalist.

c) What opens up with the disintegration of the Stalinist regimes is not a political revolution, but the opportunity for workers to reconquer political space to defend and advance the class interests of the great toiling majority.

(1) The disintegration of the Stalinist parties and weakening of the bureaucratic regimes create the possibility for the working class and the workers' movement to fight to develop, to politicize, and to start being open to the influence of revolutionary struggles the world over. It is along this road of struggle that the beginnings of a communist movement can be forged.

(2) The governments that are coming into existence throughout Eastern Europe are petty-bourgeois regimes that are bourgeois in orientation, and in this sense are not a qualitative break from their predecessors.

(a) They are staffed not only by holdovers from the nomenklatura itself, but incorporate new layers from the intelligentsia and middle classes in these countries.

(b) While being prepared to march alongside these forces in actions aimed at busting up the previous secret-police regimes, communists oppose all the new governments, which are anti-working-class politically, as were the Stalinist apparatuses they are replacing.

(3) Proletarian revolutionists put forward a communist program for the deformed and degenerated workers states, despite the fact that no revolutionary proletarian organizations exist in these countries.

(a) They speak for the interests of the working class

in the democratic and antibureaucratic struggles.
(b) They advance the perspective of the revolutionary political regeneration by the working class and its toiling allies of the economics and politics of the workers state.
(c) They point to the example of revolutionary Cuba and the revival of communist leadership through the extension of the world revolution.
(d) They advocate the restoration of genuine soviet democracy through institutions of struggle forged by the workers and toiling farmers in the course of their battles.

d) The popular explosions against the regimes in the deformed and degenerated workers states became inevitable at the point when broad layers of working people, youth, and the middle classes recognized and began acting on the basis of the following political realities:

(1) Imperialism had been weakened enough over the postwar decades that it was no longer credible that the collapse of the existing governments posed a serious threat of invasion of Eastern Europe and the Soviet Union. Workers in Eastern Europe do not believe that their mobilizations against these oppressive regimes increase the military threat by imperialism.
(a) They have absorbed the significance for their own struggles and national sovereignty of the nuclear parity of the United States and the Soviet Union.
(b) They sense that the post-Vietnam antiwar opposition in the United States is a barrier to any sustained military invasion by Washington.

(2) The evidence became unambiguous in the 1980s that the bureaucratically planned economies of these regimes — despite earlier periods of rapid industrialization — were mired in irreversible economic stagnation and social crisis.
(a) This was not just a matter of the lack of material

goods and deteriorating social welfare.

(b) The Stalinist knout could no longer force workers and peasants to produce under conditions of accelerating social inequality, bureaucratic abuse, and alienation — let alone to exercise creativity and initiative in their work.

(c) Corruption, arbitrariness, and lack of integrity in all social relations — the violence done to human culture in the broadest sense — was so deepgoing that to continue living in the old way became increasingly intolerable to working people.

(3) The regime in the Soviet Union was less and less willing to pay the political price, abroad or at home, for militarily intervening to crush popular uprisings in the Warsaw Pact countries. Working people in the Eastern and Central European workers states drew the lessons from

(a) the Polish workers uprising in the 1980s, where not only did no Soviet troops intervene (as they had in Hungary in 1956 and Czechoslovakia in 1968), but where the martial law crackdown of the Polish regime itself in late 1981 failed to crush the resistance; and

(b) the Soviet regime's 1989 withdrawal from Afghanistan, where the decade-long occupation created a worsening debacle and led to intensifying social unrest within the USSR itself.

6. The events of 1989–90 are a verification of the communist prognosis that the workers states, even those deformed from birth by Stalinist domination, would prove stronger than the bureaucratic castes.

a) The petty-bourgeois caste is not a historic ruling class.

(1) It has no historic economic role in a mode of production.

(2) This bloated layer continues to expand further and further beyond the size of an administrative bureaucracy socially necessary to the tasks of production. It

blocks any motion toward establishing new social relations of production in harmony with and leading toward a new mode of production implicit in the nationalized-property foundations of the workers states.

(3) It is a cancer weakening the workers states and their economic foundations.

b) In contrast to the regimes of the stronger capitalist ruling classes, the Bonapartist regime is weak, brittle, and unstable. These regimes have disintegrated with startling rapidity. Their explosion began after only sixty years in the Soviet Union and even less time in Eastern and Central Europe — mere blips in social history.

(1) The bureaucracy will not give up its positions without a fight. The ruling oligarchy takes whatever measures it can to preserve bureaucratic rule and privilege, including the sacrifice of entire wings of the nomenklatura in order to salvage the rest, and the incorporation of new layers into the ruling stratum.

(2) The measures taken by these regimes have not historically stabilized them. The governments have proven to be not only regimes of crisis, but regimes of permanent crisis.

(3) Gorbachev's counterreformation, embarked upon in response to the events in Poland, and his deepening Bonapartist course will accelerate, not resolve, the crisis in the USSR.

c) The workers states themselves have been shown to be stronger than the castes and their police regimes.

(1) The workers states survive and can only be overthrown in battle with the working classes.

(2) "The social revolution, betrayed by the ruling party," Trotsky explained in 1936, "still exists in property relations and in the consciousness of the toiling masses."[18]

---

18. *The Revolution Betrayed*, p. 230.

(a) More than half a century later, the first part of this assessment remains unchanged: the proletarian property relations still exist in the Soviet Union, as well as in the other deformed workers states.

(b) While the socialist consciousness of the toiling masses has been obliterated since the 1930s, and not even a nucleus of a communist vanguard exists today, bourgeois trade union consciousness and the assumption by the working class of the right to a historically defined minimal social wage remain the first obstacle that will lead to massive struggles in the workers states against the reimposition of capitalism.

(3) A counterrevolution to overturn the workers states and their nationalized property foundations cannot be carried out internally, but would require direct imperialist involvement to succeed and consolidate.

F. Disintegration of Stalinist parties

1. With the exception of the Communist Party of Cuba, nowhere in the world is a party with the name "Communist" either communist or revolutionary.

2. The Stalinist parties in the deformed and degenerated workers states are not political parties, not voluntary associations of the vanguard of a social class organized for participation in political life. They are machines for the defense and advancement of a petty-bourgeois social caste.

a) They are not "conservative" or "bureaucratic" workers' parties, but instead a "job trust" of the privileged middle-class layers in the bureaucratic apparatuses of the state, economic enterprises, trade unions, the party itself, writers' associations, and other institutions.

b) The disintegration of these apparatuses in 1989 and 1990 has been rapid and explosive.

(1) The Communist Party has already been mortally wounded in the Soviet Union.

> (a) Gorbachev's Bonapartist moves have elevated the state apparatus and posts over party structures.
>
> (b) The Communist Party has been swept from dominant positions in the Baltic states and seriously weakened in other republics.

(2) The Communist Party, or its renamed successor, has lost its monopoly control of the regimes in Poland, Hungary, Czechoslovakia, and East Germany. The CP has been formally dissolved in Romania, and is coming apart along national lines in Yugoslavia.[19]

(3) Party apparatuses throughout Eastern Europe have lost material resources, land, buildings, their press monopoly, and so on. Most have dropped the word "Communist" from their names and are attempting to take on vaguely social democratic or more explicitly nationalist trappings.

(4) These CPs have lost massive numbers of members over the past year, as

> (a) membership has become an impediment rather than a ladder to individual social and economic advancement; and
>
> (b) the apparatus's leverage to coerce other layers of the population to retain membership has broken down.

3. Outside the deformed and degenerated workers states, the Stalinist parties and youth groups are organizations fundamentally characterized by their social relationship to state power held by the petty-bourgeois castes.

a) This relationship is built on corruption and rewards

> (1) jobs in various international organizations and fronts;
>
> (2) access to travel, vacations, medical care, other perks and privileges.

b) This holds true not just for those in the party apparatuses themselves, but related "friendship" associations, youth and

---

19. A similar process resulted in the fall of the regime and party in Bulgaria later in 1990 and in Albania in 1991.

women's organizations, trade union officialdoms, and so on.

c) This relationship to the state power of the castes is the source of the Stalinist parties' separate identity from social democracy.

    (1) The difference is not in their class-collaborationist political perspectives or privileges derived from bases in municipal administrations or trade union apparatuses that they dominate; that is common to both Stalinism and social democracy.

    (2) The difference is the source of the power toward which they respectively orient (and from which they derive their political space)

        (a) the Stalinists toward the bureaucracies in the workers states;

        (b) the Social Democrats, the political expression of the bourgeoisified labor bureaucracy in capitalist countries, toward their "own" bourgeois governments.

    (3) Where the Stalinists compete with the Social Democrats solely on the plane of bourgeois electoralism and efforts at class collaboration, they become more and more marginalized, since social democracy has a much longer record of social patriotism and undivided loyalty to "their own" imperialist bourgeoisie.

    (4) The decline of Stalinist parties and regimes, however, pushes social democracy farther to the right, not to the left, and does not precipitate left-wing currents within social democracy. Instead, these developments spur class-collaborationist regroupments and the reshuffling of centrist sects in the orbit of the Stalinists and social democrats.

d) The deepening crisis of the regimes in the deformed and degenerated workers states has shaken Stalinist organizations in capitalist countries. While most are wracked by crises, these are less acute than the disintegration that has swept Communist Parties throughout Eastern Europe. The relationship of these organizations in the capitalist world to the crisis-ridden Stalinist regimes is more indirect than that of CPs in the workers states themselves.

   (1) The big majority of these parties outside the workers states have adjusted to the shifts, staking their prospects on hopes for Gorbachev's success. They continue to seek benefits from maintaining a relationship to state power, even if on a reduced basis.

   (2) Nonetheless, Gorbachev and leaders of other Stalinist parties in the deformed and degenerated workers states are less interested in links with CPs in the capitalist countries. These parties serve the caste less and less effectively as levers of diplomacy to influence capitalist ruling parties; Gorbachev and other "reformers" have access to direct relations with the imperialist rulers and their parties.

 e) A new Stalinist "Communist International" to replace the organization dissolved by Stalin in 1943 to curry favor with his World War II imperialist allies is ruled out.

   (1) Such a world organization serves no conceivable interest of the caste.

   (2) Its former components are in greater political and organizational disarray than ever before.

4. The disintegration of Stalinist parties, both inside and outside the workers states, has not given birth to currents with a clearly defined alternative political course, let alone a road forward in the fight for socialism.

 a) There is nothing for revolutionists and communists to orient toward in any of these splintering currents. While there may be individuals who can be won to communist politics, we will find and win them only in the course of broad revolutionary work, not through an orientation to fragments of Stalinist groupings.

 b) During the first ten years of the Comintern, the best layers of fighters and revolutionists were attracted to the Communist Parties.

   (1) On a world scale, this has not been the case since the

degeneration of these parties in the 1930s.

(2) Under the impact of the emergence of the revolutionary leadership of the Communist Party of Cuba in the 1960s, the best layers of fighters — especially in the Americas — did not orient toward reforming Stalinist parties but toward efforts to build new revolutionary organizations.

G. Ours is the epoch of world revolution; the dictatorship of the proletariat has proven stronger than counterrevolutionary Stalinism

1. The growing vulnerability of the international capitalist system and shattering of illusions in the stability and longevity of the counterrevolutionary Stalinist apparatuses underline the character of the epoch in which we are living in the closing decade of the twentieth century.

2. This is the epoch of world revolution: the epoch opened by the Bolshevik-led October 1917 revolution and its international extension, not the epoch of its degeneration and demise.

a) It remains the epoch of the establishment of the first dictatorship of the proletariat under communist leadership, the epoch of those workers and exploited farmers who

(1) made the October 1917 revolution or sought to emulate it;

(2) opened the struggle for national liberation and socialist revolution as a worldwide fight; and

(3) made possible in 1919 the forging of the Communist International — the first truly world revolutionary leadership — under a proletarian banner.

b) The task today remains to organize the world's toilers to move forward to the completion of the revolutionary overthrow of imperialism and the victory of the socialist revolution the world over.

3. 1990 is not, as most "opinion makers" would have it, the opening of the decade of the triumph of capitalism and bourgeois democracy, socialism having proven to be economically

unworkable and politically totalitarian.

a) The irreversible crisis of the regimes of the parasitic castes explodes the myth — originating in the mid-1930s and widely held in bourgeois and petty-bourgeois circles since then — that the Stalinist counterrevolution in the Soviet Union gave rise to a new stable historic mode of production and system of oppression.

(1) Proponents of variants of this view have often presented the regimes in the Soviet Union, and later those in Eastern and Central Europe, as virtually impregnable: a new, centuries-long social system based on unremitting repression.

(2) Some predicted its gradual convergence with an increasingly totalitarian world capitalist system — both based on growing domination by small elites over toiling populations more and more marked by their depoliticization, mediocrity, consumerism, and cultural philistinism.[20]

b) Nor is the world heading into an era marked by permanent, expanding, and perfecting bourgeois democracy.

(1) The openly bourgeois presentation of this claim — trumpeted loudly over the past year — is a rationalization for

---

20. Bolshevik leader Leon Trotsky answered the earliest exponents of this view in his 1939–40 articles and letters collected in the book *In Defense of Marxism*, published by Pathfinder. The two individuals dealt with by Trotsky were Bruno Rizzi, an Italian ex-communist who had written a book entitled *The Bureaucratization of the World*, and James Burnham, a leader of a petty-bourgeois current in the Socialist Workers Party who broke with the communist movement in 1940 under the pressure of patriotic bourgeois public opinion on the eve of U.S. entry into World War II. A few months later Burnham published a best-selling book on this topic entitled *The Managerial Revolution*. Variants of this "convergence" view have been popularized since World War II in works such as the novel *1984* by George Orwell; the novels and essays of right-wing "libertarian" Ayn Rand (and her acolytes, including the young Alan Greenspan some years before his elevation to U.S. imperialism's chief banker); and most recently in the 1994 book *The Bell Curve: Intelligence and Class Structure in American Life* by Richard Herrnstein and Charles Murray.

intensifying capitalist exploitation and oppression of working people the world over. In fact, mounting worker and farmer resistance to the consequences of the operations of capitalism will be met by the rulers with increased assaults on democratic rights and political space in the coming decade.[21]

(2) A radical petty-bourgeois version of this scenario became prominently associated in the second half of the 1980s with spokespersons for the dominant leadership of the FSLN in Nicaragua, as well as by those who look to them elsewhere in the Americas and worldwide.

(a) They have presented the Nicaraguan revolution as a "third road" between capitalism and communism — a third road that could obtain social reorganization and economic development by avoiding, not leading, the fight for the dictatorship of the proletariat.

(b) This middle way has been justified by the prognosis that the world — both "East" and "West" — is heading into a period of broader democracy, the "humanization" of foreign policy based on détente and eased international tensions, and a convergence through the "mixed economy" of market socialism with a more humane capitalism.

(c) "Sandinista" Nicaragua was portrayed as being in the vanguard of all these trends, standing against conservative and recalcitrant forces both in the "imperialist camp" (Reaganism as opposed to the

---

21. In a 1989 magazine article entitled "The End of History?" U.S. State Department official Francis Fukuyama wrote that "democratic capitalism" constitutes the "end point of mankind's ideological evolution," "the final form of human government," and "the triumph of the Western idea." Amid Gorbachev's growing talk about "universal human values," and in the wake of the fall of the first of the Eastern European Stalinist regimes in Poland, Fukuyama's article was showered with publicity by the bourgeois media at the time.

Rainbow Coalition) and the "socialist camp" (Cuba's rectification process as opposed to Gorbachev's more "enlightened" *perestroika* and *glasnost*).

(d) The defeat in Nicaragua deals a blow to this ideology in the workers movement. It is a petty-bourgeois ideology — anti-working-class and anti-Marxist at its core — whose thrust is to demand backing from the toilers for those who will make "everything better" for them, as opposed to organizing and mobilizing the workers and farmers to advance the social revolution and build a revolutionary party.[22]

c) The course of the past seven decades, reaffirmed by the events of the past year, also belie the Stalinists' claim that this is the epoch of "peaceful coexistence," "peaceful competition between social systems," the bureaucratic construction of "socialism in one country," or — à la Gorbachev — the spread of "universal human values."

(1) It is not true that revolutionary struggle by the workers and peasants against imperialism increases the danger of war.

(2) Advances in the world struggle for national liberation and socialism push back and weaken imperialism, including its political capacity to make war.

(3) While Washington continues to rely on the Stalinist regimes as a counterrevolutionary buffer against the conquest of power by the world's toilers, the Soviet government under Gorbachev is in its weakest position since the rise of Stalin to throw up obstacles to revolutionary anti-imperialist and anticapitalist struggles.

d) It is also not true, as claimed by many bourgeois and petty-bourgeois political forces (both in the imperialist countries and in the workers states themselves), that the breakdown of the regimes in Eastern and Central Europe

---

22. The FSLN's campaign slogan in the 1990 presidential campaign was, "We are winning. Everything will get better."

KHALED ZIGHARI/AP-WIDE WORLD PHOTOS

As police of the Palestinian Authority seek to restrain them, Arab youth defend themselves against assault by Israeli government troops during April 1997 protest against Tel Aviv's expansion of settlements in the occupied territories. "The exploiters have not been able to overcome the political obstacles to their capacity to carry out sustained wars, or to prevent rebellions and fights for liberation by workers and peasants of the colonial and semicolonial world."

opens a new era of "democracy."

(1) Either the working class in the deformed workers states will — through more or less protracted struggles — produce a communist vanguard that can lead the popular masses in winning the fight to establish soviet democracy, workers' and peasants' democracy; or capitalism will eventually be reimposed in blood at the hands of imperialist aggressors aided by domestic counterrevolution.

(2) There is no possibility of a stable, classless "democracy" in the deformed and degenerated workers states serving the needs and interests of "the whole people."

4. *It is imperialism that has suffered the greatest blows from the accelerating crisis of the Stalinist regimes,* which have served as its most reliable instrument for the transmission of capitalist values into the workers states and more broadly into the international workers' movement.

a) Despite the barbarities of imperialism in this century — from Hiroshima to the Nazi death camps to the saturation bombing of Vietnam — and despite the mass slaughter of working people and their vanguards by the international Stalinist murder machine, neither the exploiting classes nor their Stalinist collaborators have stopped the workers and peasants from rebounding and continuing the fight for their rights and a decent life.

(1) If workers and farmers are unable to resolve the capitalist-caused crisis facing humanity, and to defend the mighty conquests of our class since October 1917, then imperialism will impose new bloody defeats through fascism and war. While victory for the workers and exploited farmers depends on the construction of communist leadership, the direction of twentieth-century history has been toward weakening the hold of the imperialist system of exploitation and oppression, and of the world's final empire, the USA.

(2) The exploiters have not been able to resolve the

growing stagnation and vulnerability of the world capitalist system. They have not been able to impose crushing defeats on the working people and labor movements of a single imperialist country. They have not been able to overcome the political obstacles to their capacity to carry out sustained wars, or to prevent rebellions and fights for liberation by workers and peasants of the colonial and semicolonial world. And they have not been able, since 1917, to restore capitalist property relations to a single one of the countries where it has been overturned.

(3) The revolutionary internationalism of the Cuban government and Communist Party and the deepening ANC-led struggle to bring down the apartheid regime represent the wave of the future, not the last vestiges of a bygone era. And this future will be marked by class struggles, popular revolutions, national liberation movements, and civil wars.

b) The advances registered by the toilers of Eastern and Central Europe in 1989–90 against oppressive regimes have already begun to bring fighting humanity closer together.

(1) In the most immediate sense, the walls between struggles by working people in the Eastern European workers states and capitalist Western Europe have begun to crumble.

(a) This tendency has already developed the furthest in the intertwining of the prospects and struggles of workers in East and West Germany.

(b) A similar logic could be seen in the explosive struggle in Soviet Azerbaijan, which drew toilers from the USSR, Iran, and Turkey toward a common opening for workers and farmers in Eastern and Central struggle.[23]

---

23. In January 1990 Gorbachev imposed martial law in the republic of Azerbaijan, located in the southern Transcaucasian region of the former

(2) The possibility is Europe and the Soviet Union to be brought into the world revolution; to learn about, solidarize, and link up with fighting workers and farmers in Europe, North America, and throughout the imperialist world, as well as with revolutionary struggles from South Africa to Cuba and worldwide.

(3) The course, direction, and outcome of the battles that have opened in the deformed and degenerated workers states depend on their interlinkage with developments in the world class struggle, and vice versa.

c) The drawing together of struggles by working people the world over opens the way toward winning more and more revolutionists to become communists, toward rebuilding proletarian leadership and an international communist movement.

(1) The world in the making will see more Malcolm Xs, more Maurice Bishops, more Thomas Sankaras, more Nelson Mandelas, more Che Guevaras, more Fidel Castros.

(a) They will continue to be thrust forward through struggle toward the renewal of communist leadership.

(b) They will more and more recognize communism as the opposite of Stalinism and social democracy, as a road toward overthrowing world capitalism,

---

Soviet Union. Moscow's troops assaulted and occupied the capital city of Baku, killing scores of Azerbaijanis. As a pretext, Gorbachev pointed to the growing conflict between the Azerbaijani and Armenian republics over Nagorno-Karabakh, a region within Azerbaijan largely populated by Armenians. In fact, Moscow's show of force was an unsuccessful attempt to stem the disintegration of the Soviet Union.

The Azerbaijanis are a Turkic-speaking people whose historic homeland is divided between the now-independent Republic of Azerbaijan and the Azerbaijan region of northern Iran. Earlier in January 1990 protests had taken place on both sides of the border between the two regions demanding the right to travel freely back and forth and national unification. Azerbaijanis in both regions, as well as the Azerbaijani minority in Turkey, staged protests demanding the withdrawal of Moscow's troops.

not accommodation with it.

(c) They will more and more be seen by vanguard workers in all countries as part of the leadership of a common world struggle.

(2) With the breakdown of the massive Stalinist obstacles to politicization of toilers in the deformed and degenerated workers states, prospects are opened there — for the first time in many decades — for layers of them to begin being influenced and inspired by the example and by the writings and speeches of these and other revolutionary and communist leaders.

d) Marx, Engels, Lenin, Trotsky, and Guevara were not visionaries or prophets. They were revolutionary fighters, as well as scientists who generalized the hard-learned experiences along the only road forward for the workers of the world: the road toward the dictatorship of the proletariat, opening the transition to socialism and the communist future of humanity.

In face of accelerating capitalist crisis in Asia, workers employed by Hyundai Motor Co. in South Korea went on strike in mid-1998, demanding that working people not be thrown out of jobs at the behest of imperialist banks. "Intensifying interimperialist competition and the deepening instability and vulnerability of the international capitalist system converge with the prospects for a world depression and social crisis in the 1990s."

UNITE unionists join 1997 protest in New York against police beating of Abner Louima, a Haitian immigrant. "An upsurge of union resistance will give a renewed impulse to broader social struggles and increasingly proletarianize their composition. Likewise, such struggles will swell the size, and strengthen the social composition, of the emerging rank-and-file leadership of the labor movement."

PART IV

REBUILDING A WORLD COMMUNIST MOVEMENT

A. Communist Party of Cuba

1. The leadership of the Communist Party of Cuba is the first since the Bolsheviks to give communist guidance to the development of a workers state. In the face of unrelenting U.S. imperialist economic, political, and military pressures, that leadership has maintained a revolutionary course at the helm of the Cuban government for more than thirty-one years. In the process it has

   a) reknit one of the strands of communist continuity that had been broken since the Stalinist counterrevolution that destroyed the Bolshevik Party and the Communist International by the end of the 1920s; and

   b) established a current truly worthy of the name communist — the first outside of the direct continuity of the small nucleus of Bolshevik-Leninists, including the Socialist Workers Party, that had stood alone from the late 1920s through the 1950s.

2. The leadership team headed by Fidel Castro successfully bypassed the obstacle presented by a large Stalinist party and led the toilers in making a revolution and establishing a workers and farmers government.

   a) Building on that revolutionary victory, this leadership deepened popular mobilizations culminating in the expropriation of the foreign and domestic capitalists and landlords. On that foundation, a workers state was established.

   b) Unlike the workers states in Eastern and Central Europe and Asia established following World War II, the new Cuban workers state was not bureaucratically deformed from birth in a qualitative way by the domination of an increasingly crystallized petty-bourgeois caste.

c) The leadership team headed by Castro led the revolution forward in such a way that it began the construction of socialism instead of veering onto a trajectory that led toward a system worse than capitalism.

d) In the process of advancing these tasks, this leadership forged a mass proletarian communist party that follows a revolutionary internationalist course.

3. This "subjective factor" — the genuinely internationalist character of the proletarian vanguard guiding the workers state in Cuba — is the most important *objective* outcome and contribution of the Cuban revolution. The consequences for the revolution's domestic and international trajectories are inextricably intertwined.

a) Cuban communists are revolutionists of action, as modern communists have been since the revolutions of 1847–48 in Europe.[1]

b) The communist course charted by such a leadership of the working class is the fundamental precondition to advancing toward the construction of socialism on the economic foundations of a workers state; it is a precondition to catching and rectifying major errors in this process.

c) Cuba has become a powerful objective force in world politics, beyond all bourgeois or petty-bourgeois measures of its "geopolitical" or economic weight.

4. Revolutionary Cuba's policy is to conduct relations with other political forces in the world according to proletarian internationalist principle.

---

1. For a summary of the strategic conclusions the founders of the modern communist workers movement drew from those revolutionary struggles and their own active participation in them, see "Communism and the Fight for a Popular Revolutionary Government: 1848 to Today" by Mary-Alice Waters in *New International* no. 3.

a) The 1975 *Programmatic Platform of the Communist Party of Cuba* states that the party's policy is "subordination . . . of the interests of Cuba to the general interests of the struggle for socialism and communism, of national liberation, of the defeat of imperialism and the elimination of colonialism, neocolonialism and all forms of exploitation and discrimination. . . ."[2]

b) The test of the internationalist course of the Communist Party leadership in Cuba has been met above all in their deeds.

  (1) They have provided unstinting political solidarity, economic and social assistance, expertise, and military volunteers to revolutionary struggles and governments under fire by imperialism — from Vietnam to the Middle East, from Africa to the Americas.

  (2) The defeat of the South African army at the battle of Cuito Cuanavale is the latest example, with the most far-reaching consequences, of Cuban communists marshaling the resources of the dictatorship of the proletariat to advance revolutionary struggles worldwide.

c) In pursuing its internationalist course, the Communist Party of Cuba

  (1) seeks to advance an uncompromising struggle against imperialist domination anywhere in the world;

  (2) refuses to subordinate the interests of workers and peasants to the preservation of capitalist property and prerogatives;

  (3) seeks collaboration with other revolutionists of action, whether communists or not; and

  (4) approaches the ranks of fighters not as objects to be deployed, but as revolutionary leaders in becoming, with no a priori limits on what they can accomplish.

---

2. *Programmatic Platform of the Communist Party of Cuba* (Havana: Department of Revolutionary Orientation of the Central Committee of the Communist Party of Cuba, 1976), p. 120–21.

d) The internationalist course of the Communist Party of Cuba has strengthened the defense of the revolution against imperialist aggression.

   (1) Growing awareness of the international weight and historic responsibilities of the dictatorship of the proletariat in Cuba has been key to the communist vanguard's capacity to successfully organize and mobilize the workers and farmers to stand up to imperialism's pressures and attacks for more than three decades.

   (a) Willingness to make sacrifices to help others who are fighting imperialism has increased consciousness of the stakes involved in advancing the Cuban revolution.

   (b) Voluntary participation in internationalist missions reinforced awareness that only through rising communist consciousness and increasing voluntary work could the revolution advance at home.

   (2) Cuba's anti-imperialism has been bold but not reckless. Its policies have demonstrated that

   (a) by subordinating the pace and character of transforming domestic social relations to the needs of the world struggle against imperialism (e.g., the material aid and human resources devoted to helping Angola defend itself), the progress and defense of the revolution is enhanced;

   (b) the extension of the world revolution is of decisive importance to the pace and even the possibility of constructing socialism; and

   (c) the only effective way of standing up to imperialism's relentless offensive is through continuously deepening the conscious leadership and voluntary participation of working people in the economy, in politics, in the worldwide anti-imperialist struggle, and in the revolution's defense.

5. The greatest challenge and obstacle facing the leadership of the Cuban revolution since 1959 is to have triumphed in a

world in which all other mass parties standing at the head of workers states and calling themselves "communist" have been in reality Stalinist.

    a) This has been a more complex challenge for the Cuban revolution than the unrelenting pressure of U.S. imperialism.

    b) Other socialist revolutions succeeded following World War II (Yugoslavia, Albania, Korea, China, and Vietnam) through great sacrifice and courage of the workers and peasants. But the limits of the leadership resulted in the consolidation of workers states that were deformed from birth, with laws of development similar to those manifesting themselves in the Soviet Union following the Stalinist betrayal of the Bolshevik revolution.

    c) Bureaucratic castes also dominated the governments of the Eastern and Central European workers states established following the war. In the majority of these countries, the overturn of capitalist property came less in the wake of popular revolutions than through bureaucratically controlled mobilizations presided over by the Soviet army of occupation.

    d) The leaderships of all these deformed workers states followed a Stalinist course in both domestic and international policy.

6. By establishing a workers state headed by a communist leadership, the Cuban revolution reknit a strand of continuity that had been broken for decades. This was a crucial turning point in the development of the international working-class movement.

    a) For the first time since the early 1920s a revolutionary leadership at the head of a state began to *use that power* to advance a proletarian internationalist course.

    b) In the context of the advance of revolutionary struggles, the example of Cuba's revolutionary leadership has promoted the renewal of communist leadership internationally.

7. The weight of this subjective factor — a communist leadership of a workers state at the head of a broader politicized pro-

letarian vanguard — is greater now than at any previous time in the history of the Cuban revolution.

   a) The existence of a revolutionary leadership makes it possible in Cuba — unlike any other workers state — to confront and combat growing bureaucratic deformations and advance the construction of socialism. This is the historic significance of the rectification process initiated by the Communist Party in 1986 in face of mounting inequality, bureaucratism, corruption, and the resulting increase in cynicism and demoralization.

   b) This reorientation in the Cuban revolution is captured in a new watchword of the revolution: "Socialism or death!" Either forward toward socialism or backward toward the consolidation of a "system worse than capitalism" is another way of saying the same thing.[3]

   c) The success or failure of rectification will settle the life-or-death question of Cuba's capacity to move along the only road that can advance toward, rather than away from, socialism.

   d) The outcome of this class struggle in Cuba will weigh heavily on prospects for renewing communist forces worldwide.

8. The rectification process marks an effort by Cuba's communist leadership to organize the equivalent of a political revolution within the institutions and structures of the workers state, and to do so, to paraphrase Lenin, without "shaking up" the

---

3. In a speech to the second session of the Third Congress of the Communist Party of Cuba on December 2, 1986, explaining the rectification process launched some seven months earlier, Castro pointed to the example of state enterprises "that tried to become profitable by theft, swindles, swindling one another. What kind of socialism were we going to build along those lines. What kind of ideology was that? And I want to know whether those methods weren't leading us to a system worse than capitalism, instead of leading us toward socialism and communism." In *New International* no. 6 ("Important Problems for the Whole of International Revolutionary Thought"), p. 217.

worker-farmer alliance on which the state is based or the broad patriotic unity necessary to defend the revolution against Washington's implacable hostility.[4]

a) It is a response to the pressing need to revolutionize the bureaucratically warped organization of labor and the economic planning and management system modeled on Stalinist forms copied from the Soviet Union and Eastern and Central Europe.

(1) Rectification is above all a revolutionary reorientation aimed at overcoming the political obstacles to making the participation, consciousness, and self-transformation of working people the center of revolutionizing relations of production and exchange, a goal that is possible only on the economic foundations of a workers state.

(2) Rectification is the opposite of a policy that seeks a more efficient form of economic planning based on new and better ways of administering the producers through reliance on the state planning bureaucracy. The latter course could only lead to increased commodity fetishism, bourgeois values and social norms, and the demobilization, demoralization, and depoliticization of working people.

---

4. In late 1920 and early 1921, Lenin rejected Trotsky's call for "shaking up" the trade unions in order to get industrial production moving again in the aftermath of the social and economic devastation of the civil war. "For, *even if the 'shake-up' policy were partly justified*," Lenin said, ". . . it cannot be tolerated at the present time and in the present situation, because it threatens a split" within the working class and its revolutionary vanguard, the Bolshevik Party. Such a split, Lenin said, "is not just dangerous" but "extremely dangerous, especially when the proletariat constitutes a small minority of the population" and when layers of the peasantry were in open rebellion in face of war-caused famine and breakdown in production and distribution of farm tools and basic consumer goods. Under these conditions, a split would "shake and destroy the whole political edifice," Lenin said. See Lenin's *Collected Works*, vol. 32, especially pp. 43–53 and 75–80.

b) Cuba is the first workers state since the Bolshevik-led Union of Soviet Socialist Republics to attempt to follow the communist line of march that is at the heart of the rectification process.

(1) This course of organizing social labor to foster the development of social consciousness and human solidarity was explained most clearly and forcefully by Ernesto Che Guevara during the opening years of the Cuban revolution. A course diametrically opposed to that advocated by Guevara gained increasing weight, however, and a system of economic planning and management copied from the bureaucratized workers states was generalized and implemented by the mid-1970s.

(2) Central to the rectification process has been a return to the use of volunteer labor to carry out some of Cuba's most pressing social tasks. This has been done through:

(a) the relaunching of the minibrigade movement to build houses, schools, day-care centers, medical facilities, popular sports facilities, and similar projects; and

(b) the initial development of the construction contingents, which have taken on massive projects to improve Cuba's economic infrastructure and industrial capacity.[5]

(3) The reintroduction of volunteer labor has gone hand in hand with the reversal of a tendency toward greater reliance on capitalist methods, such as material incentives and wage inequalities, commodity relations among state

---

5. For a further discussion of the volunteer construction contingents and minibrigades, see "Che's Proletarian Legacy and Cuba's Rectification Process" by Mary-Alice Waters, as well as "The Politics of Economics: Che Guevara and Marxist Continuity" by Steve Clark and Jack Barnes, both published in issue no. 8 of *New International.*

enterprises, the "free" private farmers' market, the rein-
stitution of private rental housing and real estate speculation.

c) The advance of rectification has been inseparable from a
fight against growing social inequality, the consolidation
of privileged layers of the apparatus, corruption, and bureaucratic indifference and contempt for the needs and
revolutionary capacities of working people.

(1) Such counterrevolutionary tendencies are inevitably
fostered by attempts to organize the economy of a
workers state without relying on a working-class vanguard that is increasingly conscious of its revolutionary political responsibility to lead the advance toward
socialism.

(2) The first battles on this front of the rectification
process culminated in the summer of 1989 with the
trials and sentencing of former general Arnaldo
Ochoa; the de la Guardia brothers in the Ministry of
the Interior; former general José Abrantes, who had
been the minister of the interior; Diocles Torralbas,
former minister of transportation; and many others.[6]

---

6. In June-July 1989 General Arnaldo Ochoa, who was a member of the
Central Committee of the Communist Party, and three other high-
ranking officers of the Revolutionary Armed Forces and Ministry of the
Interior, including Antonio de la Guardia, were tried, convicted, and
executed for hostile acts against a foreign state, drug trafficking, and
abuse of office. At the same trial, several other Cuban army and Ministry
of the Interior officers, including Patricio de la Guardia (brother of Antonio de la Guardia) were convicted and sentenced to prison terms ranging from ten to thirty years. The following month José Abrantes, Cuba's
minister of the interior, was tried and convicted on charges of abuse of
authority, negligence in carrying out his duties, and improper use of
government funds and resources. He was sentenced to twenty years in
prison. In July Diocles Torralbas, the minister of transportation and a
member of the Central Committee for more than two decades, was convicted of misappropriation of funds for personal gain and other crimes
and sentenced to twenty years in prison.

d) Advancing the proletarianization of the Communist Party's cadres and leadership is the central challenge of the rectification process.

(1) Members of the Communist Party and Union of Young Communists have been in the vanguard of the tens of thousands of volunteers for the minibrigades and construction contingents. They have also volunteered to take jobs in sectors of the workforce in Cuba where bureaucratic leadership and policies have led to the greatest demoralization and political retreat. This registers an advance in the proletarianization of the party and its leadership.

(2) Workers, Blacks, women, and internationalist volunteers are being consciously promoted not only to become members of the party but to assume greater leadership responsibility at all levels, in all institutions.

(3) This process of making the party and its leadership more working class in composition is inseparable from conscious steps to accelerate a transition in leadership to a new generation of communists in the party.

(4) This course of "renewal or death," as it has been called in Cuba, is decisive to the progress of rectification and the future of the revolution.[7]

---

7. In a speech to the Third Congress of the Communist Party in February 1986, Fidel Castro pointed out that the previous congress in 1980 "gave the candidate list for the Central Committee a strong injection of both women and workers — steps it was magnificent to take. Now we have to continue along the same lines, adding workers, and not just workers who have become leaders but workers from the factory floor. We had to continue along this course, we had to stress three questions, three categories requiring promotion, three injections — a strong injection of women, a strong injection of blacks and of mestizos," and a strong injection of youth. Such progress, Castro said, is "a question of renewal or death." The portion of Castro's 1986 speech on the election of the Central Committee is available in *New International* no. 6, "Renewal or Death," pp. 239–53.

e) Obstacles to launching the rectification process would have been much greater if the corrosive trends that began accelerating in Cuba in the mid-1970s had not been counterbalanced to a degree by the response of the Communist Party leadership, and of millions of Cuban workers and farmers, to revolutionary advances elsewhere in the world.

(1) During the 1970s historic blows were dealt to imperialism in Southeast Asia, Ethiopia, the former Portuguese colonial empire in Africa, and Iran.

(2) Revolutions triumphed in Grenada and Nicaragua in 1979, leading to the establishment of the first workers and farmers governments in the Americas since 1959. These victories helped loosen the U.S. imperialist-imposed isolation of socialist Cuba in the region and gave a new impulse to revolutionary struggles throughout the Americas. Cuba was now one of "three giants."[8]

(3) In response to Washington's escalating military pressure in the wake of revolutionary gains in Central America and the Caribbean, millions of Cubans mobilized for the Marches of the Fighting People in 1980. That same year the Cuban government launched the Territorial Troop Militia and began a shift in its defense strategy prioritizing military training and preparedness of the entire Cuban people.

---

8. In a speech to the Federation of Cuban Women on March 8, 1980, Castro underlined the importance of the revolutionary advances in Central America and the Caribbean. "One must have a sense of history," he said, "to know . . . what revolution means here, next to the imperialist monster; yes, what the Cuban revolution and its firm, unwavering line has meant. One needs a sense of history and of realities to understand the merit of the Sandinista revolution, the merit of the Grenadian revolution. Grenada, Nicaragua, and Cuba are three giants rising up to defend their right to independence, sovereignty, and justice, on the very threshold of imperialism." *Women and the Cuban Revolution* (Pathfinder, 1981), p. 129.

(4) Hundreds of thousands of Cubans went to Ethiopia, Angola, Grenada, Nicaragua, and elsewhere as volunteers carrying out internationalist missions. The majority returned to Cuba as more steeled and conscious supporters of the communist course of the Cuban revolution.

(5) These revolutionary advances, however, also precipitated political resistance, especially within the privileged petty-bourgeois layers of the apparatus that were expanding in number and gaining ground in Cuba. The "fainthearts," as they were called, began to grow weary of the pressures from U.S. imperialism and sought respite through accommodation and retreat from the revolution's internationalist policies.

f) The advance of rectification was greatly reinforced by the Cuban government's decision in late 1987 to put the future of the revolution on the line in what became the battle of Cuito Cuanavale. The Cuban-Angolan-SWAPO victory over the South African armed forces not only changed the course of the history of Africa but gave renewed confidence and determination to the vanguard of Cuban workers, especially the youth, whose courage and capacities secured that victory and opened the door to further revolutionary advances at home.

9. For more than thirty years the example set by the course of the Cuban leadership has posed a political challenge to those claiming to be revolutionaries. The capacity to recognize the fact that a mass communist leadership of a workers state had emerged and to respond to this historic new factor in the world class struggle was an acid test.

a) The Socialist Workers Party welcomed and passed this test from the beginning.

(1) In 1960 SWP presidential candidate Farrell Dobbs and *Militant* editor Joseph Hansen visited Cuba to see the revolution firsthand and to help get out the truth about it. We sought to mobilize defense and solidarity

through the *Militant* and the SWP's 1960 presidential campaign. We printed the speeches of Cuba's leaders and built the Fair Play for Cuba Committee. The Young Socialist Alliance put identification with the Cuban revolution and its leadership at the center of its campaigns and recruitment.

(2) Our movement analyzed and explained the concrete trajectory of the new workers and farmers government, the workers state, and the evolution of the leadership in Cuba. As we did so, we built on previous political conquests and strengthened the continuity of communist theory.[9]

(3) The Cuban revolution and the SWP's response to it were the most important turning point in the post–World War II history of the communist movement in the United States. Had we failed this test, we would have been finished as a revolutionary movement.

b) An accurate appreciation of the historical place of the Cuban revolution and its leadership remains the touchstone of communist politics today. It is central to the political outlook and activity of the SWP and the international current of communist leagues of which we are part.

10. The Communist Party of Cuba has charted a revolutionary proletarian political course in spite of the obstacles erected by liberal-bourgeois and Stalinist political forces. These obstacles have had to be overcome not just once but repeatedly.

a) Maintaining this course has required proletarian principles, courage, tenacity, and discipline.

b) It meant leading the liberal-bourgeois forces in the July 26 Movement while confronting each challenge they posed in the course of the fight for power, as well as dur-

---

9. See *Dynamics of the Cuban Revolution: A Marxist Appreciation* by Joseph Hansen; *The Workers and Farmers Government* by Joseph Hansen; and *The Workers and Farmers Government in the United States* by Jack Barnes. All are available from Pathfinder.

ing the first years after the victory, as the leadership organized the workers and peasants to deepen the revolution in the class interests of the toilers.

c) It meant defeating recurrent challenges by the Stalinists to the revolution's communist course.

(1) The revolutionary leadership of the July 26 Movement had to bypass the Popular Socialist Party (PSP) in order to make the revolution.

(2) After the victory, all political currents in Cuba were tested by their deeds, as the revolutionary leadership forged a united communist organization, fusing the July 26 Movement with other prorevolution forces including the PSP and the Revolutionary Directorate.

(3) During the first years of the revolution, a substantial faction of the forces that came into the united party from the PSP, led by Aníbal Escalante, organized behind the backs of the party leadership to undermine the fusion and try to take control of the party.

(a) They used their positions to promote friends and cronies in the party apparatus.

(b) Their functioning was characterized by the bureaucratic abuse of the party ranks and nonparty workers and farmers.

(c) Their attempt to expropriate peasants' land and impose collectivization in the Escambray mountains, in violation of the agrarian reform laws and party policy, endangered the worker-farmer alliance on which the revolutionary government and party were based.

(4) As a result of the Escalante faction's activities, the very existence of the workers and farmers regime was jeopardized.

(a) The triumph of the Escalante faction would have led to the overthrow of the revolution and murder of Fidel, Raúl, Che, and other leaders.

(b) The Escalante faction was politically exposed and

defeated, however, and Stalinist forces were dealt a blow from which they never recovered.[10]

d) Political and economic policies and mechanisms copied from the Soviet Union and Eastern Europe in the 1970s and early 1980s accelerated the growth of social and economic privileges and petty-bourgeois aspirations among a vastly expanded layer of administrators and professionals in the apparatus of the state, party, unions, and other institutions.

(1) Unlike the Soviet Union, Eastern Europe, and China, however, the leadership of the Communist Party of Cuba combated and prevented the institutionalization of special stores, vacation resorts, schools, and medical and recreation facilities for a privileged elite.

(2) The Ministry of the Interior, which began to establish such caste privileges, was sharply called to order by the third party congress in 1986 and instructed to turn over all special facilities to local government units for use by the population as a whole.[11]

(3) Only with the opening of the rectification process, however, was a political course charted to reverse the motion toward institutionalized privileges for a growing social layer and to excise the cancer in the Ministry of the Interior.

e) The ongoing fight against bureaucratization in Cuba has

---

10. For further discussion of this chapter in the history of the Cuban revolution, see "The Fight for a Workers and Farmers Government in the United States" by Jack Barnes, in *New International* no. 4, pp. 135–68.

11. The Main Report to the Third Congress of the Communist Party in February 1986, presented by Fidel Castro, pointed out that the Ministry of Interior must "always set high personal standards and energetically combat all instances of complacency, corruption, vanity, disregard for the people and their principles. . . ." As an example, the report cited the Ministry of Interior's "recent decision to give the health, sports and recreational facilities, which had been built in the previous five-year period to satisfy their needs, to the provincial bodies of People's Power for the people to use."

not been at its root an "ideological" struggle, but a class conflict.

(1) Relatively privileged administrative and professional layers in Cuba comprise a disproportionate share of those attracted to Gorbachev and *perestroika* because they are attracted to bourgeois liberalism, the greater material differentiation guaranteed by the capitalist market and commodity production, and the bourgeois values of the professional middle classes in the imperialist countries.

(2) These petty-bourgeois social layers generally share a coolness if not antipathy toward Cuba's proletarian internationalist course, and a common attraction to the always-hoped-for Moscow-Washington deal that could include Cuba.

(3) These strata largely recoil from the political course of rectification: voluntary labor; the conscious promotion of workers, Blacks, women, and internationalist fighters in all institutions; the growing control by workers and farmers over the administration of the economy and state; the study of Marx, Engels, Lenin, and Castro unabridged, without "manuals of instruction"; and the entire revolutionary communist course associated in Cuba with the example of Ernesto Che Guevara.

11. Attempts to chart an alternative revolutionary course to advance toward socialism without (1) forging communist parties based on the workers and peasants and (2) establishing the dictatorship of the proletariat, a workers state, have led not only to failure but to disaster.

a) The 1980s confirm once again that there is no such thing as "reformed" let alone "revolutionary" Stalinism.

(1) In Grenada, this challenge was not met, as it had been in Cuba with the defeat of Escalante's secret faction. A counterrevolutionary faction led by Bernard Coard was able to seize control of the New Jewel Movement's Central Committee, imprison the leader-

ship of the revolution and demoralize the toilers, overthrow the workers and farmers government, crush a mass popular uprising led by Maurice Bishop that sought to reverse the counterrevolution, and assassinate Bishop and other revolutionary leaders.

(2) The political disaster in Afghanistan that resulted from the course of the PDPA leadership and its homicidal power struggles was worsened by the military intervention organized by the Soviet bureaucracy. Moscow's action effectively turned over to the reactionaries the claim to be fighting for Afghanistan's national self-determination.

(3) The Stalinist leadership of the petty-bourgeois nationalist regime in South Yemen was also torn apart in a fratricidal bloodbath in 1986 and the revolutionary democratic and secularizing momentum of the toilers was lost.

b) In Nicaragua the FSLN leadership failed in its attempt to turn "Sandinismo" into a revolutionary alternative to communism — a new road that could lead to socialism.

(1) During the second half of the decade following the 1979 triumph, Sandinismo became less and less identified in practice with the proletarian trajectory implied in Sandino's affirmation that "only the workers and peasants will go all the way."

(2) Increasingly, Sandinism was given a petty-bourgeois content by FSLN leaders heading toward conciliation with the bourgeoisie — part left social democracy, part perestroika Stalinism, part radical Rainbow Coalition liberalism (one part Olof Palme, one part Mikhail Gorbachev, one part Jesse Jackson; instead of one part Farrell Dobbs, one part Fidel Castro, one part Malcolm X).

(3) The FSLN leadership more and more retreated from organizing the working class as the leading political and social force in the revolution in alliance with the

peasants. The course increasingly became one of attempting to administer a solution to growing social and economic problems, without charting a course to break the domination of bourgeois property and social relations of production and distribution.

(4) Strengthening the workers and peasants government in Nicaragua did not depend on the rapidity with which the landlords and capitalists were expropriated, nor did it involve downplaying the decisive weight of the democratic tasks of consolidating and defending Nicaraguan national sovereignty and unification and radical agrarian reform. The acid test was advancing in a direction that promoted class consciousness, independent political organization, and the revolutionary mobilization of workers and peasants against the exploiting capitalists and landlords.

(5) Instead, the political trajectory of the revolution in relationship to the "mixed economy" became the subordination of the workers' and peasants' needs to the preservation of capitalist social relations in order to maintain the strategic political alliance being forged by the FSLN leadership with layers of the bourgeoisie and landlords.

(a) As imperialist aggression intensified, the FSLN pursued a course away from radical agrarian reform and expanding workers control in factories and workplaces; away from prioritizing the needs of exploited toilers in confronting the capitalist economic and social crisis and national reconstruction; away from advancing women's rights; and away from strengthening the volunteer, as opposed to draftee, base of the Sandinista armed forces.[12]

---

12. In relying on a draftee rather than volunteer armed forces, the Sandinista leadership adopted the course urged on them by Soviet military advisers there. In a 1997 interview, Cuban general Néstor López Cuba,

(b) The international consequence of this course was to put increasing pressure on the FSLN government to subordinate its foreign policy, including support for the FMLN in El Salvador, to securing an alliance with sections of the bourgeoisie at home as well as a truce with Washington.

(c) The FSLN leadership rejected the necessity of building a proletarian communist party from the most self-sacrificing and class-conscious vanguard of the toilers in order to consolidate and advance workers and peasants power.

(6) The evolution of the FSLN leadership's policies represents an abandonment of the political course and legacy of Carlos Fonseca, codified in his writings, including the "Historic Program" of the FSLN.

(7) The FSLN's course has pushed the big majority of the noncommunist supporters of the Nicaraguan revolution around the world further away from working-class politics.

(a) While most were disappointed by the election results in February 1990, they have been increasingly attracted to rather than repelled from the FSLN leadership's trajectory and its decisive role in the establishment of a bourgeois coalition government.

(b) The "Managua trail" has now become a road away

---

head of the Cuban military mission in Nicaragua for a number of years in the 1980s, noted that, "The Sandinistas had both Cuban and Soviet military advisers, and we didn't always agree on our advice. The Soviets argued for a large, professional, technically sophisticated, regular army. We, on the other hand, believed Nicaragua needed an army capable of eliminating the irregular forces they confronted internally, and that this could not be accomplished by a regular army. . . . It had to be fought by volunteers. That's how we defeated the bandits in the early years of the Cuban revolution." (The interview was first published in the June 22, 1998, issue of the *Militant* newsweekly.)

from rather than toward communism, the opposite of what it earlier had been for many.

12. The "Cuban road" is in fact a particular instance of what has been the trajectory of the modern communist movement since 1847: charting a course toward building the worker-farmer alliance under proletarian leadership in order to conquer state power, expropriate the exploiters, and open the building of socialism.

a) The historic political course of the communists in Cuba is not "Cuban" or idiosyncratic. It is not "Castroist." It is communist. The leadership rediscovered in practice the path pointed to by Marx and Engels and advanced by Lenin, and followed it in Cuba and in the world. They did not build a totally new road; they built a further extension on the communist road, and in so doing enriched and strengthened communist continuity.

(1) Central to the rectification process is the vigorous political defense of socialism as "the only hope, the only road for the peoples, the oppressed, the exploited, the plundered."[13]

(2) As the negative lesson of Nicaragua shows, socialism can be built only *through* establishing the dictatorship of the proletariat, not by avoiding that decisive turning point. It is only along that course, as well, that a mass worker and peasant communist cadre can be constructed.

b) The effort by Cuban communists, led by Fidel Castro as part of the rectification process, to bring to the fore the

13. Quoted from a December 1988 speech by Fidel Castro to a rally of a half million people in Havana to celebrate Armed Forces Day, the anniversary of the landing of the yacht *Granma* carrying eighty-two fighters under Castro's command to begin the revolutionary war against the U.S.-backed dictatorship of Fulgencio Batista. See "As Long as the Empire Exists We Will Never Lower Our Guard," in Fidel Castro, *In Defense of Socialism: Four Speeches on the 30th Anniversary of the Cuban Revolution* (Pathfinder, 1989), p. 30.

political example and contributions of Che Guevara helps make possible a broader, international reconquering of the program and strategy forged by Marx and Engels, Lenin, the Bolsheviks, and the first four congresses of the Communist International.

B. Building communist parties in the 1990s

1. The period we are entering will be similar in many ways to that marked by the previous deep-going international economic and social crisis, that of the 1930s, which developed on a world scale into a prerevolutionary situation.

   a) During that crisis, the labor movement came to the center stage of politics early in the 1930s in imperialist Europe, Australia, New Zealand, and North America, as well as in some of the more economically developed countries dominated by imperialism.

   b) Mounting worker and farmer resistance to the exploiters' blows provided an opportunity for the working class to recover from the defeats and setbacks it had suffered worldwide between 1923 and 1933.

      (1) In 1923 in Germany the third revolutionary workers and peasants uprising in five years posing the question of power was crushed. Mussolini's fascists came to power in Italy. The initial revolutionary wave in Europe opened by the Bolshevik-led October revolution in 1917 had been defeated.

      (2) In 1933 capitalist rule in Germany was maintained through the Nazi coup. Due to the craven class collaborationism of the Social Democrats and the frenzied factionalism of Third Period Stalinism, the Hitler movement's disciplined street-fighting units never even had to face united armed resistance by the working-class movement, which would have smashed the Nazis. Once consolidated, however, Hitler's Bonapartist police regime began to terrorize and pulverize workers organizations, paving the way for imperialist

war, the invasion of the Soviet Union, and racist exterminations.

2. The most important difference between the 1930s and today is that then the Stalinists had a choke hold on the international Communist movement by the time the world depression and generalized social crisis began.

   a) As a result of the political betrayals of the major class battles of the 1930s, the opportunity to rebound from the defeats of 1923–33 and score revolutionary victories was lost.

      (1) The failure to extend the socialist revolution beyond the Soviet republics during the prerevolutionary situation of 1918–23 was accounted for above all by the inexperience and ultraleftism of the proletarian vanguard in the newly established Communist Parties.

      (2) The failure during the mid- and late-1930s to carve out a revolutionary leadership that could lead the workers to power, halt the march of fascism, and block the imperialists' drive toward world war and the invasion of the Soviet Union can be laid directly at the feet of political betrayals by the leaderships of the world Communist movement.

   b) Communist Parties subordinated the workers movement and revolutionary national liberation struggles to the national diplomatic interests of the Soviet regime.

      (1) They pursued a class-collaborationist, Popular Front orientation toward those wings of various imperialist ruling classes that they hoped would be most responsive to the Soviet bureaucracy's needs.

      (2) They put their international murder machine to work against fighters and revolutionists who "disrupted" this course by fighting for class independence and by refusing to subordinate workers' and farmers' interests and national liberation struggles to maintaining a bloc with "democratic imperialism" and bourgeois forces.

      (3) This counterrevolutionary course resulted in devastating defeats for workers and farmers across Europe,

which, by the time of the fascist victory in the Spanish civil war in 1939, had made the invasion of the Soviet Union and the outbreak of the second world imperialist slaughter inevitable.

c) In the United States, these class-collaborationist policies took the form of subordination of the union movement and working-class battles to the imperialist Democratic Party and Franklin Roosevelt–led political coalition.

   (1) The Communist Party USA was decisive in helping to derail the evolution of the CIO, which had been born as a fighting social movement

      (a) that was based on the power of rising industrial unions;

      (b) that pointed in the direction of independent labor political action; and

      (c) whose initial blows to the Jim Crow structure and to racial and national divisions in the working class pointed toward organization of the South and desegregation of the labor movement.

   (2) With the exception of a brief ultraleft jag during the Stalin-Hitler pact, the CPUSA from 1935 on joined with the top labor officialdom and social democrats in drawing the CIO in tow behind Washington's preparations for war.

   (3) During World War II the Communist Party helped the employing class impose austerity and labor discipline on the working class to aid imperialism's war effort.

d) The size and weight of the Stalinist movement worldwide in the 1930s, combined with the social-patriotic course of the social democrats and union officialdom, blocked the development of mass revolutionary currents.

   (1) The pro-Moscow forces used all the means at their disposal from slander to assassination to throttle revolutionary developments, targeting the developing working-class vanguard. In the United States they welcomed Washington's first use of the thought-control

Smith Act against the class-struggle leadership of the Midwest Teamsters.[14]

(2) Under these conditions, there was little room for a Fidel Castro, a Malcolm X, a Maurice Bishop, or a Thomas Sankara to emerge and evolve toward communism, just as there was little room for communists such as James P. Cannon, Farrell Dobbs, and others to forge a mass revolutionary workers party.

e) The situation is strikingly different today. As we enter the 1990s

(1) Stalinist parties are everywhere in crisis;

(2) the imperialist powers have been weakened by decades of anti-imperialist struggles that have won political independence for hundreds of millions of the most oppressed and exploited peoples of the world; the road to socialist revolution has been opened for them as the only path toward economic development, political equality, and life with dignity; and

---

14. Signed into law by Franklin Roosevelt in June 1940, the Smith Act was aimed at breaking the class-struggle vanguard of the labor movement that was leading opposition to Washington's imperialist war preparations. The law provided stiff prison terms for advocating views deemed "seditious." First to be convicted under the new law were eighteen leaders of General Drivers Local 544 in Minnesota and of the Socialist Workers Party. On December 8, 1941, the day after the bombing of Pearl Harbor, the Minneapolis defendants were given sentences ranging from twelve to eighteen months in prison for "conspiring to advocate the overthrow of the U.S. government."(See *Socialism on Trial* by James P. Cannon and *Teamster Bureaucracy* by Farrell Dobbs.)

The Communist Party USA actively supported the federal prosecution and helped the Department of Justice prepare evidence for the trial. An editorial in the *Daily Worker* stated that "the leaders of the Trotskyist organization which operates under the false name of 'Socialist Workers Party' deserve no more support . . . than the Nazis who camouflage their Party under the false name 'National Socialist Workers Party.'" Following World War II, in 1949, the Smith Act was also used to railroad leaders of the Communist Party to prison. In 1958 the central provisions of the thought-control law were declared unconstitutional.

    (3) a mass proletarian communist party guides a workers state in Cuba, charting a course that strengthens rather than weakens the economic and social foundations of the dictatorship of the proletariat.

3. A second important difference from the 1930s is that the coming labor radicalization will build on the conquests of the social protest movements and working-class struggles in the 1960s and early 1970s.

    a) These include the powerful struggles for Black rights, the current manifestation of which had its origins, in fact, in the midst of World War II; the mass opposition to the Vietnam War; the new rise of the women's movement; the emergence of a politicized Chicano movement; growing awareness both in the United States and Puerto Rico of the importance of the Puerto Rican independence struggle; ongoing actions in defense of immigrants' rights, the rights of lesbians and gays and of the disabled; and rising consciousness of and opposition to nuclear power and environmental degradation.

        (1) These struggles grew out of changed conditions generated by the second world imperialist slaughter and its aftermath.

        (2) They deeply affected the working class and had a profound impact on the thinking of workers and the ranks of the labor movement.

    b) By the mid-1970s the social and political struggles of the previous fifteen years had peaked, having bumped into the objective limits imposed by the class relationship of forces and the bourgeois two-party system.

        (1) Having wrested gains that were substantial, even if skewed in their impact toward the middle class, these social movements faced limits imposed by

            (a) the consequences of the long-term weakening of the unions as a result of the institutionalization of the class-collaborationist methods of the union officialdom;

            (b) the accelerating antilabor offensive by the ruling

class, as the postwar wave of capitalist expansion came to an end; and

(c) the bourgeois ideological counteroffensive against past gains that accompanied the bosses' antilabor assault.

(2) While the social conquests won in the 1960s and 1970s have come under repeated attack, none have been substantially reversed. They remain the starting point for coming struggles.

c) An upsurge of union resistance and power in the 1990s will give a renewed impulse to broader social struggles and will increasingly proletarianize the social composition of protest actions. Likewise, such struggles will themselves reinforce union resistance and swell the size, and strengthen the social composition, of the emerging rank-and-file leadership of the labor movement.

4. A new rise of labor struggles and social protest movements will face greater opportunities in the 1990s to join forces with a fighting movement of working farmers than at any time since the 1930s.

a) In the early 1980s the worst capitalist crisis in the countryside since the 1930s forced tens of thousands of working farmers off the land.

b) Opposition to this massive expropriation was widespread, and a genuine antiforeclosure movement emerged in the Midwest and portions of the South. This movement, led by a vanguard layer of working farmers,

(1) mobilized farmers in direct action to fight the banks, monopolies, and government;

(2) built farm protest organizations comprised of working farmers;

(3) gained class-struggle combat experience;

(4) reached out for solidarity to unions and to Black and women's rights organizations; and

(5) began to look for allies internationally, as farmers were attracted to fighting peasants in Nicaragua and

farmers elsewhere in the capitalist world.

c) The high point of the farm movement of the 1980s coincided with the depths of the rout in the labor movement in the United States.

    (1) A very small layer of vanguard forces in the working-class movement actively participated in the antiforeclosure movement.

    (2) Despite the fact that many farmers or members of their families are also workers, the ranks of labor, recoiling from fights, were not able to reach out and solidarize in an organized and substantial way with the struggles of producers on the land.

d) The antiforeclosure movement declined as economic conditions on the land began to improve at the end of the 1980s.

    (1) This coincided with the break in the rout in the labor movement. The renewed resistance by the ranks of the unions opened by the Pittston and Eastern strikes came too late, however, for the rises in struggle of urban and rural working people to reinforce each other.

    (2) There continues to be a small layer of experienced vanguard farmers in the countryside, both inside and outside the existing farm protest organizations.

    (3) The coming battles in the countryside, however, will have to draw primarily upon a new generation of working farmers, who will have the opportunity to interconnect their struggles with battles by fighting workers.

5. The class structure of the Black nationality is different in the 1990s than it was in the 1960s, to say nothing of the 1930s.

a) Today, as a result of the victories won by the Black rights movement of the 1950s and 1960s, there is a substantially larger petty-bourgeois layer in the Black population. This layer has been able to integrate itself into the broader middle class to a degree that would have been unthinkable to people of all classes and races in the United States even twenty-five year ago.

b) At the same time, the large proletarian majority of the Black nationality has borne the brunt of the sharply worsening economic and social conditions of working people over the past decade. Broad layers of workers who are Black have been driven onto the knife's edge of poverty and into social conditions that are even more segregated — by race and by class — than the late 1960s or early 1970s.[15]

c) As a result of this greater social differentiation, the next upsurge in the struggle for Black rights will rapidly confront a polarization along class lines that will be sharp and deep.

(1) Petty-bourgeois layers will seek to impose their class perspectives and their organizational and political dominance in order to defend their gains against a racism that continues to be systemic and to advance their own integration into capitalist economic, social, and political institutions.

(2) Above all, they will seek to channel any broader movement for Black rights in a class-collaborationist direction — away from class combat and independent

---

15. To cite a few examples of this continuing trend, in July 1998 the official U.S. government unemployment figure for Blacks was 10.4 percent, more than two and half times the overall rate. The jobless rate for Blacks aged 16–19 was 29.9 percent, also two and a half times that for the population as a whole. The median family income of Blacks is less than 60 percent of that of whites, and the gap was substantially wider in 1996 than in 1967. Thirty percent of African-Americans live below the miserly official U.S. government poverty line. Meanwhile, one-third of Black males between the ages of 20 and 29 are either on probation, on parole, or in prison in the United States; more Black males than white males are in U.S. prisons, although Blacks make up less than 12 percent of the U.S. population.(Altogether, 5.4 million people in the United States were either on probation, on parole, or in prison in 1995 — a 200 percent increase since 1980, while the U.S. population grew less than 17 percent over that same period. With nearly 600 out of every 100,000 residents in prison, the United States has by far the highest incarceration rate in the world.)

working-class political action, away from political initiatives by workers and youth that threaten to break the mold, and away from the development of a broader communist leadership of the working class.

(3) From the outset, spokespeople from the newly arrived middle-class layers in the Black population will appeal to nationalist sentiments as part of an effort to win a social base for themselves among Black workers and youth entering the struggle against racist assaults and intensifying capitalist exploitation and oppression.

d) At the same time, any upsurge in the battle against national oppression and racist discrimination will much more quickly deepen interconnections between those struggles and any developing rank-and-file leadership in the union movement, of which workers who are Black will come to comprise disproportionate numbers as compared to Blacks as a percentage of the population.

(1) An advance in the fight for Black rights will add new power to labor struggles.

(2) A more combative union movement, moreover, will bring decisive social power into the fight for Black liberation.

(3) In the union struggles that are already breaking out today, the percentage of workers who are Black in the rank-and-file leadership is qualitatively greater than anything that was possible in the 1960s or the 1930s.

e) Several new generations of workers and youth who are Black are being attracted to the revolutionary political example and legacy of Malcolm X.

(1) Malcolm's intransigent opposition to racist discrimination and degradation, to "Americanism" in any guise, to any subordination to Washington or any of its political parties, and to imperialism's oppression of the toilers of Africa, the Americas, Asia, and the Pacific put him on a revolutionary internationalist and anti-imperialist political course while he was a

prominent figure in the Nation of Islam; it was Malcolm's refusal to retreat from this course that prepared him to end all denial as to the state of the central leadership of the Nation. This dynamic culminated in Malcolm being silenced by Elijah Muhammad in late 1963 and prepared his public break with the Nation in early 1964.

(2) As imperialism's deadly intention to silence him forever became more and more clear, Malcolm's political integrity and consistency led him to rapidly break through barrier after barrier at the end of 1964 and the beginning of 1965, and to explain the process publicly as it occurred.

   (a) Malcolm rejected his previous opposition to "mixed marriages," a reactionary legacy of the demagogic, antimaterialist foundation of politics inherited from Elijah Muhammed.

   (b) He dropped all vestiges of subtle anti-Semitic slurs that were endemic in the Nation and the broader milieus it influenced and that influenced it.

   (c) He detailed the political consequences of "personal" corruption by explaining how Elijah Muhammad's conduct (with the knowledge and connivance of much of the Nation's leadership) made a mockery of respect for women, let alone the kinds of advances for women's rights that Malcolm had seen were inseparable from social progress and revolutionary struggle everywhere in the world.[16]

---

16. The events that culminated in Malcolm being silenced and his subsequent break from the Nation of Islam were precipitated by his discovery that Elijah Muhammad had engaged in sexual relations with a number of teenage women and then, when they became pregnant, organized to suspend them from membership in the Nation on charges of "fornication." Malcolm explains in his autobiography that he learned of this from Elijah Muhammad himself in April 1963. When Malcolm refused to join with

(d) Malcolm exposed and analyzed the inevitable search by the leadership of the Nation for alliances with, and material support from, reactionary organizations; this course flowed from the social character and political limitations of that leadership. Malcolm revealed that in 1960 and 1961 he himself had been personally instructed to pursue or facilitate such alliances with the Ku Klux Klan and American Nazi Party.[17]

(e) By taking these positions and acting along these lines, Malcolm shed light on the reactionary political consequences and antiproletarian thrust of the corruption born of middle-class aspirations in a leadership pretending to speak for the oppressed — whether integrationist or separatist in its trappings.

(f) At the same time that Malcolm spoke out unflinchingly on all these matters, he deepened a united-front appeal to his followers and to other fighters, as well as to the ranks of the Nation of Islam. He pointed to the unambiguous evidence that forces bigger than the Nation — the assassination machine of U.S. imperialism — were responsible for preparing the deadly assaults to come on himself and his family.

(3) Malcolm's accelerating evolution during the last year

---

others in the Nation's chain of command to cover up this abuse — both abuse of women, and abuse of power — Elijah Muhammad decided to silence him. "When I found that the hierarchy itself wasn't practicing what it preached," Malcolm said in a 1965 interview with the *Young Socialist* magazine, "it was clear that this part of its program was bankrupt." That interview is published in full in *Malcolm X Talks to Young People* (Pathfinder, 1991), as well as in the Pathfinder pamphlet of the same name.

17. See in particular Malcolm's February 15, 1965, talk at the Audubon Ballroom in Harlem, "There's a Worldwide Revolution Going On," in *Malcolm X, February 1965: The Final Speeches* (Pathfinder, 1992).

of his life toward secular political organization, anti-capitalism, and then socialism placed him on a trajectory that converged with that of other revolutionaries and communists worldwide.

(a) He reached out to establish common ground with the communist leadership of Cuba, both in Africa and on occasions when its most prominent representatives, Fidel Castro and Che Guevara, traveled to the United States.

(b) He sought collaboration with communists in the United States organized in the Socialist Workers Party and Young Socialist Alliance.

(4) As class battles intensify in the 1990s, working-class fighters of all nationalities, skin colors, and languages will be drawn to Malcolm's political legacy as they move toward proletarian internationalist and anti-capitalist perspectives.

(a) These young revolutionists will become cadres and leaders not only of renewed struggles against all manifestations of racist and national oppression, but also of the working-class movement and communist parties.

(b) This fact underlines the importance of the efforts by communists to keep Malcolm's writings and speeches in print and to expand their circulation to the broadest possible layers of fighters and revolutionists among workers and farmers in the United States and worldwide.

(5) Middle-class misleaders of the Black nationality more and more drape themselves in the mantle of Malcolm X in an effort to build a base for themselves among young people attracted to his example. At the same time, these petty-bourgeois layers fear working-class youth — whether Black, white, or other — and hold them in contempt, echoing bourgeois propaganda about the "dangers of the underclass." (Some also

romanticize the "underclass," at a safe distance, projecting onto Black youth their own bourgeois misogyny and brutality.)

(a) Some of these middle-class forces attempt to distort Malcolm's political evolution by portraying his last year as a retreat from revolutionary positions as he supposedly converged toward the perspectives of Martin Luther King, or even toward liberalism. Ignoring Malcolm's outspoken opposition to both the Democratic and Republican parties, these liberals project their own political course and rhetoric onto Malcolm and seek to present him as a forerunner of Jesse Jackson's Rainbow Coalition.

(b) Many of these and other petty-bourgeois political currents practice the politics of demagogy in the name of nationalism (and sometimes "Marxism," as well). In marked contrast to their own conduct and example, Malcolm emerged as a revolutionary of integrity who knew from the bottom up the conservatizing and ultimately bourgeois character of the corruption of depending on income derived from hustles or organized crime; who became impervious to middle-class aspirations and resentments; to red-baiting, race-baiting, and Stalinist blandishments, let alone racism (anti-Haitian, anti-Asian, etc.), anti-Semitism, anti-woman bigotry, or similar self-serving demagogy of any kind.

(6) Malcolm X provides living proof of the capacity of revolutionary-minded fighters from the ranks of the working class to broaden their scope and move toward communism and revolutionary leadership of the highest historic caliber. His example reinforces the judgment that the experienced leading cadres of the SWP who are Black are forerunners of a much

broader communist leadership development that will come out of deepening struggles and political clarification.

(a) Given the greater class differentiation in the Black nationality today, nationalist-minded fighters emerging from a new burst forward in the fight for Black liberation will rapidly reach out toward a broader world view, toward Marxism. They will have a better chance than the Black Panther Party generation of avoiding the trap of confusing Stalinism with Marxism.[18]

(b) The wider the struggles against racism, the more self-sacrificing the commitment to fight for Black liberation, and the broader the reach of the labor movement and its vanguard to embrace these struggles, the greater will be the opportunities for influence, recruitment, and renewal of the cadres of the Socialist Workers Party and Young Socialist Alliance.

(c) In the United States, as in other imperialist countries, "nation time" and the socialist revolution will triumph together.

---

18. Founded in 1966 in Oakland, California, in response to a cop killing of a sixteen-year old Black youth, the Black Panther Party for Self-Defense over the next several years attracted thousands of young Blacks and others repelled by the evils of racism and looking for strategies that addressed the source of the oppression they were fighting. In their search for anticapitalist solutions, however, the leadership of the Black Panthers instead found Stalinism, which at the time still had substantial reserves worldwide. By the end of the 1960s, the combination of thug methods, class-collaborationist illusions, and ultraleft adventures the Panthers absorbed from Stalinism left them wide open to deadly disruption operations by the FBI and other police agencies. Some twenty Panthers were killed, either directly by cops — as in the case of Fred Hampton, murdered in his bed in 1969 by the Chicago police — or in shoot-outs with cops or each other urged on by government provocateurs. Numerous other Panthers were framed up and railroaded to prison.

C. A fraction of the international working class and its fighting vanguard

1. SWP cadres are a fraction of the working class, of its vanguard fighters, and of the emerging rank-and-file leadership in the unions.

  a) Communist workers have no "trade union strategy" separate from the broader revolutionary proletarian strategy reflected in actual mass work that flows from the dynamics of the class struggle and from efforts to advance the fight for a workers and farmers government.

    (1) Communists in the unions seek to collaborate with all fighting union members in using the most *effective* tactics to advance the working-class struggle and to increase the experience and self-confidence of the rank-and-file leadership.

    (2) Communists support and advance tactics that enable the ranks to bring their weight to bear in using union power and reaching out for solidarity on that basis.

    (3) This is the opposite of the officialdom's course of reliance on expanding forms of collaboration with the employing class, which rots out union power and demoralizes and depoliticizes militants. No part of the course of the officialdom coincides with a revolutionary orientation.

  b) Workers who are communists participate in labor battles to advance the fight for the transformation of the unions into revolutionary instruments of struggle as part of a course toward socialist revolution.

    (1) One element of this fight is the perspective of a class-struggle left wing in the union movement.

    (2) The approach to tactics that flows from the communist strategy is captured in the program adopted in 1938 when the working-class organization bearing the continuity of communism in the United States took the name Socialist Workers Party: "All methods are

good which raise the class consciousness of the workers, their trust in their own forces, their readiness for self-sacrifice in the struggle. The impermissible methods are those which implant fear and submissiveness in the oppressed in the face of their oppressors. . . ."[19]

2. SWP cadres are a fraction of the revolutionaries who are fighting to advance the worldwide struggle against imperialist oppression and capitalist exploitation.

    a) Our collaboration with other fighters is not based on ideological criteria — including whether or not they are communists.

        (1) We proceed from deeds that reflect determination to fight imperialism instead of searching for some accommodation with it.

        (2) We are shoulder to shoulder with those — at whatever their current level of resistance — who refuse to subordinate the interests of workers and farmers to any layer of the capitalist exploiters.

        (3) We are in continuity with fighting men and women throughout history who have said no to exploitation and oppression rather than sink down on their knees.

    b) It is only from fighters, from revolutionists of action, that communists will be forged in the course of struggle. And it is only from within the working class that the mass political vanguard of these fighters can come.

    c) The lesson from over 150 years of political struggle by the modern workers movement is that, more and more, to become and to remain a revolutionist means becoming a communist.

3. SWP cadres are a fraction of communists in the world.

    a) We are linked to communist political continuity

        (1) from Marx and Engels and the international Com-

---

19. *The Transitional Program for Socialist Revolution* by Leon Trotsky (Pathfinder, 1977), p. 148.

munist League current they helped found in 1847;

(2) through Lenin, the Bolsheviks, and the first five years of the Communist International;

(3) to Trotsky and the communists who fought to continue Lenin's course against Stalin's insistence on the possibility of building socialism in one country and reaching a long-term accommodation with the imperialist rulers;

(4) to the forging of a communist leadership in Cuba and the renewal of the communist vanguard on a mass scale for the first time since the early 1930s; and

(5) the link with the Bolshevik-Leninist legacy that is manifested in the international communist current we are part of.

b) We recognize the indispensability of the communist program — the generalization of the experiences and lessons of the struggles of the international working class — and the decisive weight of that program as a weapon of the working class in the socialist revolution.

(1) The political continuity and clarity of an international communist vanguard is necessary because the program and strategy the working class need to advance the revolutionary struggle for national liberation and socialism cannot be generated automatically out of any given strike or single political fight by workers and farmers.

(2) Communism generalizes the lessons of the workers movement

(a) from a broader historical vantage point than that of any particular struggle (it sees the present as history; it uses the lessons of the past reflected through present living experience);

(b) from a broader geographical framework (that of the international class struggle); and

(c) from the relations among *all* classes in modern society as seen from the standpoint of the working class.

(3) Only communist cadres who are tried and tested in working-class struggle will have the necessary *experience* and will have *earned* the respect of fellow fighters that will assure them and their publications the kind of hearing without which layers of the workers vanguard cannot be won to the communist program and party.

D. The communist strategy of party building today

1. The "six points" outlined in the 1988 letter by Mary-Alice Waters, "The Communist Strategy of Party Building Today: A Letter to Comrades in Sweden," are central to forging communist forces in the 1990s.[20]

   a) These six points — the turn to industry, political centralization, weekly rhythm of working-class political life, expansion of broad propaganda work built around Pathfinder, youth recruitment, and proletarian internationalism under the banner of the new International — summarize the course of action necessary today for the Socialist Workers Party to carry out effective mass work as a component of fighting workers and of international communist forces.

   b) This strategy also marks the only road today that can advance us toward the longer-term, broader convergence of communist forces in the world.

2. The collective experience over the past three years of the SWP and each of the communist leagues with whom we collaborate convinces us that we must see ourselves *as part of* — and to an increasing degree see our activity as *determined* by — the growing international centralization that results from this strategy. This is especially true for the SWP, which has the greatest weight because of its political continuity, experience, and size.

   a) More and more we have had similar rhythms and political priorities in our activities around such work as our orien-

---

20. Reprinted elsewhere in this issue.

tation toward fighting coal miners, the Eastern strike solidarity campaign, Mark Curtis defense work, Cuba solidarity work, and anti-apartheid activity.

b) The promotion of Pathfinder literature and expansion of Pathfinder distributors and bookstores has played and continues to play the pivotal role in increasing the impact and strengthening the foundations of our common propaganda arsenal.

(1) Pathfinder publications have become more and more central tools in our collaboration with other revolutionaries and communists around the world.

(2) Each communist organization has faced the challenge of taking greater political responsibility for leading the professionalization and expansion of Pathfinder promotion and sales and its integration into all aspects of our work — based on a growing international centralization of this effort.

c) Through the weekly international circulation of the *Militant* and increased collaboration of workers internationally in its production and financing, we have taken further steps toward making the *Militant* the political organizer and centralizer of our work.

(1) Distribution of *Perspectiva Mundial, Lutte ouvrière, New International,* and *Nouvelle Internationale* as supplements to the *Militant* has strengthened our ability to reach diverse working-class forces in many countries.[21]

(2) Through our weekly sales, including at plant gates,

21. In 1991 the first issue of *New International*'s Spanish sister publication, *Nueva Internacional,* was produced, and in 1993 the first issue of the Swedish-language *Ny International.* The French-language bimonthly *Lutte ouvrière* changed its name to *L'internationaliste* in January 1991 and ceased publication in the spring of 1992 in order to allow the communist movement to focus its editorial resources in French on the translation of *Nouvelle Internationale,* as well as Marxist books and pamphlets published by Pathfinder.

and through international subscription and renewal drives, we have begun to build up a long-term readership of working-class fighters around the world for whom the *Militant* and our other publications are indispensable weapons.

d) This international collaboration in implementing the party-building strategy that centralizes our work, summarized in the six points, is the road toward increasing our collective striking power.

(1) It is the opposite of a programmatic regroupment of revolutionary organizations based on a checklist of political points, or "principles," of agreement and disagreement.

(2) It is the opposite of centralization that flows primarily through executive bodies made up of leaders selected from parties in various countries (whether chosen by the parties themselves on a federative basis, or elected by a sovereign international congress).

(3) It increases our mutual responsibility in working with other revolutionists and communists; it strengthens proletarian discipline and norms as we do so.

3. The communist movement is part of the fighting vanguard of the international working class, not a component of an ambiguously classless political "left." This dictates a double axis of political work:

a) We fight to maximize united action (e.g., Eastern/Pittston labor solidarity work, Cuba defense, the anti-apartheid movement, battles for Black and women's rights). Our fight against sectarianism and factionalism, and for unity in action, is an expression of the fact that communists are the only political current that has no historic interests separate and apart from those of the working class.

b) Within the battle to promote united action, as the *Communist Manifesto* says, communists also represent and prepare for the *future* of the workers movement. We advance a communist political perspective. This allows militant workers to begin to politically differentiate us from all the varieties of petty-bourgeois currents within the workers movement.

(1) Socialism is not a set of ideas that can be tacked on to trade unionism, nationalism, feminism, and in that way advance the historic interests of the working class.

(2) Such spontaneous, partial, and ultimately bourgeois or petty-bourgeois forms of consciousness are a reflection of the initial radicalization of vanguard fighters and at the same time an expression of the fact that these fighters have not yet crossed the bridge to communism.

(3) The conclusion that the conquest of power and the construction of socialism by workers and farmers is the necessary foundation for eradicating all forms of exploitation and oppression and transforming human relations requires a leap by workers in political consciousness. Progressive struggles and social protest movements have to be seen from the perspective of this line of march of the working class toward power.

(4) This advance in consciousness can only be the result of experiences in struggle combined with generalizing the lessons of these struggles as part of the history of workers' fight for emancipation.

4. The divergence between communists and petty-bourgeois currents within the world working-class movement is widening and sharpening.

a) Communists are not part of the "anti-Stalinist left," "progressives," "democratic forces," or "Marxist-Leninists": all these labels have been appropriated by various petty-bourgeois currents that include one or another combination of Stalinists, social democrats, and anti-Marxist radicals or liberals.

b) We are not part of the "Trotskyist movement," or the Fourth International, currents that emerged from the 1980s on a trajectory rejecting a communist course toward building parties of worker-bolsheviks who are part of the fighting ranks of the working class.

c) We do not orient toward any wing of Stalinist parties (including the South African Communist Party or Communist Party of the Philippines); nor to other Stalinist or centrist layers who see perestroika as part of the road forward (such as the *Guardian* or *Frontline*);[22] nor to those who rationalize Stalinist repression by falsely identifying it with the dictatorship of the proletariat (such as the Workers World Party).

d) We are diverging from all "left" or "progressive" organized oppositional currents in the union movement. We are further away then ever from those who trail after one or another wing or figure in the officialdom, seeking posts to "be in a better position" to transform the unions.

5. Because communists are part of the growing resistance by vanguard fighters in the working class, we can and do find ourselves singled out as targets by antilabor forces.

a) We are targeted not because of ultraleft or sectarian mistakes, nor because we are way out ahead or to the left of fighting workers, but because we are part of the resistance.

(1) Cops, employers, and right-wingers are not primarily going after the communists, but the broader vanguard of fighting workers of which we are part.

(a) We often end up in the line of fire because, unlike most other militants, we are also members of an identifiable revolutionary political organization.

(b) As individuals, we become known for our involvement in fights on a wide range of fronts, on and off the job.

---

22. The *Guardian* and *Frontline* were the publications of two currents in the broader Stalinist milieu that at various times during the 1970s and 1980s oriented toward one or another component of the bureaucratic caste of the Chinese workers state. Both subsequently dissolved as part of the post-1990 disintegration of world Stalinism.

(c) Sometimes we simply find ourselves targeted as one among other fighters.

(2) In fighting back against such attacks, we often have to take on responsibilities that are disproportionate to our size and general influence in the workers movement today.

(a) If we are politically confident in explaining that the rights and interests of all fighters are at stake, then broader layers of workers, farmers, and democratic-minded people increasingly take up the fight as their own.

(b) By responding in a timely way to moves by rightists and antilabor forces to close down the space of the workers vanguard, *more* space can be *won* for the revolutionary movement, as broader democratic circles see the fight as their own (e.g., Pathfinder Mural, Grenada Pathfinder book ban, Northern Ireland arrest of Pathfinder sales representative Pete Clifford).[23]

---

23. In the year or so prior to the drafting of this resolution, members and supporters of the Socialist Workers Party and communist leagues in other countries had won support from a broad range of prominent organizations and individuals in responding to several government and right-wing attacks on political rights. In November 1988 members of Parliament, the National Council of Civil Liberties, and others had protested the detention without charges of Pathfinder sales representative Peter Clifford in British-occupied Northern Ireland; Clifford was interrogated and held for twenty-four hours under the so-called Prevention of Terrorism Act before being released to continue his sales trip.

In early 1989 the U.S.-imposed government in Grenada banned 86 books by Fidel Castro, Malcolm X, Nelson Mandela, Karl Marx, and others published or distributed by Pathfinder; protests were issued by several members of the U.S. Congress and British and Canadian parliaments, the PEN American Center writers' organization, the Oilfields Workers' Trade Union of Trinidad, and many others.

In December 1989 the six-story Pathfinder Mural on the wall of the Pathfinder Building, pictured on the cover of this issue of *New International,* was vandalized by right-wingers who hurled paint bombs, defacing

(c) As the class polarization deepens, it becomes more and more essential to combine political defense with appropriate security measures to protect the activities of the communist movement, measures that will help *politically* educate and gain support from rank-and-file leaders.

b) In the Mark Curtis frame-up the cops initially went after Curtis, not the SWP.

(1) Mark Curtis was representative of other young workers like him who were resisting the brutal offensive of the packinghouse bosses, fighting for the rights of fellow workers who were immigrants, organizing against racist cop harassment, and opposing restrictions on women's rights.

(2) Curtis supporters have drawn expanding forces into the fight, from Iowa to every corner of the globe, raising the political price the rulers must pay for their continuing imprisonment of Curtis and maximizing space for him to carry out communist work.

(3) This politically centralized international campaign to explain the context of the frame-up and win support for Curtis's freedom has been organized from within the working-class movement, with Curtis as an active

---

its lower portion. The assault came just weeks after the formal unveiling of the mural, and shortly after the publication in the *New York Post* of an editorial headlined, "Off the Wall — That's Where It Belongs." The *Post* editorial concluded with the provocative call to action, "The mural should be removed." And ultrarightist demagogue Patrick Buchanan wrote in his syndicated column: "Ironic, is it not? In East Europe, the victims of communism tear down images of Marx and Lenin; in the arts capital of America, their portraits go up [and] Fidel Castro rises over the Westside Highway." Artists, trade unionists, and many others from New York and around the United States and the world immediately condemned the defacement, including Mayor-elect David Dinkins, who issued a statement urging apprehension of those responsible for the attack. Another paint bomb attack on the mural in March 1991 also met with a broad range of protests.

communist fighter, not just a man appealing for justice. The defense campaign has been central to deepening the proletarianization and advancing the international development of the communist leagues.

c) The Workers League disruption effort is likewise aimed against the fighting vanguard of the working class. Since 1977 we have had to wage a battle to help others recognize the activities of this antilabor outfit from this perspective and politically confront the challenge to reach out and bring broader forces into the fight against it.

(1) We had to learn to explain the stakes for democratic rights and for the labor movement in rejecting the cop-baiting slander campaign against the SWP (the smear of Joseph Hansen, George Novack, Jack Barnes, and the "Carleton 12" as FBI agents) and in turning back the assault on freedom of political association posed by the Workers League-initiated lawsuit against the SWP filed by Alan Gelfand.[24]

---

24. As a central part of its harassment and disruption operation against the Socialist Workers Party and other vanguard fighters in the labor movement, the Workers League in 1975 launched a broad public slander campaign charging that the leadership of the Socialist Workers Party was controlled by double agents of the U.S. government and Moscow's secret police. In addition to veteran SWP leaders Joseph Hansen and George Novack, other targets of this cop-baiting included current SWP national secretary Jack Barnes, *New International* editor Mary-Alice Waters, and several other party members who had been won to the communist movement in the early 1960s while students at Carleton College in Northfield, Minnesota. For a detailed reply to this international frame-up effort, see *Healy's Big Lie: The Slander Campaign against Joseph Hansen and George Novack*, an Education for Socialists publication published by Pathfinder.

In 1979 a Workers League cadre named Alan Gelfand — who had been working as an agent of that organization within the SWP and was subsequently expelled — filed a lawsuit seeking federal court action to remove the leadership of the SWP on the basis that it was dominated by police spies; the aim of the suit was to tie up SWP leadership time and drain the party's financial resources. Federal judge Mariana Pfaelzer al-

(2) Our goal is not and has never been for the SWP alone to combat and defeat the Workers League. That would be a self-defeating and damaging retreat toward sectarian politics. We seek to win broad forces within the labor and progressive movements to draw on their own experiences to recognize the Workers League's antilabor attacks for what they are and respond appropriately to the attacks on the political rights of unionists and other fighters, as well as the threats to their physical safety.

(3) Through growing experiences with Workers League disruption of labor battles (e.g., the Arizona copper miners' strike 1983–84, Hormel 1985–86, paperworkers 1987–88, Pittston 1989, the Domsey ILGWU strike in Brooklyn 1990), growing numbers of workers have come to see their own fight against this disruption and our fight as one and the same struggle. This awareness also exists among a small but increasing layer of workers internationally, based on their experiences with outfits associated with the Workers League in other countries (e.g., International Communist Party in Britain, Socialist Labor League in Australia, and remnants of groups in Canada and New Zealand).

(4) It is along these lines that we and other Mark Curtis Defense Committee supporters are taking on the Workers League international disruption and deepening the understanding of the stakes in this international defense effort.

d) The Pathfinder Mural and its defense have generated a wide response. This is an expression of the place that Pathfinder and our movement are carving out as part of a

---

lowed this abusive legal action to drag on for ten years before ruling in late 1989 that Gelfand's case "is groundless and always was," and had been conducted "in large part to generate material for political attacks on the SWP by the Workers League."

broader vanguard of fighters and revolutionists in the U.S. and world class struggle.

(1) The mural is recognized around the world as a major work of public art in its own right, the product of an extensive international collaborative effort.

   (a) It has enabled our movement to take national and international initiatives with an impact beyond our current size, resources, and weight in the labor movement.

   (b) It has the special value of presenting in a highly effective visual manner the political character of Pathfinder. It is an invaluable weapon for our movement both to promote Pathfinder and reach out to broader forces.

   (c) Its very existence, maintenance, and breadth of support open the minds of revolutionists in other countries to a more accurate appreciation of the political possibilities in the class struggle in the United States today.

(2) The attacks against the mural are part of the deepening polarization around artistic freedom and freedom of expression generally (e.g., censorship as a precondition for government funding of the arts; the indictment of the director of the Cincinnati Arts Center for the Mapplethorpe exhibit; the death warrant against Salman Rushdie, etc.).[25]

---

25. In 1989 the U.S. Congress adopted legislation prohibiting the National Endowment for the Arts from funding works deemed "obscene or indecent" according to criteria outlined in the bill. In face of widespread public opposition to such censorship, Congress the following year dropped the restriction from its three-year appropriation for the NEA.

In October 1990 Dennis Barrie, director of the Contemporary Arts Center in Cincinnati, Ohio, was found not guilty of obscenity charges brought against him by the city government several months earlier stemming from an exhibit of works by photographer Robert Mapplethorpe.

In February 1989 the government of Iran issued a death warrant

(3) The mural — and the speaking tours by Cuban painter Aldo Soler and by other artists from Nicaragua, El Salvador, and South Africa who participated in the project — are examples of how a workers party can collaborate with revolutionary-minded artists to advance communism among broader layers of students and working people, including coal miners, airline workers, farmworkers, and farmers.

E. Struggle for a proletarian party

1. The Socialist Workers Party has conquered the turn to industry.[26]

a) A high and stable percentage of cadres are in the party's ten national industrial union fractions.

(1) From its base in the industrial unions, the party has made the working class its political milieu — organized and unorganized, employed and unemployed, native born and immigrant, farmworkers and urban workers.

(2) The axis of the party's work — from the sales of its press and publications, to political campaigns, to participation in broad struggles — is within the working class and unions.

(3) The party as a whole passed the test of becoming fully part of the key labor battles of 1989–90 as part of the developing vanguard of working-class fighters.

b) Every branch of the SWP today is a turn branch.

(1) A large majority in every branch of the party are in national union fractions or jobs committees.

---

against novelist Salman Rushdie, declaring his book *The Satanic Verses* blasphemous to Islam. As of mid-1998 Rushdie remained in hiding under police protection in the United Kingdom.

26. The Socialist Workers Party's turn to the industrial unions in the latter half of the 1970s, and its experience in carrying out this strategic orientation over the subsequent two decades, are dealt with extensively in *The Changing Face of U.S. Politics: Working-Class Politics and the Trade Unions* by Jack Barnes (Pathfinder, 1981, 1994).

(2) The life and weekly rhythm of a party structured around workers in union fractions is now the experience of the big majority of cadres.

    (a) This is a precondition for the party to organize and lead all of its cadres, whether in industry or not, in disciplined activity around a common political perspective.

    (b) It is the foundation for the party's readiness for class combat.

    (c) It is the solid basis on which the party can gain political homogeneity and come to democratic decisions, take unanticipated initiatives as well as make difficult shifts and retrenchments, and resolve debates over our course and tactics.

c) The SWP's conquest of the turn is registered in the expanding concentric circles of workers who are friends of the party, who have grown to know and respect us on the job, in the union, and through our broader political work.

    (1) These friends include union activists who subscribe to our press and are eager to be quoted in the *Militant* about how useful the paper is to their work; who make occasional financial contributions and come to a party function; who work with us around strike solidarity or come to a united-front activity we are building.

    (2) This gain increases the party's leverage in the unions and broader politics.

2. The SWP consolidated the turn during the later part of the third "dog days" in the history of our movement.

a) The first dog days (1929–33) are described by Jim Cannon in *History of American Trotskyism*.[27]

---

27. In 1928 James P. Cannon and other founding leaders and cadres of the Communist Party were expelled by the Stalinist leadership for their defense of the revolutionary internationalist course of the Communist International and its national parties during Lenin's time; those expelled regrouped as the Communist League of America (CLA). Shortly thereaf-

b) The second dog days came in the 1950s.
    (1) By the close of that period, we had lost the national industrial fraction structure of the party.
    (2) The depth of that retreat is registered by the fact that even with the initial growth of the Young Socialist Alliance from its founding in 1960 — and the upturn in recruitment of younger forces under the impact of the Cuban revolution, the upsurge in the struggle for Black rights, and the initial opposition to the expanding war in Vietnam — the party's net loss in membership did not bottom out until the fall of 1967.
c) The third dog days began with the retreat of the labor movement in the wake of the 1981–82 recession, followed by the all-out rout that began to be broken only in 1986. Internationally, the momentum of the revolutionary advances of the second half of the 1970s (Grenada, Nicaragua, Iran, independence for the former Portuguese colonies in Africa, defeat of U.S. imperialism and unification in Vietnam) was slowed, as imperialism mounted its counteroffensive and landed heavy blows.
    (1) Since the onset of the third dog days, the party has experienced a major drop in membership.

---

ter, Stalin ordered an ultraleft turn that further disoriented the majority of the ranks of the CP, including some who had initially been open to Cannon and his comrades. "In those dog days of the movement we were shut off from all contact," Cannon said in a series of 1942 talks, later edited and published as *The History of American Trotskyism (1928–38): The Record of a Participant*. "... Those were the hardest days of all in the thirty years that I have been active in the movement — those days from [1929 until 1933], the years of the terrible hermetically sealed isolation, with all the attendant difficulties. Isolation is the natural habitat of the sectarian, but for one who has an instinct for the mass movement it is the most cruel punishment" (pp. 115, 119). The "dog days" came to an end with the initial rise in labor resistance and struggles by farmers and youth in 1933–34 and the CLA's turn toward these openings, which a few years later culminated in the strikes, factory occupations, and other battles that built the industrial unions as a militant mass social movement in the United States.

(2) We have organized a retreat from the previous number, range, and variety of branches (Albany, Albuquerque, Cincinnati, Dallas, Denver, Gary, Harrisburg, Indianapolis, Iron Range, Lincoln, Louisville, New Orleans, San Antonio, San Diego, Seaside, Tidewater, Toledo).

(3) We gave up district committee structures (Chicago/Gary, Baltimore/D.C., Northern California Bay Area, New York/New Jersey).

d) Given the new union and working-class resistance in 1989–90, confirming the break in the rout signaled earlier by the struggles in the packinghouses, we are now coming out of — but are not yet out of — this third dog days of the communist movement in the United States. How quickly we will come out will be determined by the evolution of the class struggle over the next year.[28]

3. Over the past decade the party had to face up to and meet

---

28. Contrary to expectations in 1990, the third "dog days" did not end for the working class in the United States (and in the majority of other imperialist countries) until the renewed rise in resistance in the working class and layers of the oppressed in 1997–98. The year following adoption of this resolution was marked by the U.S.-organized military buildup and murderous war against Iraq between August 1990 and March 1991. While the outcome of the war was a debacle for Washington, the patriotism and triumphalism promoted by the U.S. rulers before, during, and after the largely uncontested assault on Iraq dampened working-class combativity in the United States.

The U.S. capitalist economy fell into a recession during the eight months of the war buildup and war in late 1990 and early 1991.The subsequent upswing in the capitalist business cycle was so sluggish that official unemployment continued rising over the following year, peaking at 7.5 percent in 1992. Annual economic growth as of the end of 1997 averaged 2.18 percent for the 1990s, barely half the 4 percent average during the quarter century prior to the 1974–75 world recession.

The political effects of the war-caused triumphalism and the onset of deflationary conditions stretched out labor's retreat for more than another half decade. During this period the party continued to decline in membership and consolidated its forces in eighteen cities, thirteen fewer than at the time this resolution was written.

political challenges that were indispensable to conquering the turn.

a) The turn was conquered by cadres who are increasingly politically self-confident; who are footloose and ready to move where needed; who view their jobs as political assignments; whose financial commitment reflects a broader subordination of their personal lives to the building of a proletarian party; and who exemplify the fact that revolutionary centralism and the proletarian discipline that flows from it are preconditions for effective participation in the class struggle.

b) While leading the necessary elements of a retreat, we did so in such a way as to extend the structure and functioning of a turn party, and to enable the party to take bold initiatives in response to developments in the class struggle.

(1) We continued to assign a substantial percentage of the elected national leadership to the field in the industrial fractions and branch leaderships.

(2) We paid political attention to maintaining jobs committees in every branch; to continuing the effort to have multifraction branches; to keeping the perspective of weekly plant-gate sales; to not retreating from provisional membership; and to advancing our work with active supporters in branches strong enough to do so.

(3) We carried through the turn in a democratic, inclusive, and even-handed way. As a result, a minority of the leadership and membership who could not tolerate functioning in a revolutionary centralist proletarian organization carried out a split in 1983, one that politically strengthened the party rather than weakening it.

(4) We organized a national effort in relation to two industrial fractions that could not otherwise have been sustained given the decline in membership and the retrenchment in the number of branches:

(a) *An orientation toward resistance in the coalfields:* In early 1987, at a point when the turn was in the greatest danger of being reversed from the effects of the rout of the labor movement, the National Committee estimated that the packinghouse battles over the previous year marked a break in that pattern. The NC reaffirmed the party's orientation to fighting coal miners, took special measures to strengthen the UMWA fraction and the seven coalfield branches, and rejected nearly unanimously a proposal to begin exempting one or more of these branches from this orientation.

i) This was reinforced by further special measures in 1989 to take advantage — in both the West and East — of the new political openings around the Pittston strike and the broader resistance among miners.

ii) These centralized efforts laid the basis for the SWP's collaboration with other communist leagues to advance common work with fighting coal miners outside the United States. The first major step has been the decision by the Communist League of Britain to construct a fraction in the National Union of Mineworkers, to strengthen its coal branches, and to put the coal orientation at the base of party building there.

(b) *The UFCW fraction and Iowa District:* In response to the wave of packinghouse struggles in the Midwest in 1986–87, we took the steps necessary to establish a UFCW packinghouse fraction, including setting up three new branches (Des Moines, Iowa; Austin, Minnesota; and Omaha, Nebraska) and an Iowa District in early 1987. We recognized and acted on the fact that the viability of the national packinghouse fraction depends on a solid

Midwest branch base for the party in these and surrounding states.

(5) The regional active workers conferences in spring 1987 and two rounds of regional political conferences in 1989 were important in continuing to organize the cadres of the party to advance toward conquering the turn along these lines.[29]

c) The party recognized and addressed the differential pressures on cadres who are women as the relationship of class forces in the 1980s was registered in the retreat and rout of the unions, the decline of the women's liberation movement, and the capitalist ideological offensive against the gains women had previously won.[30]

(1) These pressures were exacerbated by the slow pace of recruitment and increasing average age of cadres in the party.

(2) We recognized that the disproportionate pressure on women to retreat from party leadership was not a product of alleged greater sexism encountered by women working in industry.

(a) The qualitative increase in the percentage of women who are wageworkers and the percentage of the

---

29. Coming out of an active workers conference in Pittsburgh in July 1998, the Socialist Workers Party took steps to rebuild a fraction in the United Mine Workers and to strengthen its fractions in the United Food and Commercial Workers and the Union of Needletrades, Industrial and Textile Employees (formed in 1995 through a merger of the ILGWU and ACTWU). During the retreat of the labor movement earlier in the 1990s, the party lost its UMWA fraction through layoffs and sharply curtailed hiring opportunities in the mines, while its UFCW and UNITE fractions grew disproportionately small relative to several other of its union fractions. With the pickup in labor resistance in 1997–98, the party turned toward new opportunities to once again strengthen its work in these strategically important sections of the working class and labor movement.

30. See the introduction by Mary-Alice Waters to *Cosmetics, Fashions, and the Exploitation of Women* by Joseph Hansen, Evelyn Reed, and Mary-Alice Waters (Pathfinder, 1986).

workforce that is female — combined with the broad political impact of the fight for women's equality — continues to weaken the hold of reactionary antiwoman prejudices, to increase the weight of working-class leaders within the fight for women's emancipation, and to advance women within the broader leadership of the unions and class struggle.

(b) The party's turn to the industrial unions has been and remains key to advancing the self-confidence and leadership capacities of communists who are female. It continues to transform the consciousness of the communist movement as a whole — male and female — toward a political appreciation of women not as a sex, but as worker-bolsheviks and fellow leaders. It was decisive in allowing the party to emerge relatively unscathed from the rout of the middle-class-led feminist movement.

(3) The party consciously organizes to maximize the number of women serving on leadership bodies and shouldering major public and internal responsibilities. We reject, however, attempting to compensate for the greater pressures on cadres who are female by maintaining a fixed percentage of women in leadership positions — including by a de facto "quota" system, however disguised.

(a) We recognized that despite our subjective wishes, the effects of women's oppression in capitalist society will continue to weigh more heavily on women as they grow older. It is not a failure of the party that the percentage of women on leadership bodies of the Young Socialist Alliance is and will continue to be generally higher than on party leadership committees. It is not a failure of the party that the percentage of women on branch leadership committees is and will continue to be generally higher than in the national and central party leadership. It is not a failure of the party if the percentage of women on the National Committee declines somewhat in a period when the labor movement is in retreat, recruitment is slow, and our cadre is aging.

(b) All these tendencies register where we are in the history of the evolution of women's fight for emancipation, the class struggle, and the building of proletarian parties. To deny these social realities would inexorably lead to weakening the national leadership of the party and destroying the ongoing, long-term process of cadre development.

(c) Recognizing that the pressures on us are due to weighty social and historical factors is not an excuse for lack of consciousness, indifference, or a failure to continuously work to lessen the obstacles facing cadres who are women and who are taking on greater leadership responsibilities. That is a permanent obligation of a communist organization, and one that the SWP has met better than any.

(4) There are two measures against which we should gauge the progress of the party in continuing to advance the leadership confidence and capacities of cadres who are women.

(a) The party would be losing ground unnecessarily if the percentage of women in industry began to drop in relationship to their percentage in the membership.

(b) We would be losing ground if we stopped demanding of female cadres elected to leadership committees that they take on the whole range of tough jobs and responsibilities entailed in party leadership.

d) As part of conquering the turn, the party was able to confront and discuss out to the end the incompatibility of all forms of race-baiting with the construction of a proletarian communist party and leadership, and to codify this conquest in a printed report with near unanimous agreement in the membership.

(1) This is the first time in the history of the workers movement anywhere that race-baiting has been dealt with politically and has been uncompromisingly rejected as a destructive, antiproletarian method of functioning.

(2) The SWP's accomplishment is a political acquisition that will serve the entire international communist and national liberation movements, since race-baiting is not an isolated phenomenon and has a corrosive dynamic that tears apart any revolutionary — or progressive — organization. It corrupts the objective development of leadership and blocks a relationship among cadres who are political equals from ever developing.

(3) The poison of race-baiting has long been endemic to the Communist Party USA and the circles it influences both in the United States and internationally. Our rejection of this petty-bourgeois practice has better armed us as communists to confront this corruption. Race-baiting is brought into social protest movements, solidarity groups, and political organizations by the Stalinists and other individuals, currents, and cliques pretending to represent the interests of oppressed nationalities.

(a) Race-baiting has become the stock-in-trade of such layers, who use it against the proletarian wing and young forces in efforts to bureaucratically maintain or gain control of political or social protest organizations. (Our experiences in the National Black Independent Political Party richly demonstrated to us the development of this dynamic.)[31]

   (b) Failure to combat and overcome race-baiting will
       corrupt any leadership development in organiza-
       tions of the workers movement and oppressed na-
       tionalities. It will reinforce all forms of racism
       (against Haitians, Asians), anti-Semitism, and reac-
       tion, which it can become a bridge to and cover for.

e) The above two political acquisitions of the communist
   movement could only have been accomplished by a politically homogeneous party whose cadres in their big majority were part of the ranks of the working class and were
   in the process of conquering the turn. At the same time,
   without these accomplishments the turn could not have
   been conquered.[32]

4. We face numerous challenges in structuring the leadership
of a party that has conquered the turn, as part of an international communist movement whose component organizations
are at different stages in conquering the turn.

a) The size and scope of the New York–based propaganda
   apparatus (the editorial operation, its business and pro-
   motions work, the printshop, the periodicals) make sense
   only from the standpoint of accepting responsibilities as
   part of an international communist movement.

   (1) The apparatus is out of proportion to the size and re-
       sources of the SWP alone and is not sustainable over
       time by a single organization of our character.

   (2) This current structure is understandable and sup-

31. See *The National Black Independent Political Party* (Pathfinder, 1981), as
well as the 1985 resolution of the Socialist Workers Party, "The Revolutionary Perspective and Leninist Continuity in the United States," in *New
International* no. 4, pp. 73–75.

32. For fuller discussion of these questions of proletarian leadership, see
"Preparing the Election of the National Committee" by Mary-Alice Waters and "Race-Baiting and Communist Leadership" by Mac Warren, both
available in *Background to "The Changing Face of U.S. Politics and "U.S. Imperialism Has Lost the Cold War"* (Pathfinder, 1998).

portable only if seen in its transitional dual character.

    (a) It is the propaganda apparatus of the SWP, which must become proportionate to the size, resources, and leadership capacities of the party.

    (b) It is an international propaganda apparatus in becoming, organized and proportioned to meet the needs and to draw on the resources of a world movement.

(3) Our goal is not for each of the communist leagues to emulate the apparatus in New York, gradually relieving the SWP of its "international" responsibilities.

    (a) Instead, we will take growing collective responsibility for this propaganda apparatus, the expansion of which makes it possible for our work to reflect the centralizing application of the communist strategy of party building today summarized in the "six points."

    (b) More and more, this will be the concrete challenge before us in advancing the international movement.[33]

b) The party has adjusted its structure and the organization of the leadership to meet the needs imposed by a period of slow recruitment, rising average age of the membership, and the decelerated pace of the kind of political experiences in mass work that rapidly push forward transitions in leadership.

(1) Branch organizers working full-time jobs in industry have become the norm under the prevailing conditions in the class struggle and current stage of party building.

---

33. See "Extending the Arsenal of Communist Propaganda and Reconquering the Apparatus through Revolutionary Centralism," a report by Mary-Alice Waters adopted by the June 1991 convention of the Socialist Workers Party. It is available in the Education for Socialists booklet, *Pathfinder Was Born with the October Revolution* (Pathfinder, 1998).

(2) A high percentage of the total party cadre have had the experience of taking assignments in the print-shop and national apparatus.

    (a) This percentage would be smaller in a period of more rapid recruitment and membership growth.

    (b) The experience of comrades coming from industry, into the apparatus, and then back into fractions, has been and continues to be a major factor advancing our political homogenization and proletarian character.

(3) We continue to maintain a substantial percentage of the national leadership in the field, in the leadership of the branches and industrial union fractions. The combined process of assigning leadership out of the apparatus and into the field, and drawing leaders from the branches and fractions into assignments and responsibilities at the center, strengthens and broadens the party's national cadre.

    (a) It maximizes and homogenizes the experience of the broad party leadership.

    (b) Under the objective conditions we face, it facilitates the assimilation of younger generations of the cadre into national leadership responsibility.

c) The fundamental structure and orientation of the party's national industrial union fractions remain as outlined in the 1985 report by Joel Britton for the National Committee adopted by the SWP convention.[34] Our participation in the Eastern and Pittston battles confirms

    (1) that fraction leadership develops through leadership in the working-class struggle, in mass work; and

    (2) that this is the road that maximizes leadership renewal of a communist party.

---

34. See "Building the Party's Nine National Industrial Fractions" by Joel Britton, in *Background to "The Changing Face of U.S. Politics" and "U.S. Imperialism Has Lost the Cold War"* (Pathfinder, 1998).

d) With the conquest of the turn, fraction-building plant-gate sales are more important than ever as a regular aspect of the weekly rhythm of party members.

   (1) These weekly sales, led by the branch executive committees, allow the membership as a whole to keep in touch with factories, mines, and mills where we want to build fractions. They help build and politically reinforce the industrial fractions that we have already established.

   (2) In addition, these sales provide a way to reach out on a weekly basis to industrial workers at factories where we do not have fractions.

e) Branch jobs committees are permanent and living institutions, under the direction of the branch executive committees.

   (1) They help to diversify and adjust fraction priorities and keep on top of job openings, in order to advance our perspective of building multifraction branches.

   (2) The jobs committee is just as important when the entire branch membership is currently employed in target industries as when a number of members or provisional members are looking for work. Adjustments and new challenges (including efforts to bring in new members or collaborate with the Young Socialist Alliance) are never many months away.

f) An acid test of a proletarian branch is the degree to which it keeps its eyes politically on the worker-farmer alliance in becoming.

   (1) We are always probing ways to reach out and collaborate with working farmers and their organizations; helping to mobilize union and other support behind farmers' struggles and to draw working farmers into strike support and other labor solidarity activities; and seeking to broaden the readership of the *Militant* and Pathfinder books, pamphlets, and magazines among rural toilers.

(2) We continue to pay close political attention to farm-workers and their struggles and organizations. Agricultural wageworkers are an important bridge between city and countryside, between the labor movement and nonunion rural toilers as a whole.

(3) Experience shows that the possibility exists to deepen farm work and strengthen our parties through broadening our international collaboration.

g) As part of deepening the proletarianization of the party, we have made progress in organizing comrades who are not party members as part of the communist movement.

(1) Provisional members

(a) The party's decision in 1989 to lengthen provisional membership to six months is a result of our experiences in conquering the turn. This lengthening of provisional membership helps open up more widely recruitment to the proletarian party, whatever the current job of potential members.

i) Experience indicates that six months is necessary to permit sufficient time for the party to carry out its responsibilities to help prospective members make the transition to becoming part of a cadre whose lives are subordinated to the rhythms and priorities of a proletarian party.

ii) For prospective members, this adjustment is not only a matter of political education. Above all it is needed to facilitate the transition from their previous job and rhythms of functioning to life as an industrial worker organized in a union fraction and as part of a branch with a weekly rhythm of activities.

iii) The SWP is different from any organization that any provisional member has ever been in; it has different rhythms and priorities. This is true not just for students or nonindustrial workers, but for workers whose previous experience is as a member of an industrial union.

iv) Party membership changes the relationship between the personal and the political: where you work, your income and what you do with it, even limits on your friendships (no cops, foremen, etc.).

v) The provisional membership period must allow sufficient time for prospective members to be integrated into the branch jobs committee in order to have a good shot at getting into one of the party's ten national industrial union fractions.

vi) Finally, enough time needs to be allowed for branches to organize an initial program of reading and discussion covering the party's history and ideas.

(b) The decision to become a constitutional member of the party is a weightier one than becoming a provisional member.

i) Payment of the constitutionally required initiation fee marks the point at which an individual ceases to be a provisional member and shoulders not only the responsibilities but also the full rights of party membership.

ii) Acceptance of the full rights of party membership is the biggest responsibility of all. Your vote counts, and you share full decision-making responsibility for the course that all members of the communist movement will carry out.[35]

---

35. In 1995 the Socialist Workers Party concluded that provisional membership was for the moment no longer the most effective way for party branches to guide workers and youth in making the transition to the proletarian rhythms and habits of party membership. Given the smaller size

(2) Active supporters

    (a) Clarity on norms of party membership frees us to recognize the different rhythm of political life and sustainable responsibilities of supporters who are not members, so that we can work with them fully as an organized group of comrades, as part of a common communist movement.

    (b) The party's active supporters are organized as a national formation.

        i) They are active supporters of the Socialist Workers Party, not of a particular branch. They are voted in as active supporters by a branch executive committee that is then responsible for the organization of their political work.

        ii) To be an active supporter is not an informal or simply self-designated relationship to the party; it is a category of membership in the communist movement. There is a definable membership list established by vote, as with party membership.

    (c) Active supporters carry out regular political work under the party's direction. They are not just financial contributors or occasional forum-goers. Active supporters assist the party in drawing on the help and financial assistance of this broader layer of friends and supporters.

---

of most branches, the distinction between the candidacy period and party membership was increasingly being blurred in practice, and fewer branches were able to sustain the six-month education program for provisional members. The 1995 SWP convention ended the candidacy period and voted to have each branch organize a class series aimed at facilitating the recruitment, education, and integration of new members. In addition, the attraction of a small layer of young people to the communist movement in 1994–95, and the launching of a new socialist youth organization on that basis, opened another training ground for potential recruits to the Socialist Workers Party.

(d) All monthly sustainer pledges from active supporters, whatever they may be, go directly to the national party treasury.

(e) Like party members, active supporters work at and enjoy politics, but unlike members they do not subordinate personal priorities to the rhythm of a workers party.

  i) Active supporters are free of the responsibility for the branches' decision-making discussion and debates. They do not have access to party internal mailings, bulletins, or discussions. They do not participate in making its decisions. They support the party as an organization that they are attracted to and judge on the basis of its public work and its press.

  ii) Active supporters are not members of the industrial union fractions and party committee structures.[36]

  iii) The *Militant* is the weekly political organizer of the active supporters.

(f) Like party members, active supporters are organized to carry out political activity structured around the communist strategy of party building, but they do so in a selective — not rounded — way decided on and organized by the party (Friends of the Pathfinder Mural, circulation drives and election campaigns, bookstore work, Militant Labor Forum organization, Mark Curtis and other defense efforts, Cuba and South Africa solidarity work, strike support activity, etc.).

(g) Above all the work of active supporters includes systematic fund raising from friends of the party

---

36. See "Party Membership and Active Supporters," letters by Jack Barnes and Joel Britton, in *Background to "The Changing Face of U.S. Politics" and "U.S. Imperialism Has Lost the Cold War."*

and from active supporters themselves, which they organize and review with party leaders as part of their periodic meetings.

(3) Young Socialist Alliance[37]

---

37. In March 1992 the National Committees of the Socialist Workers Party and Young Socialist Alliance held a joint meeting to discuss how best to take advantage of opportunities for youth recruitment to the communist movement. Over the previous decade, as the labor movement both in the United States and worldwide suffered blows, the YSA had declined in size, and the median age of its membership and leadership had risen beyond the norm for a revolutionary youth organization. The joint leadership meeting decided that the next step in winning a new generation to proletarian politics, while maintaining the continuity of the communist youth movement embodied in the Young Socialist Alliance, was to dissolve the YSA "into a movement of young people who are actively organizing support to the socialist alternative in [the 1992 U.S. presidential campaign] to the bipartisan candidates of war, racism, and depression and who are engaged in actions of social protest and other political activity along with members of the Socialist Workers Party."

Less than two years later, in early 1994, groups of revolutionary-minded young people from several U.S. cities began collaborating to rebuild a communist youth organization. At meetings in Chicago, Illinois, in April 1994 and Oberlin, Ohio, in August of that year, they initially took the name Socialist Youth Organizing Committee and later the Young Socialists. On the basis of further common political activity and experience, delegates from Young Socialists chapters across the United States held their first convention in Minneapolis, Minnesota, in April 1996 and adopted a statement of political and organizational principles. In the fall of that same year, the SWP National Committee and the YS National Committee decided to organize joint fractions of their members in the industrial unions. The YS held its second convention in Atlanta, Georgia, in March 1997, and has called its third convention for Los Angeles at the end of November 1998.

Revolutionary-minded youth from other countries participated in this process from the outset, working to build Young Socialists groups in Australia, Canada, France, Iceland, New Zealand, Sweden, the United Kingdom, and elsewhere.

"The history of this century has shown that before large workers' struggles become generalized and begin building on and reinforcing each other, layers of youth start rebelling against the most brutal and dehumanizing consequences of capitalism's economic and social contradictions," SWP national secretary Jack Barnes explained to participants in

    (a) There is a difference in the rhythm of activity, experience, and life of the YSA and the SWP.

        i) The SWP is built around the rhythms of a party of industrial workers. The YSA, on the other hand, is an organization not only of young workers but also of nonparty high school and college youth.

        ii) Given the conquest of the turn by the SWP, this gap between the two organizations is substantial compared to most of the thirty-year history of the YSA. It is a weightier political step for a YSA member to join the party today. This underlines the importance of party cadres working politically with the YSA membership, bringing party history to YSA members and discussing the ideas contained in our basic arsenal of books.

    (b) Above all, our central task is to help recruit to the YSA. Party members must help reach out by speaking on campus and attracting contacts to classes and activities organized by the YSA.

5. Working to maximize political homogeneity is a permanent axis of the challenge to forge proletarian parties.

  a) From heterogeneous personal backgrounds and origins that together strengthen the collective experience of a communist cadre, all members come to identify with the line of march of the working class.

    (1) The political homogeneity of the party cadres does not come without effort. It is won by a cadre that takes its class struggle experiences seriously and

---

the 1994 Chicago gathering. ". . . Those we can win to the revolutionary movement right now are not large in numbers, but they are spread all over the United States." See "Imperialism's March Toward Fascism and War" in *New International* no. 10, esp. pp. 219–35 and 317–33.

See also the "Young Socialists Manifesto" at the opening of this issue of *New International.*

works to conquer a common political understanding of them, enriching Marxist theory in the process.

(2) This is the only basis on which varying assessments of new conjunctures and tactics can be resolved through common experience and democratic discussion, resulting in authoritative decisions on our course and collective action to advance party work.

b) As part of our adjustment to the slowing pace of recruitment and leadership transition over the past period, we have had to make a conscious retreat on two institutions central to deepening the political homogeneity of the party and world movement.

(1) We have not organized a session of the party leadership school since 1986.

(a) A revolutionary workers party must pay particular attention to homogeneous leadership education. That is why the reestablishment of the leadership school in 1980 went hand in hand from the outset with our decision to lead the party into industry.[38]

(b) Our retreat on the leadership school since 1986 has slowed the homogenization not only of the SWP leadership, but of an international communist leadership, as well.

(c) The hiatus in the regular sessions of the leadership school has also weakened centralized attention through the branches to the education of party cadres in Marxism. As a permanent aspect of the party's activities, such education is vital to advancing political homogeneity. The Lenin class series organized by every branch in the first half

---

38. See "Educating the Leadership of a Proletarian Party" in *The Changing Face of U.S. Politics* by Jack Barnes, pp. 372–87, as well as pp. 149, 161–62, and 191–92 in that book.

of the 1980s was integral to our political advance as a turn party.[39]

(2) We have not produced a new issue of *New International* since mid-1987.

(a) Although we have continued to conquer important political and programmatic questions — such as those dealt with in this draft resolution — we have repeatedly had to postpone the concentrated work required to get these acquisitions into print in a publicly usable form.

(b) The *New International* remains the single best source for cadres and other fighters to read and study the political perspectives and program around which our forces are being forged internationally.

(3) Not having the leadership school or new issues of *New International* feeds depoliticization, political shallowness, and slows down leadership transition. Our challenge in the year ahead is to organize ourselves to reestablish these two weapons that remain central to advancing politically.[40]

c) Fighters come to the revolutionary workers movement rebelling against authority. In meeting the challenge of politically leading the assimilation of these young fighters into the party, communists value and reinforce their in-

---

39. The syllabus for that class series, "Lenin's Conception of the Class Forces and Strategy in Making the Russian Revolution (1902–1917)," is available in *Two Study Guides on Lenin's Writings*, an Education for Socialists publication available from Pathfinder.

40. Since this resolution was adopted in August 1990, five more issues of *New International* have been published, including this one. In addition, the Spanish-language *Nueva Internacional* was launched and four issues have appeared, as well as two more issues of the French-language *Nouvelle Internationale*, and two issues of the Swedish-language *Ny International*. Issues of these three publications containing Spanish, French, and Swedish translations of the articles in this issue of *New International* are scheduled in 1998.

dependent, increasingly self-confident, and critical attitude toward bourgeois and petty-bourgeois traditions,
norms, and values.

(1) At the same time, inside the communist movement,
cadres learn above all respect for the proletarian political continuity, traditions, norms, and values that
are the most dearly paid-for conquests of the modern
revolutionary workers movement.

(a) We learn to appreciate the profoundly radical
character of being part of an organization that
uses lessons from the communist movement of
the 1930s and political contributions of Trotsky as
a guide to daily political practice; that checks and
corrects these guides against those of Lenin, the
Bolsheviks, and the Communist International;
and that checks Lenin, as he himself always did,
against Marx, Engels, and the conquests of the international communist and workers organizations
of which they were founding leaders.

(b) In this sense, the communist movement is the most
traditional and conservative movement, and simultaneously the most radical and revolutionary.

(2) Taking and using this communist tradition is a collective political act that combines

(a) organized Marxist education (through classes,
books and pamphlets, political magazines and
newspapers) that constantly deepens the politicization of party cadres;

(b) encouragement and help in developing the habit
of reading the Marxist classics and party history;
and

(c) common experiences in the class struggle through
party branches and union fractions, leading to
discussions and decisions on our course.

(3) Above all, workers come to a revolutionary organization to find disciplined functioning that can render the

struggles of their class effective against what seems to be the insuperable powers of the class enemy.

d) The Socialist Workers Party is the oldest communist party in the world.

   (1) It is through the SWP that the fundamental continuity of a politically homogeneous international communist movement has been registered. That continuity has developed in a cumulative way through an unbroken braiding of leadership generations with political and organizational continuity going back to the origins of the Communist International.

   (2) This fact places responsibilities on the SWP as part of a world movement that can only be met if we recognize that this unbroken communist continuity is and will continue to be an international conquest, a conquest that has come only through international collaboration.

6. A more than ten-year offensive by the employers has failed to drive the labor movement from center stage of politics in the United States. This fact, which was our starting point, can only be accurately assessed by recognizing the great weight of its potential impact on the world relationship of class forces. By seeing it as a central fact of international politics, we can reach out to fellow workers worldwide to collectively meet the responsibilities and make the communist gains that it portends.

The fight for Black freedom

Malcolm X Talks to Young People

"I for one will join in with anyone, I don't care what color you are, as long as you want to change this miserable condition that exists on this earth"—Malcolm X, Britain, December 1964. Also includes his 1965 interview with the *Young Socialist* magazine. $10.95

Fighting Racism in World War II

C.L.R. James, George Breitman, Edgar Keemer, and others

A week-by-week account of the struggle against racism and racial discrimination in the United States from 1939 to 1945, taken from the pages of the socialist newsweekly, the *Militant*. $20.95

Marx and Engels on the United States

Karl Marx and Frederick Engels

Articles and letters from 1846 to 1895 examine the rise of U.S. capitalism, the historic conflict with a system based on slave labor, the impact of the frontier and free land, and the challenges facing the emerging working-class movement. Indispensable for understanding the economic roots and consequences of the Civil War and the class structure and conflicts of the United States today. $15.95

Leon Trotsky on Black Nationalism and Self-Determination

Drawing on lessons from the October 1917 Russian revolution, Trotsky explains why uncompromising opposition to racial discrimination and support to Blacks' struggle for national self-determination are an essential part of the strategy to unite the working class to make a socialist revolution in the United States. $10.95

From Pathfinder. Write for a catalog.

$\mathcal{G}et$ $\mathcal{Y}our$

PATHFINDER READERS CLUB CARD NOW!

$\mathcal{B}$ooks by revolutionists written in the heat of political battles. That's the world that opens up to members of the Pathfinder Readers Club. Build up your library by choosing from more than 500 titles by Karl Marx, Frederick Engels, V.I. Lenin, Leon Trotsky, Rosa Luxemburg, Ernesto Che Guevara, Fidel Castro, Malcolm X, Farrell Dobbs, James P. Cannon, Joseph Hansen, George Novack, Evelyn Reed, Nelson Mandela, Thomas Sankara, Maurice Bishop, Eugene V. Debs. Pathfinder lets these and other revolutionary leaders speak in their own words.

- Readers Club members receive a **15 percent discount** on books and pamphlets in the Pathfinder catalog at any Pathfinder bookstore around the world.

- You get **even higher discounts** on special selected titles and new releases.

- And membership costs only **US$10 a year**.

To get your Readers Club card anywhere in the world, contact the Pathfinder bookstore nearest you (see front of magazine for distributors' addresses), or send US$10 to Pathfinder, 410 West Street, New York, NY 10014.

Further reading

The Politics of Chicano Liberation

OLGA RODRIGUEZ AND OTHERS

Lessons from the rise of the Chicano movement in the 1960s and 1970s. Presents a fighting program for those determined to combat divisions within the working class based on language and national origin. $15.95

An Action Program to Confront the Coming Economic Crisis

A Program for International Working-Class Struggle Today

How a program to fight for jobs and affirmative action, and to combat imperialism's pillage of the Third World, is crucial to uniting working people internationally. $3.00 Also available in Spanish, French, Icelandic, and Swedish.

Maoism vs. Bolshevism

The 1965 Catastrophe in Indonesia, China's 'Cultural Revolution,' and the Disintegration of World Stalinism

JOSEPH HANSEN

Following the Chinese revolution of 1949, many workers and youth in Asia and elsewhere—inspired by that historic blow to imperialism—were politically misled by the Mao Zedong leadership. These articles, reports, and resolutions by Joseph Hansen explain the communist alternative to Mao's Stalinist course, which in 1965 paved the way for a bloody CIA-backed coup in Indonesia. $10.00

Black Music, White Business

Illuminating the History and Political Economy of Jazz

FRANK KOFSKY

Probes the conditions in the jazz world breeding the contradiction between the artistry of Black musicians and control by largely white-owned business of the means of jazz distribution—the recording companies, booking agencies, festivals, clubs, and magazines. $15.95

Write for a catalog.

The Changing Face of U.S. Politics
Working-Class Politics and the Trade Unions
JACK BARNES A handbook for workers coming into the factories, mines, and mills, as they react to the uncertain life, ceaseless turmoil, and brutality of capitalism in the closing years of the twentieth century. It shows how millions of workers, as political resistance grows, will revolutionize themselves, their unions, and all of society. $19.95 Also available in Spanish and French.

Background to "The Changing Face of U.S. Politics" and "U.S. Imperialism Has Lost the Cold War"
JACK BARNES, JOEL BRITTON, AND MARY-ALICE WATERS Reports and resolutions of the Socialist Workers Party on trade union policy, proletarian leadership versus clique functioning, the poison of race baiting in the workers movement, and the membership norms of the revolutionary party. A companion to *The Changing Face of U.S. Politics* and 1990 SWP political resolution published in this issue of *New International.* $7.00

The Struggle for a Proletarian Party
JAMES P. CANNON A founding leader of the Socialist Workers Party defends the centrality of proletarianization within the political and organizational principles of Marxism in a polemic against a petty-bougeois current in the party. The debate unfolded as Washington prepared to drag U.S. working people into the slaughter of World War II. $19.95

Background to "The Struggle for a Proletarian Party"
JAMES P. CANNON AND LEON TROTSKY The challenges faced by the Socialist Workers Party in deepening its involvement in the organizations and struggles of the industrial workers class in the late 1930s. The SWP must "orient in practice the whole organization toward the factories, the strikes, the unions," writes Leon Trotsky in a 1937 letter to party leader James P. Cannon. $6.00

Socialist trade unionists talk about the *Militant* newsweekly and revolutionary books and pamphlets with coal miners during sale at West Virginia portal, May 1997. "We are striving for consistent, professional communist work in the unions accompanied by the *deepening* proletarianization of the experience and composition of the party and its leadership."

THE COMMUNIST STRATEGY OF PARTY BUILDING TODAY: A LETTER TO COMRADES IN SWEDEN

by Mary-Alice Waters

New York, New York
May 30, 1988

Dear Comrade,

Your letter indicates that you are planning to attend the Oberlin conference and party convention in August [1988]. I am very glad that you will be there, since that is by far the best way for you to get an accurate view of what the SWP is doing, what we think communists around the world should be doing today, and why. The resolution we will be discussing and voting

---

This letter from Mary-Alice Waters, editor of New International *and a leader of the Socialist Workers Party, was sent to a member of a group of communist workers in Sweden in May 1988. In March of that year, Waters had been part of an international leadership delegation that visited Sweden to meet with these comrades.*

This letter formed the basis of the section entitled "The Communist Strategy of Party Building Today" in part IV of the 1990 SWP political resolution featured elsewhere in this issue, "U.S. Imperialism Has Lost the Cold War." The letter was published along with the resolution in the party's internal bulletin for discussion in SWP branches and by delegates to the party convention that year. In addition to adopting the general line of the political resolution as a whole, delegates approved a brief separate resolution adopting and summarizing the main points of this letter.

As is often the case, the letter written in the course of a real political struggle to clarify ideas and set a course of action is richer and more concrete than any brief telescoped resolution. The letter is what party members and Young Socialists return to when discussing what became known as "the six points." It should be read as an integral part of the resolution, "U.S. Imperialism Has Lost the Cold War."

on, together with the reports and debate at the convention itself, as well as the parallel workshops, classes, rallies, and informal discussions, will all focus on precisely these decisive questions.[1]

Of course, we will be discussing these issues from the perspective of communist workers in the United States, but not as "American communists." As you know, we don't think we should be doing one thing and comrades in Sweden or Mexico or Grenada something else. To the best of our ability we start not from "United States politics" but from world politics and the need to reconstruct a world communist leadership. We try to advance a strategy to move in that direction, one that is in harmony with the events unfolding day by day among the toilers of the world and their vanguard. We apply that strategy in everything we do, and think other communists should do the same. But the one thing you won't get from us is tactical advice on how to do this in Sweden (or anywhere else).

THIS IS IMPORTANT, because several times in your letter you interpret things that one member of the international leadership delegation that visited Sweden a couple months ago said, or you think he said, as tactical advice about how to fight to win others to a communist course of action, and tactical suggestions on what you should be doing to build a communist party in Sweden today. I'm confident that such advice was the furthest thing from that comrade's mind.

I will send you the package of materials that all our branches are using for a preconvention educational series. It is based on articles that have appeared in the *Militant* over the last year, and it would be useful for you and other comrades in Luleå (whether they are coming to the SWP convention or not) to

---

1. The resolution discussed and adopted by the 1988 SWP convention, "What the 1987 Stock Market Crash Foretold," is printed in issue no. 10 of *New International.*

read and discuss these.[2] The political resolution that we are in the process of drafting will develop the same major themes: the character of the creeping crisis we have been living through, its differential impact on layers of the toilers around the world, and the nature of the economic and social crisis announced by the October stock market crash and its implications for workers and farmers; the lines along which a world communist movement will be reconstructed; the character and tasks of small communist nuclei today — what we must do to meet the challenges we already face and to consciously prepare for those that are coming.

If you work your way through this preliminary education series, the resolution and the convention itself will be much richer for the comrades who are attending.

In addition to the SWP convention, there will also be a meeting at Oberlin of groups of comrades from various countries who have been part of the international organization of book launchings of *Che Guevara and the Cuban Revolution* over the last year. The work centralized by Pathfinder to increase circulation of communist literature internationally, and especially the political launching and promotion of its new collection of Che's writings and speeches, has been an extremely valuable experience — one that no group of sects or Stalinist organizations could have had — and we all want to politically assess it. I'm sure those groups involved want to leave Oberlin organized internationally to build on those successes in the coming months with the launching of several new books that will be out shortly, including *The Economic Thought of Ernesto Che Guevara, Thomas Sankara Speaks*, and a new collection of Malcolm X speeches.[3]

---

2. Luleå is a city with a large steel mill close to the iron ore mining area of northern Sweden. Several members of the group of communists to whom this letter was addressed lived and worked in Luleå at the time.
3. *Che Guevara and the Cuban Revolution*, the most comprehensive collection in English of the writings and speeches of this revolutionary leader,

That is the kind of international organization that will come out of discussions at Oberlin this summer, and any comrades who are interested in doing this will take part in the discussion.

You REFER TO six points that a member of the delegation raised in his discussion with you in March. Although I didn't hear what this comrade said, I am quite sure I know what he was referring to, because these are points we have discussed in the SWP leadership as well. Comrades in the leadership of the Revolutionary Workers League in Canada, the Communist League in Britain, the Socialist Action League in New Zealand, and others have had similar discussions.[4] You will find they are taken up in our coming resolution.

Your recapitulation of the six points is not quite right, and certainly any idea that they are preconditions to be realized before August 1988 is nonsensical, as you indicate. Your comment that it is not obvious how to realize them in such a time perspective is a humorous understatement.

The six points we are talking about *are* the concrete foundation for communist activity today, however. They flow from the need to meet an *objective* situation unfolding in the world. Serious progress on them *is* a precondition for increased international communist organization and more effective common

---

was published in October 1987 to coincide with the twentieth anniversary of the death in combat of Guevara and other comrades in Bolivia. Supporters of Pathfinder organized public launchings of the book, with a broad array of speakers and messages, in fifteen cities in Australia, Canada, Iceland, New Zealand, Sweden, the United Kingdom, and the United States. Over the next two years, Pathfinder book launchings were held around the world for *Che Guevara: Economics and Politics in the Transition to Socialism* by Carlos Tablada (translated from the Spanish book "The Economic Thought of Ernesto Che Guevara"); *Thomas Sankara Speaks*; and *Malcolm X: The Last Speeches.*
4. The Revolutionary Workers League and the Socialist Action League subsequently changed their names to Communist League in Canada and Comunist League in New Zealand.

activity, and that organization and activity would be the most important by-product of real progress on the six points.

What are the six points?

First and foremost is the turn. We all face the challenge to move forward in the construction of organizations of communist workers, carrying out consistent communist (as opposed to radical and trade unionist) political activity in the party's milieu, which is the industrial working class — employed and unemployed, native-born and immigrant, organized and unorganized. We are striving for consistent, professional communist work in the unions accompanied by the *deepening* proletarianization of the experience and composition of the party and its leadership.

The second point is the need for *political centralization* to build a turn party. Practice has shown us more concretely what is involved in this. The turn cannot be carried out by individuals getting jobs in industry, or by a group of union fractions alone, or by a minority within a party whose majority is not communist in practice. The turn can only be real if it is the axis of work for an *organization* whose leadership is striving for political homogeneity and centralization, carrying out (in a particular country) an international political orientation.

A proletarian organization can't be built without consistent work to develop nationally coordinated and centralized fractions in various industries and industrial unions. It can't be done without having both strong, politically well-rounded, and confident branches *and* fractions. The two have some different tasks, but through the common political content of their work, they mutually reinforce each other.

The turn cannot be initiated or advanced at key points in its development unless the central political leadership takes the direct role in leading it.

As you can tell from reading the reports in the *Militant* on the series of Active Workers Conferences we organized over a period of several months last year, we in the SWP have found this point to be our biggest challenge. The turn is never conquered once and for all time. Even with a relatively strong and politically homogeneous party that initiated the turn over a decade ago, we found that under the pressures of the employers' offensive of the last years we were actually being pushed back from the turn. We had to reorganize ourselves, consolidate a number of branches, and reconquer essential political aspects of building a turn party.

We had to accept the possibility that leading the party forward to reconquer ground given up under pressure in the recent years could well divide the cadre or leadership. But we knew that if we defaulted on reconquering the turn and drifted toward branches and fractions that functioned with increasing decentralization, and thus less and less political homogeneity, divisions would be inevitable — and, under those conditions, far deeper and more destructive to the possibility of building a proletarian party.

Our experience on this has been to some degree paralleled by the organizations in New Zealand and Canada. In Britain the comrades have discovered that while many thought they had organized themselves to carry out the turn within the Socialist League, it was an illusion. Not because they didn't try, and they were well qualified to try, but because *it can't be done without a communist organization.*[5]

I'm not familiar with what you are doing in Sweden, or what discussions you have had in Luleå in the recent period. Nor, as I said above, am I offering tactical advice. But the one thing I know for sure you are not doing is building a turn party, or deepening the turn within the Socialist Party of Sweden, because it can't be done.

---

5. Supporters of the turn to industry and other communist policies in the United Kingdom were expelled from the Socialist League in January 1988, one week before a national convention at which their platform would have had the majority. Those expelled went ahead with the scheduled convention, which had been undemocratically canceled, and took the name Communist League.

The third point has to do with the need for a weekly rhythm of branch and fraction political life. The rhythm of our political work — like most things in this society — is dictated by the capitalist organization of production. The schedules we and our political milieu are obligated to keep are decided for us by the need to sell our labor power.

One of the first things that always happens when a party or branch is getting demoralized and starting to move away from a proletarian orientation is someone proposes that weekly branch meetings are too much, that "workers" don't have time to come to meetings that often. A decision is made to hold branch meetings only every other week, or sometimes even less often. Once the weekly norm is abandoned, an irreplaceable basis for the disciplined life of a centralized, combat party has been destroyed. Weekly forums, classes, plant-gate sales, regular fraction meetings, and recruitment work all rapidly disappear. Because we *do* organize our lives on a week-by-week basis, and if the party isn't organizing our political work according to that rhythm, something else will.

THE PUBLIC activity of a communist party has to be built around the regular use of a weekly paper. A biweekly or less frequent paper simply cannot furnish that rhythm, nor can it respond rapidly enough to political developments to orient the party and its supporters. That is why comrades in countries outside the United States have found that using the *Militant* as the central organizer of a weekly schedule of activities has been so important in the last period. It increases the value of less frequent publications and allows them to concentrate on their strengths. The *Militant* is the only weekly communist paper in English that exists at the moment (and there's no communist paper of any frequency in many other languages). We've been making some progress on using it more effectively.

In the SWP we supplement the use of the *Militant* with our other regular propaganda tools. We use *Perspectiva Mundial* and *New International* this way, as well as pamphlets sometimes. Comrades in other countries use those publications and *Nouvelle Internationale*, as well as their own biweekly or monthly papers, which are substantially smaller than the *Militant.* Comrades in Britain, Australia, and Iceland as yet have no regular publications of their own, and have found — even in Iceland, where English is not the first language — that they are able to use the *Militant* with greater success than they had originally thought.

T HE FOURTH POINT is the expansion of our communist propaganda work built around Pathfinder Press and Pathfinder Bookstores, or Pathfinder international (not "Pathfinder International") as it can be described more and more accurately.

It is on this that we have had the most concrete common experience the last year, from which we have all learned a great deal about what is possible. Yet we are just beginning to see the present possibilities and obligations of Pathfinder in historical perspective, as part of the reconstruction of a communist world movement.

It's hard to really accept and act on the fact that given our small size and resources, there are a growing number of irreplaceable tasks on a world scale that *only* Pathfinder will do. We can see that we are a long way from realizing the potential. Fortunately, Pathfinder's circle of friends and allies is expanding internationally, from the Caribbean to the Pacific, because others also need — and are beginning to see — what Pathfinder alone can do.

Our propaganda work built around Pathfinder has no boundaries, by definition. Whether it's Che and the Cuban revolution, or the 1987 stock market crash and the deepening crisis anticipated by workers everywhere, or the relevance of the discussions in the Communist International for workers and farmers today, we are talking about questions that are vital to the future of working people in every country.

And expanding communist propaganda wherever we can in the world today is our most elementary task. In fact, except for Cuba, where the existence of a mass communist party that politically dominates a revolutionary workers and farmers regime opens up some additional possibilities, propaganda work, properly understood, is the only thing open to communists today: everything we do is aimed at winning broader support among working people for a proletarian internationalist perspective.

Given the character and scope of the expansion of Pathfinder over the last year, we are obligated to pay special attention to it. That's why we agreed to host for Pathfinder a postconvention meeting at Oberlin this summer to internationally organize our next steps forward. It's a meeting the participants have all earned. It comes out of the dynamic of what we have conquered in practice in the last twelve months.

The fifth point is the youth. This is a question of political orientation, not an organizational question. We're not talking about setting up youth groups, organizing youth commissions or whatever. In fact, by looking at the youth question politically and assessing experiences internationally, we can avoid premature organizational steps of that kind.

In everything we do our attention is directed above all towards those fighting young workers who are the communist cadres of the future. It is these young fighters, as well as students who are attracted towards working-class battles and are open to joining a proletarian organization, who we are trying to reach with communist propaganda. That is who we are trying to recruit. They are the ones — in their overwhelming majority members of no politically centralized organization — who will be most deeply affected by the cataclysmic events that are coming, and will be the most determined combatants.

Our political orientation to the youth is especially important given the increasing average age of all our forces, and the increasing pressures this brings to adapt to the rhythms and norms of the society in which we live, including the unions of which we are members. Our success will be measured by our ability to find the way to a new generation, and win them to a communist party.

The sixth point could perhaps be called "under the banner of the new International."

The world communist organization that originated in Lenin's time was destroyed by Stalinism. The continuity of world communism was kept alive for a substantial period through the Bolshevik-Leninist opposition and the Fourth International, despite whatever weaknesses and errors. When the International was founded in 1938 it was accurate to say, as the Transitional Program does, that outside the ranks of the Fourth International there was not "a single revolutionary current on this planet really meriting the name."[6] But with the 1959 victory of the Cuban revolution and the subsequent forging of a communist leadership in Cuba that continues to advance, that statement definitely ceased to be true.

THE "ACID TEST" of the Cuban revolution has always been the test of recognizing the place of the communist *leadership* in Cuba and acting on that understanding.

The historical balance sheet is clear. The majority leadership of the forces that are organized through the United Secretariat of the Fourth International have responded to this test more like an ultraleft sect than a communist leadership. As SWP leader Joe Hansen pointed out, this was just as true during the

---

6. The Fourth International, which the Socialist Workers Party helped found and lead, was forged by communists around the world who sought to maintain the continuity of the course of the Bolshevik Party and Communist International as they had been led by V.I. Lenin until his death in 1924. Its founding program — "The Death Agony of Capitalism and the Tasks of the Fourth International" by Bolshevik leader Leon Trotsky, which was discussed and adopted by the Socialist Workers Party for submission to the founding congress — is printed in *The Transitional Program for Socialist Revolution* by Trotsky (Pathfinder, 1977).

years of the guerrillaist deviation as it is today.[7] They always engaged in small-group politics. They were always *competing* with the Cuban leadership, striving to displace it by a Trotskyist leadership organized by the United Secretariat.

This erroneous political stance toward the Cuban Communist Party has been further codified since 1979 by the response of the United Secretariat majority to the revolutionary victories in Grenada and Nicaragua. The 1981 resolution of the International Executive Committee on Cuba and the 1985 world congress resolution, "The Present Stage of Building the Fourth International," codify these positions. I would add that the response of the United Secretariat to the communist leadership emerging within the African National Congress over the last decade has been similar. Grotesque as it may be, they see it as a threat, too, as a competitor.

The reconstruction of a world communist movement will not pass through the Fourth International (United Secretariat), to say nothing of other currents that call themselves Trotskyist or some variant of the Fourth International. It will shatter the United Secretariat forces even further. That is why we say (and have said throughout the transitional period we have been going through the last half decade) that we march under the banner of the new International. We are seeking to deepen collaboration with communists who have been forged through different historical experiences from ours, and, in the process, we will win whatever forces we can who are ready to break from Trotskyism in order to become communists.

We do not say, nor do we believe, that there are no communists in the Fourth International. A number of individuals who are today part of the various groupings that make up the majority in the United Secretariat will be part of the reconstruc-

---

7. See *The Leninist Strategy of Party Building: The Debate on Guerrilla Warfare in Latin America* by Joseph Hansen (Pathfinder, 1979), as well as Hansen's *Dynamics of the Cuban Revolution: A Marxist Appreciation* (Pathfinder, 1978).

tion of the communist movement on a world scale. But it would be a fatal political mistake to *orient* to them, as opposed to charting a communist course of action internationally and consistently pursuing it. Only by doing so will we affect those who can be won — there and elsewhere.

It is important to note that we are not the only ones within the United Secretariat who recognize that the Fourth International is being shattered by its political incapacity to meet the challenges faced today. A significant portion of the French section, for example, states unequivocally that it is a mistake to try to build a communist party today. They believe the balance sheet of 1968 to 1988 proves that those striving to create a Leninist party were chasing a blue unicorn. They conclude the Ligue Communiste Revolutionnaire should recognize that fact and regroup with others to build a centrist party, before it's too late even for that.

The German section has already divided between those who joined the Greens (designating it the party of the present and future German working class) and those who fused with the ex-Maoist Communist Party of Germany. The Mexican Partido Revolucionario de los Trabajadores doesn't pretend that adherence to the Fourth International is a condition of membership.

The historical crisis of the Fourth International is a fact recognized by a majority of forces within the United Secretariat. But, as the above few examples demonstrate, diametrically counterposed answers are given concerning the political roots of the crisis and the course communists must chart today.

BRIEFLY STATED, those are the six points. As you can see, there is nothing new in them. If you go back and reread the turn report adopted at the 1979 world congress of the Fourth International (and other articles on the turn in the book *The Changing Face of U.S. Politics*), the minority report on Nicaragua presented at the world congress, "Their Trotsky and Ours," the political resolution we adopted at the last SWP convention, the major articles in *New International*, the discussion pieces in the *Militant* I referred to earlier — it's all there. It's especially important to note what the turn report says will be the consequences of *not* carrying out the policies outlined.[8]

In all that material we're talking about the turn, about communist propaganda work, and about the Leninist strategy of party building today that can only be understood and conquered through practical work along these lines.

There is no way you can advance on one of the six points without striving to move forward on all of them. Of course, in practice, we all move forward unevenly — and necessarily so. But any attempt to develop one aspect of a communist orientation while ignoring or rejecting the others will result in being pushed backward on all fronts. Progress on the six points, based on the foundation of the turn, is the test by which we must measure whether or not communist nuclei have conquered enough common ground to be truly politically homogeneous, cutting across national borders, laying the objective basis for international organization.

You refer to the "framework of communist convergence," which is a term that has been used in various things we and other comrades have written. This is one of the points the delegates discussed at the Communist League convention in Britain last January, and we discussed at one of our recent National Committee meetings. The more we talked about it, the more we came to agreement that it's not a good term, because

---

8. "The Turn and Building a World Communist Movement," the report by Jack Barnes adopted by the 1979 world congress of the Fourth International, can be found in *The Changing Face of U.S. Politics* (Pathfinder, 1981, 1994). The minority resolution on Nicaragua, "Nicaragua: How the Workers and Farmers Government Came to Power," and a report on that resolution by Jack Barnes, are printed in issue no. 9 of *New International*. "Their Trotsky and Ours" by Jack Barnes is published in issue no. 1 of *New International*. The political resolution adopted by the 1985 SWP convention, "The Revolutionary Perspective and Leninist Continuity in the United States," is printed in issue no. 4 of *New International*.

it creates more ambiguities and problems than it solves. To the extent that there is a convergence of communist forces on a world scale, i.e., to the extent the term has any meaning in the world today, it is simply the by-product of what different communist organizations are doing. In the process they find themselves moving in the same direction.

Communist convergence is not a goal we set, a pot of gold at the end of the rainbow. Nor is it an imaginary embryo organization. We're not part of some "communist convergence current" that includes the ANC, and the Cuban CP, the FSLN, or who knows what other revolutionary groups that are sometimes designated to be part of the convergence. The Cuban CP is not our leadership, let alone the ANC, the FSLN, or anyone else. We chart a communist course in practical collaboration with other organized forces who we find traveling the same road and who are at the same *historic stage* of experiences, organization, and size.

In the process we will also find ourselves working with others — like ANC cadres, FSLNers, and Cuban CPers — on specific campaigns and projects where the political trajectories of revolutionaries — and of communists — at very different stages of experience, organization, differentiation, and size come together.

I T SHOULD BE EMPHASIZED that the point of departure for everything I've said above is not an evaluation of the Fourth International or any of its components. We start from the world we live in, the complications of that world, and set a political course for communists. Only then is it relevant to look at how well any organization, including the Fourth International and its sections, measures up.

Since you ascribe nothing but political disorientation to the leadership of the Fourth International, there is no need to add anything to what I've said about the United Secretariat. I'll put it aside.

I do want to restate the opinion of the SWP leadership on the Swedish section, however.[9] We do not think it can be reformed into a communist organization. In this I am again not saying anything new. This was the judgment we expressed at the time of the last world congress, after a number of comrades from our leadership had visited Sweden and gotten a firsthand look at the work of the section. You seem to be coming to a similar view when you say, "more and more we have also come to realize that we have lost the battle for the SP."

It is not only the Swedish Socialist Party that is no longer reformable. The same holds true for every section of the Fourth International except Canada and New Zealand, and the sympathizing section in the United States. The experience of the last decade has provided ample proof of the fact that no section was able to carry out the turn, deepen its proletarian internationalist composition and leadership, and move forward in constructing a communist party without a political battle and deep-going split. The great failure of those comrades in the leadership of various European sections who initially supported the turn was their total default and unwillingness to *lead* when it became evident that moving forward in the construction of a proletarian party would necessarily entail a split. *Not* splitting with old friends and the familiar, comfortable swamp of competing cliques was more important to them than being communists.

But there is something special about the role of the Swedish party in this political struggle that took place between 1979 and 1982. Those were the four key years. It was the SP leadership that, on behalf of the International Executive Committee majority, led the counterrevolution on the turn. Following the 1979 world congress at which the Swedish leadership, like many others, voted for the turn report, the Swedish section had a chance to begin transforming itself into a communist

---

9. At the time, the comrades to whom this letter was sent were members of the Socialist Party, the Swedish section of the Fourth International.

party. That, of course, would have resulted in a split, including with leading comrades who had become trade unionists. But by the time of the 1982 meeting of the International Executive Committee that possibility had been closed off. That is six years ago already.

The counterrevolution led by the Swedish section played an important role in the fate of the Fourth International. Tom Gustafsson, one of the central leaders of the SP, was the United Secretariat majority reporter for the turn counterrevolution at the 1982 IEC meeting. Basing his report largely on the Swedish experience, he chided the French for dragging their heels and argued with them that the "American (brutal) turn" couldn't be defeated simply by opposing and rejecting it. It could only be done by conceding the need to proletarianize the composition of our sections and organizing to get a substantial minority of comrades into industrial jobs and unions, while carrying out a political course — in the unions and in party work — that was the negation of the turn. It is what I call the "Swedish turn."

The "Swedish turn," however, was no more a form of the turn than the panda's "thumb" is a form of thumb. It's not a detour, an alternate, more difficult route on the same historical course of evolution. It's an obstacle and then a deadly trap, one that blocks off and prevents a turn party from being built.

This is important, because what happened in Sweden was the most corrupting kind of experience of all for communists trying to lead a real turn. It made the fight *more* difficult in Sweden than it was even in Britain, for example. It means that comrades in Sweden trying to build a turn party have a greater handicap to overcome, more to unlearn because of the character of the party created by the "Swedish turn."

I don't mean to imply that Sweden was the only place where this kind of model "turn-counterrevolution-in-the-name-of-the-turn" took root. The "Belgian turn" played a similar role, and there may be some others.

The biggest error of judgment made by comrades in Sweden was not that you didn't see what was happening. You did, and helped others of us to appreciate the depth of the political corruption. But for a while after 1982 you kept hoping that some external factors would change all this, that maybe the experiences of the Fourth International would bring weight to bear to reverse the course of the Swedish party. But just the opposite happened. The Socialist Party "led" for the Fourth International in this regard and the Fourth International leadership reinforced the Swedish counterrevolution on the turn.

THIS COMES TO THE HEART of the matter. *The impact of world events cannot transform a party that has institutionalized a counterrevolution on the turn.* It is only by understanding this fact that you can appreciate the depth of the problem. The SP cannot today be pushed towards becoming a communist organization through some outside influence.

This is the point in your letter that I most disagree with, if I understand you correctly. You state, "the situation now is that the SP differs in some ways from other European sections of the Fourth International. A more positive attitude to the ANC is not just opportunism. We think that comrades in the leadership and in the party have been influenced by the Sandinistas. There is no reason to overestimate these positive traits and we cannot know how they will stand up against a factional and sectarian offensive from the United Secretariat. But this is the situation *now.*"

I agree with you that it is not just opportunism. Moreover, working to aid, and being attracted towards, the Nicaraguan revolution and the mass struggle against apartheid in South Africa is positive no matter who does it. On some political questions related to the revolutionary developments in Nicaragua and South Africa, some comrades in the leadership of the SP may well have more correct positions than those that prevail in the United Secretariat. I believe the same is true in other sections of the Fourth International.

There are, however, literally millions of people in the world

today who support the ANC or are influenced by the Sandinistas. But that doesn't necessarily bring them closer to being
communists. For many it is just the opposite, in fact. They support Sandinismo and the FSLN because they believe it is an alternative to communism. They try to counterpose the "Nicaraguan road" to the "Cuban road." To some degree that is the
case even in the United Secretariat.

Similarly, as you probably know well from your experiences
in Sweden, there are countless liberal and social democratic
forces that give massive support to the ANC, precisely because
they hope that by doing so they will be able to influence the
course of the South African revolution and block the development of communist leadership within the ANC.

We are all for massive aid to the ANC and the Sandinistas,
no matter what the motives. Experience has shown that the
revolutionists in South Africa and Nicaragua are quite capable
of handling "friends" who have different strategic objectives.
The more liberals, radicals, social democrats, ultralefts, and
whatever involved in practical help the better.

BUT WE HAVE a different starting point: reconstructing a
communist leadership on a world scale. Simply having a positive attitude towards the ANC or being influenced by the Sandinistas is not necessarily a step forward along that line of
march. Proletarian internationalist work carried out by a
communist organization does make you *more* communist. But
if Nicaraguan or South African solidarity work isn't an inseparable aspect of building a communist party to begin with, it
doesn't make you more communist to do it, anymore than it
does the tens of thousands of others doing radical solidarity
work, including participation in work brigades, going to international conferences, etc. It doesn't make that work less immediately useful, either.

Being *politically* attracted towards the leadership of the Cuban revolution is, for many, something of a different order, I

believe, than being pro-ANC, or pro-FSLN. This is even more true today, given the clear course of the central leadership on rectification.[10] It's harder to be attracted to the Cuban CP without taking a step towards communism, and that is why you're not going to see a "pro-Cuban" shift in the SP or in the Fourth International.

But even being "positive" toward or "influenced" by the Cuban CP doesn't necessarily push you closer to being a communist. We all know plenty of Stalinists who are "positive" toward the Cuban CP. No one is ever won to communism simply by being attracted to, or influenced by, ideas. They must be expressed and concretized in the practice of a proletarian organization — even if it's only a nucleus — in the country in which you engage in politics. Even Marx and Engels didn't become communists until they were recruited by cadres of a revolutionary workers party. It is the only way. You become a communist through consciously led revolutionary working-class practice.

Under the pressure of big world events, small parties claiming to be revolutionary will shatter. What will be decisive to winning forces from them, in addition to winning other, more important forces, will be the existence of an independent and self-confident communist nucleus, however small, that is acting as if it intends to become a communist party, that can reach for those workers who are shaken by the big events — wherever they come from — and show them a way forward. That is what has always happened at every big turning point in the history of the communist movement.

It will happen again under the impact of the economic and social crisis that has been announced, and we won't have to wait for the twenty-first century for this to begin to unfold.

I'm not talking about how to act on this understanding. I'm

---

10. For a discussion of the rectification process in Cuba, see the opening section of Part IV of "U.S. Imperialism Has Lost the Cold War" elsewhere in this issue.

302   *Mary-Alice Waters*

not *proposing* anything. I'm stating a historical fact that one either agrees with or not, and acts on or not. And I will add what I consider another fact, confirmed by rich historical experience. If communists stay too long inside an organization they agree cannot be transformed into a proletarian party, sooner or later they will be incapable of leaving it (even if they leave it organizationally someday). Every year that goes by you only get one year older, and slightly less flexible, slightly less capable of unlearning what you thought you had learned about building a proletarian party by acting as a loyal opposition minority.

Setting off on your own certainly does not guarantee you will develop into a communist organization. But failing to do so, at some point, guarantees that you won't.

You STRESS THAT a party cannot be built without major events in the world class struggle. Of course, those are the only times rapid growth of a communist organization can occur. But another point is more fundamental. If the hard work of building a communist workers organization is not begun *before* these events, it will be next to impossible for a *communist* organization to be created out of them.

One point you made about the Socialist Party that I agree with completely is that it is not a small social democratic party, or a reformist party. You give part of the answer when you point out that there is no room for such a formation in Sweden. I would say that is true elsewhere, too.

The problem remains what it has always been since the Swedish section was formed at the beginning of the 1970s. Despite right-wing errors, its trajectory is that of an ultraleft sect that is trying to find a way to advance as part of a "revolutionary left" current. This will always breed a certain amount of trade union politicking, electoral illusions, and — more and more — adaptations to "national characteristics." Another point in your letter that I think is not quite accurate is your reference to the "attempted split at the world congress" that failed. It is true that some in the leadership of the International tried to organize a split leading up to the 1985 world congress and were bitterly disappointed when we prevented it from being consummated and codified by a world congress vote.

While the form and timing of the planned split operation failed (which bought a little more time and space for communists to organize and fight, and politically reorient to face the reality of the Fourth International), the split was *in fact* qualitatively deepened. The day following the world congress, the proposal we made to the leadership that Jack Barnes and I move to Paris and share responsibilities for the day-to-day leadership was rejected. The International Executive Committee for the first time demonstratively *excluded* all SWP comrades from the United Secretariat Bureau. Moreover, the Canadian section, the only other section in the Western Hemisphere that shared the same views as the SWP, was excluded even from the United Secretariat.

Since then, the de facto split has been total, and its forms have continued to spread. A body called the United Secretariat now meets three or four times a year, without a quorum present for much of its deliberations, to take up an agenda with few meaningful political points. The real discussions take place elsewhere.

One thing on which you indicate concern is that your course in Sweden might affect the status of the Communist League in Britain in relation to the Fourth International. I don't think this should worry you. Nothing you do there can have any bearing on this question. It has already been decided. It was the United Secretariat Bureau that forced the split and organized to recognize the minority of the British section. The United Secretariat codified it with no hesitations a few weeks later. It's not that the British comrades haven't decided *how* to fight their expulsion; it's that there is nothing meaningful they *can do*. The next meeting of the IEC will ratify the United Secretariat's actions, if not go beyond them. There will literally be *no interest* in the point. Many IEC members will demonstratively walk out of the room when the point comes on the agenda, or sit reading a novel until it comes time to vote. Then they will confirm that the Communist League is not a section or sympathizing organization of the Fourth International.

The fight in the Socialist Party in Sweden will not center on the Communist League of Britain. It will be over counterposed political orientations in the Swedish class struggle, starting from the meeting to launch *Che Guevara and the Cuban Revolution*, increased distribution of Pathfinder literature, distributing the *Militant*, collaborating with others doing the same things internationally, including the Communist League, and the centrality of such activities to building a turn party.

The "British question" in fact is a stalking horse for the only real international issue, the "SWP question." That's how bad things are in the Fourth International. The British comrades were really expelled for the affront of selling the *Militant*, not a "British paper," as one member of the British International Socialist Group disdainfully heckled. Or for becoming "Big Macs," as a United Secretariat member suavely depicted their sin. To recognize as sections only those who do *not* sell the *Militant* will take a little longer — but not much. When that vote takes place there will also be little interest in it, on either side. It will only reflect, and accurately so, a political reality that is much larger and more fundamental.[11]

Other than the obvious things you say a member of the international leadership delegation referred to during our trip to Sweden in March, such as organizing to expand interna-

11. In May 1989 the group of communists in Luleå and other cities to whom this letter was addressed held a conference and voted to form the Communist League in Sweden. A year later, in June 1990, the Socialist Workers Party and communist leagues or groups of revolutionists in Australia, Canada, France, Iceland, New Zealand, and Sweden previously affiliated to the United Secretariat of the Fourth International each decided to formalize what had already been the reality for some time and terminate these links, whether fraternal or statutory. See *New International* no. 7, pp. 10–12 and *The Changing Face of U.S. Politics: Working-Class Politics and the Trade Unions* by Jack Barnes, pp. 202–3.

tional propaganda work around Pathfinder, international organization can only be posed as a by-product of concrete communist activity along the lines I've been discussing. It can only come out of the real convergence of communist groups that are able to conquer this trajectory as internationalist, turn organizations. The truth is that no such set of organizations exists today, and that is why it's accurate to speak of the six points as preconditions.

They are the same everywhere. And we must all judge our own parties — whether they have five members or five hundred members — by the same yardstick, that is, how well we are measuring up to what is required of us by the political challenges we face. That is how we expect individual members of the SWP to judge the SWP. It is no different anywhere else in the world.

We will get a chance to discuss all this at greater length during the Oberlin conference this summer, but I wanted to reply to some of the most important things you raised in your letter without waiting. This letter has turned out longer than I thought it would when I began. I hope it will prove useful.

I also hope you will be able to convince even more comrades from Luleå to come to Oberlin. It's not too late.

L AST YEAR'S OBERLIN conference was marked above all by its internationalist character. Out of discussions there came the course we charted toward greater international use of the *Militant*, toward Pathfinder expansion, and toward the book launchings of *Che Guevara and the Cuban Revolution*.

This year's convention and conference will be marked more than anything else by what we accomplish in reconquering the political centrality of the turn as the underpinning of everything we do. This will provide the basis for another qualitative step forward in the use of our communist propaganda tools as an integral part of a course toward deepening proletarianization and internationalism. Out of this understanding will also come momentum toward a course that can achieve a potentially new level of international political homogeneity.

This is not only important for smaller groups. It is equally important for the SWP. Since the turn perspective was defeated in the Fourth International, the reality is that we have not been part of an international organization either. But there is no internationalism without international organization, and advancing along the lines we are talking about will deeply affect the SWP too.

Comradely,
s/ Mary-Alice
Mary-Alice

New International

A MAGAZINE OF MARXIST POLITICS AND THEORY

There will be new Hitlers, new Mussolinis. That is inevitable. What is not inevitable is that they will triumph. The working-class vanguard will organize our class to fight back against the devastating toll we are made to pay for the capitalist crisis. The future of humanity will be decided in the contest between these contending class forces. $14.00

Jack Barnes
"Imperialism's March
toward Fascism and War"

Also available in Spanish, French, and Swedish.

During the 1990–91 Gulf war, Washington slaughtered some 150,000 Iraqis. But the outcome did not bring the dawn of the "new world order" trumpeted by the U.S. rulers at the time. Instead it held a mirror to the growing world capitalist disorder, accelerated its contradictions, and sounded the opening guns of sharpening conflicts and class battles to come. $12.00

Also available in Spanish, French, and Swedish.

New International

New International

A MAGAZINE OF MARXIST POLITICS AND THEORY

Their Trotsky and ours
COMMUNIST CONTINUITY TODAY
by Jack Barnes

LENIN AND THE COLONIAL QUESTION
by Carlos Rafael Rodríguez

The 1916 Easter rebellion in Ireland: Two views
by V.I. Lenin and Leon Trotsky

1

$8.00

New International

A MAGAZINE OF MARXIST POLITICS AND THEORY

THE WORKING CLASS FIGHT FOR PEACE
by Brian Grogan

ARISTOCRACY OF LABOR
by Steve Clark

ARSENAL OF MARXISM
SOCIAL ROOTS OF OPPORTUNISM
by Gregory Zinoviev

2

$8.00

New International

A MAGAZINE OF MARXIST POLITICS AND THEORY

1848 TO TODAY
Communism and the fight for a popular revolutionary government
by Mary-Alice Waters

'A nose for power': Preparing the Nicaraguan revolution
by Tomás Borge

National liberation and socialism in the Americas
by Manuel Piñeiro

3

$8.00

New International

A MAGAZINE OF MARXIST POLITICS AND THEORY

THE CRISIS FACING WORKING FARMERS
by Doug Jenness

THE FIGHT FOR A WORKERS' AND FARMERS' GOVERNMENT IN THE U.S.
by Jack Barnes

Land reform and farm cooperatives in Cuba

4

$9.00

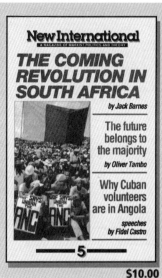

The Rise and Fall
of the Nicaraguan Revolution

SOCIALIST WORKERS PARTY RESOLUTIONS
AND ARTICLES BY JACK BARNES, STEVE
CLARK, AND LARRY SEIGLE
Lessons for fighters everywhere from the
workers and peasants government that
came to power in July 1979. Based on ten
years of journalism by working-class
activists from inside Nicaragua, this special
issue of *New International* magazine
recounts the achievements and worldwide
impact of the Nicaraguan revolution. It
then traces the political retreat of the
Sandinista leadership that led to the
revolution's downfall at the end of the 1980s. Includes the "Historic
Program of the FSLN." $14.00 Also available in Spanish in *Nueva
Internacional* no. 3.

Sandinistas Speak
*Speeches, Writings, and Interviews
with Leaders of Nicaragua's
Revolution*
TOMÁS BORGE, CARLOS FONSECA, DANIEL
ORTEGA, AND OTHERS.

The best selection in English of historic
documents of the FSLN, and speeches and
interviews from the opening years of the
1979 Nicaraguan revolution. Includes
"Nicaragua: Zero Hour" by FSLN founder
Carlos Fonseca. $13.95

FROM PATHFINDER

John Coltrane and the Jazz Revolution of the 1960s

FRANK KOFSKY

An account of John Coltrane's role in spearheading innovations in jazz that were an expression of the new cultural and political ferment that marked the rise of the mass struggle for Black rights. $23.95

What Working People Should Know about the Dangers of Nuclear Power

FRED HALSTEAD

Why the labor movement should demand that all nuclear power plants be shut immediately and why the disposal of radioactive wastes poses a danger to human beings for centuries to come. $3.00

Farmers Face the Crisis of the 1990s

DOUG JENNESS

Examines the deepening economic and social crisis in the capitalist world and how farmers and workers can unite internationally against the mounting assaults from the billionaire bankers, industrialists, and merchants of grain. $3.50

Thomas Sankara Speaks

The Burkina Faso Revolution, 1983–87

Peasants and workers in the West African country of Burkina Faso established a popular revolutionary government and began to combat the hunger, illiteracy, and economic backwardness imposed by imperialist domination. Thomas Sankara, who led that struggle, explains the example set for all of Africa. $18.95

See front of magazine for addresses.

The state

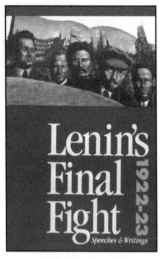

Lenin's Final Fight
Speeches and Writings, 1922–23
V.I. LENIN
In the early 1920s Lenin waged a political battle in the leadership of the Communist Party of the USSR to maintain the course that had enabled workers and peasants to overthrow the tsarist empire, carry out the first socialist revolution, and begin building a world communist movement. The issues posed in his political fight remain central to world politics today. $19.95
Also available in Spanish.

The Revolution Betrayed
What Is the Soviet Union and Where Is It Going?
LEON TROTSKY
In 1917 the toilers of Russia carried out one of the most profound revolutions in history. Yet within ten years a political counterrevolution by a privileged social layer whose chief spokesperson was Joseph Stalin was being consolidated. This classic study of the Soviet workers state and its degeneration illuminates the roots of the crisis shaking Russia today. $19.95
Also available in Russian and Spanish.

The Truth about Yugoslavia
Why Working People Should Oppose Intervention
GEORGE FYSON, ARGIRIS MALAPANIS, AND JONATHAN SILBERMAN
Examines the roots of the carnage in Yugoslavia, where Washington and its imperialist rivals in Europe are intervening militarily in an attempt to reimpose capitalist relations. $8.95

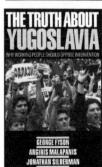

and revolution

The Origin of the Family, Private Property, and the State
FREDERICK ENGELS

How the emergence of class-divided society gave rise to repressive state bodies and family structures that protect the property of ruling layers, enabling them to pass along wealth and privilege. Engels discusses the consequences for working people of these class institutions—from their original forms to their modern versions. $16.95

State and Revolution
V.I. LENIN

On the eve of the October 1917 Russian revolution, Lenin reaffirms the views of Marx and Engels—and lessons from the 1905 and February 1917 revolutions—on the need for workers to overthrow the state of their oppressor and establish their own government and state. Progress Publishers $4.95

For a Workers and Farmers Government in the United States
JACK BARNES

Explains why the workers and farmers government is "the most powerful instrument the working class can wield" as it moves toward expropriating the capitalists and landlords and opening the road to socialism. $7.00

The Workers and Farmers Government
JOSEPH HANSEN

How experiences in revolutions following World War II in Yugoslavia, China, Algeria, and Cuba enriched communists' theoretical understanding of revolutionary governments of the toilers. $7.00

The Cuban revolution

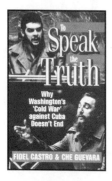

To Speak the Truth
WHY WASHINGTON'S 'COLD WAR' AGAINST
CUBA DOESN'T END
Fidel Castro and Che Guevara
In historic speeches before the United Nations
and UN bodies, Guevara and Castro address
the workers of the world, explaining why the
U.S. government so hates the example set by
the socialist revolution in Cuba and why
Washington's effort to destroy it will fail. $16.95

In Defense of Socialism
FOUR SPEECHES ON THE 30TH ANNIVERSARY OF
THE CUBAN REVOLUTION, 1988–89
Economic and social progress is possible with-
out the dog-eat-dog competition of capitalism,
Castro argues, and socialism remains the only
way forward for humanity. $13.95

U.S. Hands off the Mideast!
CUBA SPEAKS OUT AT THE UNITED NATIONS
Fidel Castro, Ricardo Alarcón
The case against Washington's 1990–91 war
against Iraq, as presented by the Cuban gov-
ernment at the United Nations. $10.95

How Far We Slaves Have Come!
SOUTH AFRICA AND CUBA IN TODAY'S WORLD
Nelson Mandela, Fidel Castro
Speaking together in Cuba in 1991,
Mandela and Castro discuss the unique
relationship and example of the struggles
of the South African and Cuban peoples.
$8.95 Also available in Spanish.

and world politics ▬▬

Women and the Cuban Revolution
BY FIDEL CASTRO, VILMA ESPÍN, AND OTHERS
Edited by Elizabeth Stone
The transformation of women's economic
and social status in Cuba since the 1959 rev-
olution. $13.95

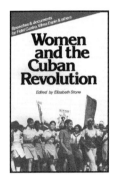

Che Guevara: Economics and Politics in the Transition to Socialism
Carlos Tablada
Quoting extensively from Guevara's writings
and speeches, this book presents the interrela-
tionship of the market, economic planning,
material incentives, and voluntary work in the
transition to socialism. $17.95 Also available in
Spanish and French.

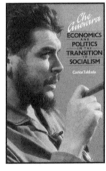

The Second Declaration of Havana
In February 1962, as the example of Cuba's
socialist revolution spread throughout the
Americas, the workers and farmers of Cuba
issued their uncompromising call for a conti-
nent-wide revolutionary struggle. $4.50 Also
available in Spanish, French, and Greek.

Dynamics of the Cuban Revolution
Joseph Hansen
How did the Cuban revolution come about?
Why does it represent, as Joseph Hansen
puts it, an "unbearable challenge" to U.S.
imperialism? What political challenges has it
confronted? Written with a polemical spirit
and political clarity as the revolution
advanced. $20.95

From Pathfinder. See front of magazine for addresses.

READINGS FOR REVOLUTIONARIES

Europe and America
TWO SPEECHES ON IMPERIALISM
Leon Trotsky

In two speeches in the mid-1920s, Trotsky explains why the emergence of the United States as the dominant imperialist power is the decisive factor in world politics. He describes the sharpening conflicts between Washington and its European rivals and highlights the revolutionary prospects for the workers of the world. $6.00

Lenin's Struggle for a Revolutionary International
Articles and letters from the political battle led by V.I. Lenin within the leadership of the international workers movement for a revolutionary course in the years leading up to and during World War I. Part of the Pathfinder series, The Communist International in Lenin's Time. $32.95

Maurice Bishop Speaks
THE GRENADA REVOLUTION AND ITS OVERTHROW, 1979–83
Speeches and interviews by the central leader of the workers and farmers government in the Caribbean island of Grenada. With an introduction by Steve Clark. $20.95

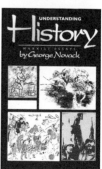

Understanding History
George Novack

How did capitalism arise? Why and when did this system of exploitation exhaust its once progressive role? Why is revolutionary change fundamental to human progress. $15.95